LOST BEAUTIES
OF THE
ENGLISH
LANGUAGE

BY
CHARLES MACKAY
LL.D.

BIBLIOPHILE BOOKS

This edition published by
Bibliophile Books
18 New Concordia Wharf
London, SE1 2BB
England

Bibliophile Books 1987

Distributed in the U.S.A. by Marboro Books

ISBN 0-900123-40-0

Printed in the United States of America
M 9 8 7 6 5 4 3 2

" Ancient words
That come from the poetic quarry
As sharp as swords. "
Hamilton's Epistle to Allan Ramsay.

INTRODUCTION.

MANY learned and interesting works have been written on the origin, growth, and present state of the English language, but, as far as the author of the present work is aware, none has been written to point out the many losses which it has suffered, and which it is still suffering, from time, corruption, and change of literary fashion. Of all the languages of the world, the English has the greatest power of assimilating to, and incorporating with itself, the useful words — whether of trade, sentiment, poetry, or science—with which it comes into contact, in the cosmopolitan developments of society, which are the great characteristics of the present age.

The English is essentially a living and a growing speech. All the languages of antiquity have had their tender infancy; their passionate youth; their careful maturity; their gradual, though it may be imperceptible, decay, and, finally, their death. After death has come the apotheosis of a language, if it has been worthy of such honour—or burial in the books, which, like the remains or memorials of ancient heroes, become the sacred treasure of newer ages. All languages pass through these stages in their career. Sanscrit, Gaelic, Greek, and Latin are familiar examples of the death and sanctity of great and mighty tongues that were once living powers to sway the passions and guide the reason of men. In their ashes even yet live the wonted fires that scholars love to rekindle. The languages of modern Europe that have sprung directly from the Sanscrit and Celtic, may all be said to have passed their infancy and youth, and to have reached maturity, if not old age. The Celtic languages—all sprung from an ancient Oriental root, and which include Scottish and Irish Gaelic, Manx, Cymric, and Breton—are in the last stage of vitality, destined to disappear, at no very remote period, into the books, which will alone preserve their memory. Were it not for Victor Hugo, and some recent borrowings from the English, it might be said that French had ceased to expand, and had become stereotyped into a form no longer to be modified. Spanish, Portuguese, and Italian hold their own ; and that is all that can be said of them. German, and the languages sprung from the same root and stem, contain within themselves such immense resources, and are so continually evolving new compounds, as to free them from that reproach of stagnation which may not unjustly be applied to the other great tongues which we have enumerated. But English—which, taken all in all, may be considered by far the richest, though not the most beautiful or the most sonorous, of all the languages spoken in our day—is yet in its vigorous youth, and cannot be accused of exhibiting any symptoms of decay. It is doubtful whether it have yet reached the full maturity of its prime, or whether the mighty nation now existent in America, or the as mighty nation which is destined yet to arise in Australia, will not, as time rolls on, and new wants are created, new circumstances encountered, and new ideas evolved out of the progress of science and civilization, add many thousands of new words to our already copious vocabulary. Other languages are dainty in the materials of their increment; but the English is, like man himself, omnivorous. Nothing comes amiss to its hungry palate. It does not live on air and honey-dew, or even on bread, like more delicate organisations. All nature—all the languages of the earth—administer to its wants. It borrows, it steals, it assimilates what words it pleases from all the points of the compass, and asks no questions of them, but that they shall express thoughts and describe circumstances more tersely and more accurately than any of the old words beside which they are invited to take their places. Saxon, Celtic, Greek, Latin, French, Arabic, Turkish, Persian, have all helped it; and the once despised, but beautiful, dialect of its Scottish sister has given it many poetical words, which it is not likely to part with. But if English is thus perpetually growing and gaining, it is at the same time perpetually losing. Were it not for the noble translation of the Bible, and for Chaucer, Gower, and the poets of the Elizabethan age, it would have lost still more than it has of its early treasures, and would have been Latinised to an extent that would have impaired its vigour, emasculated its passion, and deprived it of that sturdy vernacular which is the richest element in its blood, and best serves to build up its bone and muscle. If few languages now spoken in the world have gained so much as the English from the progress of civilization, it must be admitted, at the same time, that few have lost so much, and lost it without necessity. It has been said that a good carpenter is known as much by the shape as by the quantity of his chips; and the chips that the English tongue has thrown off since the days of *Piers Ploughman* to our own, betoken, both by quality and quantity, what a plethora of wealth it possesses, and what a very cunning carpenter Time has proved in working with such abundant materials.

It is one of the current assertions which, once started on high authority, are very rarely questioned, that the writings of Chaucer are a " well of pure English undefiled."

Chaucer's well, limpid and beautiful as it is, and undefiled as grammarians and critics may please to consider it, is not so much a fountain as a double stream. Chaucer, though so ancient in our eyes, was a neologist, and strove rather to increase the wealth of the written English, of which he was so great a master, by the introduction of words from the Norman-French, little understood by the bulk of the people, though familiar enough to the aristocracy, for whom he mainly wrote, than to fix in his pages for ever the strong simple words of his native Anglo-Saxon. The stream of native English in his writings runs pure and cool; the stream of Norman-French runs pure and bright also; but the two currents that he employed in his song never thoroughly intermingled, and at least nine-tenths of the elegant Gallicisms which he employed found no favour with successive writers; and few of them have remained, except in the earlier poems of Milton. If we really wish to discover the true "well of English undefiled," where the stream runs clear and unmixed, we must look to the author of *Piers Ploughman* rather than to Chaucer. We shall there find a large vocabulary of strong words, which are plain to all men's comprehension—preserved in the Bible, and in the common speech of the peasantry, and, notably, in that living branch of the old English language which is known as the Scottish dialect.

No such systematic attempt as that made by Chaucer to popularise words of French origin, was essayed by Scottish writers of that time; not even by King James I.—the illustrious author of the *King's Quair.* Yet, in consequence of the friendly intercourse long subsisting between France and Scotland—an intercourse that was alike political, commercial, and social—a considerable number of words of French origin crept into the Scottish vernacular, and there established themselves with a tenacity that is not likely to be relaxed as long as the language continues to be either written or spoken. Some of these are among the most racy and characteristic differences between the English and the Scotch. It will be sufficient to cite : to *fash one's self*, to be troubled with or about anything— from *se fâcher*, to be angered ; *douce*, gentle, good-tempered, courteous—from *doux*, soft ; *dour*, grim, obdurate, slow to forgive or relent—from *dur*, hard ; *bien*, comfortable, well to do in worldly affairs—from *bien*, well ; *ashet*, a dish—from *assiette*, a plate ; a *creel*, a fish-basket—from *creille*, a basket ; a *gigot* of mutton—from *gigot*, a leg ; *awmrie*, a linen-press or plate-cupboard—from *armoire*, a movable cupboard or press ; *bonnie*, beautiful and good—from *bon*, good ; *airles* and *airle*-penny, money paid in advance to seal a bargain —from *arrhes*, a deposit on account ; *brulzie*, a fight or dispute—from *s'embrouiller*, to quarrel ; *callant*, a lad, a brave boy—from *galant*, a lover or a gallant youth ; *braw*, fine—from *brave*, honest and courageous ; *dool*, sorrow—from *deuil*, mourning ; *grozet*, a gooseberry (which is a popular English corruption from *gorse*berry)—from *groseille; ; taupie*, a thoughtless, foolish girl, who does not look before her to see what she is doing—from *taupe*, a mole ; *haggis*, the Scottish national dish—from *hachis*, a hash ; *pawn*, peacock —from *paon; caddie*, a young man acting as a porter or messenger—from *cadet*, the younger born ; *spaule*, the shoulder— from *epaule*, &c.

The Scoto-Saxon and Old English words derived immediately from the Dutch, and following the Dutch rules of pronunciation, are exceedingly numerous. Among these are *wanhope*—from *wanhoop*, despair ; *wanchancie, wanlust, wanrestful*, and many others, where the English adopt the German *un* instead of *wan*.

The English and Scottish words derived from the Gaelic are apparent in the names of places and in much of the colloquial phraseology of everyday life. Among the first, *ben, glen, burn, burnie, strath, bog, corrie, crag* or *craig*, and *cairn*, will recur to the memory of any one who has lived or travelled in Scotland, or is conversant with Scottish literature. *Gillie*, a boy or servant ;

grieve, a land-steward or agent, are not only ancient Scottish words, but have lately become English. *Loof*, the open palm, is derived from the Gaelic *lamh* (pronounced *laff* or *lav*), the hand ; *cuddle*, to embrace—from *cadail*, sleep ; *whisky*, from *uisge*, water ; *clachan*, a village—from *clach*, a stone ; *croon*, to hum a tune—from *cruin*, to lament or moan ; *bailie*, a city or borough magistrate—from *baile*, a town ; *tinder*, from *teine*, fire ; *sonsie*, fresh, healthful, young, good-looking—from *sonas*, good fortune ; *grove*, an assemblage of trees—from *craobh*, pronounced *craov*, a tree ; *fallow*, lying uncultivated, from *falamb*, pronounced *fallav*, empty—may serve as specimens of the many words which the Scoto-Saxon and Anglo-Saxon languages owe to the Gaelic or Celtic stock that originally possessed these islands.

Four centuries ago, the English or Anglo-Saxon, when Chaucer, Gower, and Lydgate were still intelligible, had a much greater resemblance to the Scoto-Saxon than it has at the present day. William Dunbar, one of the earliest, as he was one of the best, of the Scottish poets, and supposed to have been born in 1465, in the reign of James III. in Scotland, and of Edward IV. in England, wrote, among other poems, the " Thrissel and the Rose." This composition was equally intelligible to the people of both countries. It was designed to commemorate the marriage of James IV. with Margaret Tudor, daughter of King Henry VII. of England—that small cause of many great events, of which the issues have extended to our time, and which gave the Stuarts their title to the British throne. Though Dunbar wrote in the Scotch of the *literati*, rather than in that of the common people, as did King James I. at an earlier period, when, a captive in Windsor Castle, he indited his beautiful poem, " The King's Quair," to celebrate the grace and loveliness of the Lady Beaufort, whom he afterwards married ; the " Thrissel and the Rose" is only archaic in its orthography, and contains no words that a commonly

well-educated Scottish ploughman cannot at this day understand, though it might puzzle some of the writers of leaders
for the London press to interpret it without the aid of a
glossary. Were the spelling of the following passages moder-
nised, it would be found that there is nothing in any subsequent
poets, from Dunbar's day to our own, with which it need fear a
comparison, either in point of poetry or of popular comprehension :—

> " Quhen Merché wes with variand windis past,
> And Apryll haddé, with her silver shouris,
> Tane leif at nature, with ane orient blast,
> And lusty May, that mudder is of flouris,
> Had maid the birdis to begyn thcir houris
> Among the tender odouris reid and quhyt,
> Quhois harmony to heir it was delyt.

> " In bed at morrowe, sleiping as I lay,
> Methocht Aurora, with her crystal een,
> In at the window lukit by the day,
> And halsit me with visage paile and grene,
> On quhois hand a lark sang fro the splene,
> ' Awauk, luvaris ! out of your slummering !
> See how the lusty morrowe dois upspring !' "

Many of the popular authors of that century did not, like
Dunbar, confine their poetic efforts to the speech of the learned,
but wrote in the vernacular of the peasantry and townspeople.
The well-known poem of " Peblis to the Play " is the earliest
specimen of this class of literature that has come down to us.
This composition scarcely contains a word that Burns, three
hundred years later, would have hesitated to employ. In like
manner the poem of " Christ's Kirk on the Green," written
more than three hundred years ago, made use of the language of the peasantry to describe the assembly of the lasses
and their wooers that came to the " dancing and deray," with
their gloves of the " *raffele* richt " (right doeskin), their " shoon
of the *straitis* " (coarse cloth), and their

> " Kirtles of the *lincum* light,
>   Weel pressed wi' mony plaitis."

The author's description of " Gillie " is equal to anything in Ramsay or Burns, and quite as intelligible to the Scottish peasantry of the present day :—

> " Of all their maidens mild as meid
>   Was nane sae gymp as Gillie ;
>   As ony rose her rude was reid,
>   Hir lire was like the lily.
>   Bot zallow, zallow was hir heid,
>   And sche of luif sae sillie,
>   Thof a' hir kin suld hae bein deid,
>   Sche wuld hae bot sweit Willie."

Captain Alexander Montgomerie, who was attached to the service of the Regent Murray in 1577, and who enjoyed a pension from King James VI., wrote many poems in which the beauty, the strength, and the humour of the Scoto-Saxon language were very abundantly displayed. The " Cherry and the Slae " is particularly rich in words that Allan Ramsay, Walter Scott, Robert Burns, and Christopher North have since rendered classical, and is, besides, a poem as excellent in thought and fancy as it is copious in diction. The description of the music of the birds on a May morning may be taken as a specimen :—

> " The cushat croods, the corbie cries,
>   The Coukoo couks, the prattling pies
>   To keckhir they begin.
>   The jargon o' the jangling jays,
>   The craiking craws and kecklin' kayes,
>   They deaved me with their din.

> " The painted pawn with Argus e'es
>   Can on his mayock call ;
>   The turtle wails on withered trees,
>   And Echo answers all.
>   Repeting, with greting,
>   How fair Narcissus fell,
>   By lying and spying
>   His schadow in the well."

Time was within living memory when the Scotch of the upper classes prided themselves on their native Doric ; when judges on the bench delivered their judgments in the broadest Scotch, and would have thought themselves guilty of puerile and unworthy affectation if they had preferred English words or English accents to their own ; when advocates pleaded in the same homely and plastic tongue ; when ministers of religion found their best way to the hearts and to the understanding of their congregations in the use of the language most familiar to themselves, as well as to those whom they addressed ; and when ladies of the highest rank—celebrated alike for their wit and their beauty—sang their tenderest, archest, and most affecting songs, and made their bravest thrusts and parries in the sparkling encounters of conversation, in the homely speech of their childhood. All this, however, is fast disappearing, and not only the wealthy and titled, who live much in London and in England, begin to grow ashamed of speaking the language of their ancestors, though the sound of the well-beloved accents in the mouths of others is not unwelcome or unmusical to their ears, but the middle-class Scotch are learning to follow their example. The members of the legal and medical profession are afraid of the accusation of vulgarity that might be launched against them if they spoke publicly in the picturesque language of their fathers and grandfathers ; and even the clergy are unlearning in the pulpit the brave old speech that was good enough for John Knox (though he was the greatest Angliciser of his day, and was publicly accused of that fault), and many thousands of pious preachers who, since his time, have worthily kept alive the faith of the Scottish people by appeals to their consciences in the language of their hearts. In ceasing to employ the "unadorned eloquence" of the sturdy vernacular, and using instead of it the language of books, and of the southern English, it is to be feared that too many of these superfine preachers have lost their former hold upon the mind, and that they have sensibly weakened the powers of persuasion and conviction which they possessed when their words were in sympathetic unison with the current of thought and feeling that flowed through the broad Scottish intellect and language of the peasantry. And where fashion leads, snobbism will certainly follow ; so that it happens even in Scotland that young Scotsmen of the Dundreary class will sometimes boast of their inability to understand the poetry of Burns and the romance of Scott on account of the difficulties presented by the language ! —as if their crass ignorance were a thing to be proud of !

The English and Scotch languages are both mainly derived from the Teutonic ; and five or six hundred years ago, may be correctly described as having been Anglo-Saxon and Scoto-Saxon. Time has replaced the Anglo-Saxon by the modern English, but has spared the Scoto-Saxon, which still remains a living speech. Though the children of one mother, the two have lived apart, received different educations, developed themselves under dissimilar circumstances, and received accretions from independent and unrelated sources. The English, as far as it remains an Anglo-Saxon tongue, is derived from the Low German, with a mixture of the Scandinavian and Icelandic ; while the Lowland Scotch, or Scoto-Saxon, is indebted more immediately to the Dutch, Flemish, and Danish, both for its fundamental and most characteristic words, and for its inflection and grammar. The English, like the Teutonic, bristles with consonants. The Scotch is as spangled with vowels as a meadow with daisies in the month of May. English, though perhaps the most muscular and copious language in the world, is harsh and sibilant ; while the Scotch, with its beautiful terminational diminutives, is almost as soft as the Italian. English songs, like those of Dibdin, Moore, and Campbell, however excellent they may be as poetical compositions, are, for these reasons, not so available for musical purposes, as the songs of Scotland. An Englishman, if he sings of a "pretty little girl," uses words

deficient in euphony, and suggests comedy rather than sentiment; but when a Scotsman sings of a " bonnie wee lassie," he
employs words that are much softer than their English equiva-
lents, express a tenderer idea, and are infinitely better adapted to
music. The principal components of the Scoto-Saxon tongue are
derived, first from the Teutonic, comprising many words once
possessed by the English, but which have become obsolete in the
latter; secondly, words and inflections derived from the Dutch,
Flemish, and Norse; thirdly, words derived from the French, or
from the Latin and Greek through a French medium; and fourthly,
words derived from the Gaelic, which is indubitably a branch
of the Sanscrit. As regards the first source, it is interesting to
note that in the glossary appended to Mr. Thomas Wright's
edition of those ancient and excellent alliterative poems, the
"Vision" and "Creed" of *Piers Ploughman*, there occur about
two thousand obsolete English or Anglo-Saxon words, many of
which are still retained in the Scoto-Saxon of the Scottish Lowlands; and that in the Glossary to Tyrrwhitt's edition of
Chaucer, there occur upwards of six thousand words which need
explanation to the modern English reader, and full one half of
which need no explanation whatever to a Scotsman. Even
Shakespeare is becoming obsolete to his countrymen, and uses
upwards of two thousand four hundred words, which Mr.
Howard Staunton, his latest, and in many respects, his most
judicious editor, thinks it necessary to collect in a glossary for
the better elucidation of the text. Many hundreds of these
words are perfectly familiar to a Scottish ear, and require no in-
terpreter. It appears from these facts, that the Scotch is a far
more conservative language than the English, and that although
it does not object to receive new words, it clings reverently and
affectionately to the old. The consequence of this mingled
tenacity and elasticity is, that it posesses a vocabulary which
includes for a Scotsman's use, every word of the modern
English language, and several thousand words which the English

people never possessed, or have suffered to drop into desuetude. In addition to this conservancy of the bone and sinew of the language, the Scoto-Saxon possesses an advantage over the modern English, in having reserved to itself the power, while retaining all the old words of the language, to eliminate all harsh or unnecessary consonants. Thus it has *lo'* for love : *fa'* for fall ; *wa'* for walk ; *awfu'* for awful ; *sma'* for small ; and many hundreds of similar abbreviations, which detract nothing from the force of the idea or the clearness of the meaning, while they soften the roughness of the expression. No such power resides in the English or French, though it was once inherent in both languages. Very little of it belongs to the German, though it remains in all those European tongues which trace their origin to the Platt-Deutsch. The Scottish poet or versifier may write *fa'* or *fall* as it pleases him, but his English compeer must write "fall" without abbreviation. Another source of the superior euphony of the Scoto-Saxon is the single diminutive in *ie*, and the double dimunitive in *kie*, which may be applied to any noun in the language, as *wife, wifie, wifikie*, wife, little wife, very little wife ; *bairn, bairnie, bairnikie*, child, little child, very little child ; *bird, birdie, birdikie ;* and *lass, lassie, lassikie*, etc. A few English nouns remain susceptible of diminutives, though in a less musical form, as *lamb, lambkin ; goose, gosling*, etc. The beauty of the Scottish forms of the diminutive is obvious. Take, for instance, the following lines :—

> " Hap and row, hap and row,
> Hap and row the feetie o't ;
> It is a wee bit wearie thing,
> I downa bide the greetie o't."

Endeavour to translate into modern English the diminutives " feetie" and " greetie," and the superiority of the Scottish or old English for poetical purposes will be obvious.

But the old Scottish language, though of later years it has become unfashionable in its native land, survives not alone on the tongue, but in the heart of the " common" people (and where is there such a common or uncommon people as the peasantry of Scotland ?), and has established for itself a place in the affections of those ardent Scotsmen who travel to the New World and to the remotest parts of the Old, with the *auri sacra fames* to lead them on to fortune, but who never permit that particular species of hunger—which is by no means peculiar to Scotsmen—to deaden their hearts to their native land, or to render them indifferent to their native speech, the merest word of which, when uttered unexpectedly under a foreign sky, stirs up all the latent patriotism in their minds, and opens their heart, and, if needs be, their purse, to the utterer. It has also, by a kind of Nemesis or poetical justice, established for itself a hold and footing, even in that English language which affects to ignore it ; and, thanks more especially to Burns and Scott, and to the admiration which their genius has excited in England and America, has engrafted many of its loveliest shoots upon the old trees of the Anglo-Saxon and English language. Every year the number of words that are taken like seeds or grafts from the Scottish conservatory, and planted in the fruitful English garden, is on the increase, as will be seen from the following anthology of specimens, which might have been made ten times as abundant if it had been possible to squeeze into a wine-glass a whole gallon of hippocrene. Many of these words are recognised English, permissible both in literature and conversation ; many others are in progress and process of adoption and assimilation ; and many more that are not English, and may never become so, are fully worthy of a place in the dictionary of a language that has room for every word, let it come whence it will, that expresses a new meaning, or a more delicate shade of an old meaning than the existing forms of expression admit. *Eerie*, and *gloaming*, and *cannie*, and *cantie*, and *cozie*, and *lift*, and *lilt*, and *caller*, and *gruesome*, and *thud*, are all of an ancient and a goodly pedigree, and were, the most of them, as English in the fifteenth century as they ought to be in the nineteenth."

Since the days of *Piers Ploughman*, the spoken language of the English and Scottish peasantry has undergone but few changes as regards words, but very many changes as regards terminations and inflections. On the other hand, the language of literature and polite society has undergone changes so vast that uneducated people are scarcely able to understand the phraseology that occurs in the masterpieces of our great authors, or the Sunday sermons of their pastors, delivered, as the saying is, "above their heads," in words that are rarely or never employed in their everyday hearing. Among this class survive large numbers of verbs as well as of inflections that ought never to have been allowed to drop out of literature, and which it only needs the efforts of a few great writers and orators to restore to their original favour.

Among the losses which the English language has undergone are, firstly, the loss of the plurals in *n* and in *en*, and the substitution of the plural in *s;* secondly, the present participle in *and*, for which we have substituted the nasal and disagreeable *ing;* thirdly, the loss of the French negative *ne*, as in *nill*, for " I will not;" *nould*, for " I would not;" *n'am*, for " I am not;" and of which the sole trace now remaining is " willy-nilly;" and, fourthly, the substitution of the preterite in *d*, as in lov*ed* and admir*ed*, for the older and much stronger preterite formed by a change in the vowel sound of the infinitive and the present, as in run, ran ; bite, bit ; speak, spoke ; take, took ; and many others that still survive. And not only has the language lost the strong preterite in a great variety of instances where it would have been infinitely better to have retained it, but it has lost many hundred preterites altogether, as well as many whole verbs, which the illiterate sometimes use, but which Literature for a hundred and fifty years has either ignored or despised. Of all the nouns that formerly formed their plural in *n*, as the German or Saxon nouns still for the most part do, very few survive—some in the Bible, some in poetical composition, some in the common conversation of the peasantry, and some, but very few, in polite literature. Among them may be mentioned "oxen," for oxes; "kine," for cows; "shoon," for shoes; "hosen," for stockings; "een," for eyes; "housen," for houses; and the words, as common to the vernacular as to literature, "men," "women," "brethren," and "children." In America, the word "sistern," as a companion to brethren, survives in the conventicle and the meeting-house. "Lamben" and "thumben," for "lambs" and "thumbs," were comparatively euphemistic words; but thumbs and lambs, and every noun which ends with a consonant in the singular, are syllables which set music, and sometimes pronunciation, at defiance. What renders the matter worse is, that the *s* in the French plural, from which this perversion of the English language was adopted, is not sounded, and that the plural is really marked by the change of the definite article, as *le champ, les champs.* Thus in borrowing an unpronounced consonant from the French, in order to pronounce it we have adulterated our language with a multitude of sibilations alien to its spirit and original structure. The substitution of *s* for *eth* as the terminal of the present person singular of every verb in the language is an aggravation of the evil. If this change had been repudiated by our forefathers, a grace much needed would have been retained in the language.

Gradually, too, the English language ha lost the large number of diminutives which it formerly possessed, and which, as already remarked, are still common in the Scottish dialect. The English diminutives in ordinary use in the nursery are many, but are chiefly employed in the pet names of children, as "Willie," for little William; "Annie," for little Anne; and so forth. The diminutives belonging to literature are abnormally few.

Among other losses, the plural in *en* of the present tenses of all the verbs is greatly to be lamented. We lov*en* and we smil*en* would serve many rhythmical needs, and administer to many poetic elegancies that the modern forms do not supply.

"The persons plural," observes Ben Jonson in his *English*

Grammar—a work by no means so well known as his poetry—
"keep the termination of the first person singular. In former
times, till about the reign of King Henry VIII., they were
wont to be formed by adding *en;* thus, 'loven,' 'sayen,' 'com-
plainen.' But now (whatsoever is the cause) it hath quite
grown out of use. Albeit (to tell you my opinion) I am per-
suaded that the lack thereof, well considered, will be found a
great blemish to our tongue."

But of all the losses which the language has sustained, not
alone for poetry, but for oratory, that of many useful verbs,
some of which are still existing in Scottish parlance, and of the
ancient preterites and past participles of many old verbs of
which the infinitives and present tenses still hold their places,
is the most to be deplored. This loss began early; and that
the process is still in operation in the present day, is manifest
from the fact that many preterites written in the best books and
spoken in the best society forty years ago, are dropping out of
use before our eyes. We constantly find *bid* for *bade*—"I
bid him now;" "he *bid* me yesterday;" *dare* for *durst*—"I
told him I *dare* not do it;" *need* for *needed*—"it was clear to me
a year ago that he *need* not perform his promise;" *eat* for *ate* or
ett—"he *eat* his dinner;" *bet* for *betted*—"he *bet* me a thousand
to one." The verbs *to let, to cast,* and *to put,* seem to have
enjoyed no preterite during the last two hundred years in England, though in Scottish literature, both of the past and the
present, their preterites are as common as their infinitives and
present tenses. *Must,* in English, is equally devoid of the
infinitive, the preterite, and the future; while *can* has a preterite, but neither infinitive nor future. For what reasons these
and similar losses have occurred in English and in other modern
languages might be interesting to inquire, though it might possibly lead us into metaphysical mazes were we to ask why an
Englishman who may say "I can" and "I could," must not say
"I will *can*," but must resort to the periphrase of "I will be

:able," to express power in futurity ; or why the sense of present
·duty and obligation implied in the words " I must" cannot be
·expressed by the same verb if the duty be bygone or future, as
I "*musted*," or "I will *must*," but have to be translated, as it were,
into " I was obliged," or " I shall be obliged," to do such and
:such a thing hereafter.   These, however, are losses or imper-
ifections, whatever may be their occult causes, which can never
·again be supplied, and which it is useless to lament.

One of the most grievous of the losses which the language has
·suffered, is that of the preterites and past participles of ancient
·verbs that are still in use, and of many good English verbs in
all their tenses which, without reason, have been left for verna-
·cular use to the people of the north of England and Scotland,
:and have not been admitted to the honours of modern literature,
·except in the poems of Robert Burns, Miss Blamire, and the
·novels of Sir Walter Scott and John Galt.   These preterites
ought not to be lost—many of them are not dead, but sleeping
— many only need the fostering care of a few writers and
·speakers of genius and influence to be revived—and most of
them formed the bone and pith of the language of our fore-
:fathers, and make the beauty and strength of the Bible in many
·of its noblest passages.

What should we say if an English nobleman, of ancient and
·illustrious lineage and great wealth, had in the cellars and
·vaults of his castle, hundreds of coffers and oaken chests filled
·to the lid with coins of the purest gold, stamped with the image
:and superscription of bygone kings, if he would never use nor
look at any portion of his wealth ?   What, also, should we say
·of him if, in want of gold for his daily needs, he persisted in
·borrowing it from strangers at usurious interest, rather than
·touch his antique treasures ?   We should say he was unwise, or
at the least eccentric, and that it was questionable whether he
·deserved to possess the great wealth which he had inherited.
Every master of the English tongue, whether he be poet, orator,

or great prose writer, is in the position of this supposed noble-man if he will not study the ancient words of the language, and revive to the extent of his ability such among them as he finds to be better adapted to express strong as well as delicate shades of meaning than the modern words which have usurped their places. To the poets more especially, and, if there be none left in our day (which we should be very sorry to assert), to the versifiers, who are not likely ever to fail us as long as there are hopes and fancies in the hearts of young men and women, this is a matter of special concern. The permissible rhymes of the modern English tongue are not very abundant; and such as exist, if not as well worn as love and dove, breeze and trees, heart and dart, are far too familiar to come upon the ear with any great charm of novelty. The dactylic rhymes are still fewer, as every one who has tried his hand at versification is pain-fully aware. It is the poet, more than the prose writer, who strengthens as well as beautifies the language which he employs. It is true that language first makes literature; but literature, when once established among a people, reacts upon language, and fixes its form—decides what words shall and what words shall not be used in the higher forms of prose and poetical composition. Old English—such as it is found in *Piers Plough-man* and his successors as far downwards as the poets and dramatists of the Elizabethan era, and as late as Milton and Dryden—is a passionate rather than an argumentative language; and poets, who ought to be passionate above all else, otherwise they are but mere versifiers, should go back to those ancient sources if they would be strong without ceasing to be correct and elegant. The words that were good enough for Shake-speare and his contemporaries ought to be good enough for the greatest writers of our day. But Shakespeare himself, as already observed, is to a very considerable extent becoming obsolete.

The intercourse between Great Britain and the United States of America has of late years so greatly increased, and the interchange of thought between readers and writers on both sides of the Atlantic has become so intimate and incessant, as to have produced a marked effect, not only on the familiar language of Englishmen, but on English literature and, more especially, that of the newspaper press. Ever since the colonization of the first thirteen colonies, which proclaimed their independence nearly a century ago, the United States have received vast accessions of immigrants from the British Isles, who carried along with them to the new country of their adoption, not only the literary language of books, but the language of the peasantry —of what are called the common people ; of people who used the rough and rustic speech of the counties—as distinguished from the more cultivated and more copious speech of London and of books—and who introduced into the current phraseology of everyday life many hundreds of words that literary men would consider obsolete, archaic, or provincial, and, therefore, to be avoided ; but which were quickly adopted by the less fastidious writers for the American press, who cared less for fine writing than for making a strong impression on the minds of those whom they addressed. By dint of repetition in print, these old English—and all but forgotten—words have become part of the ordinary speech of the Americans, and are fast making their way back again to the land of their birth, stamped with the acceptance and approbation of a country that no longer aims in its literature to be a copyist. These Americanisms, as they are erroneously called, are making themselves at home in the old country, and adding to the wealth of that great and expansive language which promises to be the one all-pervading language of the civilized world—or, at least, to share that honour with the Spanish and the German, and to predominate largely over both.

Lest it may be objected that all the archaic words—reviving and revivable—that are introduced into the following pages, are not " beauties " in the strictest sense of the word, it may be claimed that if not beauties, they are utilities—or may be made so—and that everything which is useful is beautiful in its degree. Every country has its literary and its popular language ; but if ever there were a language in the world, from which literature might advantageously borrow from the language of the people— of the past ages and of the present—it is the English.

Let us conclude with the observations of Frederick Schlegel, in his lectures on the " History of Literature :"—

" The care of the national language is at all times a sacred trust and a most important privilege of the higher orders of society. Every man of education should make it the object of his unceasing concern, to preserve his language pure and entire, to speak it, so far as is in his power, in all its beauty and per- fection. . . . . A nation whose language becomes rude and barbarous, must be on the brink of barbarism in regard to everything else. A nation which allows her language to go to ruin, is parting with the last half of her intellectual independence, and testifies her willingness to cease to exist."

[The author has to return thanks to the Messrs. Blackwood, of Edinburgh, for permission to reprint the substance of the above introduction and many " Lost Preterites," which origi- nally appeared in *Blackwood's Magazine*, in a paper with that title.]

LOST BEAUTIES
OF THE
ENGLISH
LANGUAGE

Abear, to tolerate, or endure: This word survives among uneducated people, and is a better form of expression than its modern synonym 'bear.' It is more correct to say of a man, that you cannot *abear* him, than to say you cannot bear him, for bear may mean to 'carry.' Abear is found in Chaucer, Spenser, and Shakespeare.

Abrook, the intensitive or augmentative of 'brook,' to 'bear,' or 'abear,' to tolerate, endure.

Acold, very cold.

> 'The owl, with all his feathers, was *acold*.'—*Keats.*
>
> 'Poor Tom's *acold*.'—*Shakespeare.*

Adle, stagnant water that smells badly. From the same root, 'addled,' a rotten egg.

Afeard, struck with fear—a more purely English word than its synonym afraid, which is a corruption of the French *effrayé*, frightened.

> A soldier, and *afeard*?—*Shakespeare.*

Aforetime, of old time; in the days of old; auld lang syne.

Aftermath, the pasture after the grass has been mowed; a second mowing or crop.

Aftertale, a postscript sometimes added when the tale or story is, or ought to be, ended.

Afterword, a postscript to a letter; or appendix to a book.

Agasp, gasping for breath.

Agg, to irritate: whence, by corruption, to 'egg on,' to excite.

Agore, gory, bloody.

Aidle, to earn one's bread indifferently well. 'I *aidle* my keep.'

Airt, the quarter from which the wind blows.

> 'Helter skelter from a' *airts*,
> In swarms the country drives.'—*Stagg's Cumberland Ballads.*

> 'Of a' the *airts* the wind can blaw,
> I dearly lo'e the west,
> For there the bonnie lassie lives.
> The lass that I lo'e best.'—*Robert Burns.*

Alder, } the genitive plural of all; a prefix formerly used to
Aller, } intensify the meaning of an adjective in the superlative degree,—as if to better the best, and heighten the highest: in which sense it is still employed in modern German, and all the Teutonic languages. In Wicliffe's Bible, the Almighty is called the Alder-Father, and the Alder-Creator. Pope, in his Universal Prayer, says, 'Father of all,'—a phrase much less forcible than the one word of our ancestors.

Alderbest, best of all.

> That all the best archers of the north
> Sholde come upon a day,
> And they that shoteth *alderbest*
> The game shal bere away.—*Ballad of Robin Hood.*

Alderelde, extreme old age.

Alderfirst, first of all.

> Then Tonda forthwith *alderfirst*
> On the Christen smote wel fast.—*Guy of Warwick.*

> Placebo came and eke his frendes some,
> And *alderfirst*, he bade them all a bone.—
> Chaucer : The Merchant's Tale.

Alderforemost, the foremost of all.

> William and the Emperor went *alderforemost.*—*William and the Werwolf.*

> For though they make semblant fairest,
> They will beguile you *alderforemost.*—*The Seven Wise Masters.*

Alderhighest, highest of all.

> And *alderhighest* took Astronomie.—*Lydgate's Poems.*

Alderlast, last of all.

>And *alderlast* how he in this citie
>Was by the sonne slaine at Tholouse.—*Bochas.*

Alderlest, least of all.

>Love,—against the whiche who so dependith,
>Himselven most, him *alderlest* availeth.—*Chaucer: Troilus and Creseide.*

Alderliefest, dearest of all; best beloved of all.

>Mine *alderliefest* Lorde and brother dear.—*Chaucer: Troilus and Creseide.*
>With you mine *alderliefest* sovereign.—*Shakespeare: King Henry VI.*

Aldermost, greatest, or most of all.

>But *aldermost* in honor out of soule,
>They had a relicke highte Palladion.—*Chaucer: Troilus and Creseide.*

Aldertruest, truest of all

>I humbly do request
>That by your means our princes may unite
>Their love unto mine *aldertruest* love.—*Greene's Works.*

Alderwisest, wisest of all.

>And truliche it sitte well to be so,
>For *alderwisest* have therewith been pleased.
>*Chaucer: Troilus and Creseide*

Alderworst, worst of all.

>Ye don us *alderworst* to spede
>When that we have most nede.—*Guy of Warwick.*

Allwholly, entirely.

Amiddleward, in the midst of.

>The lady took and smote with main,
>Right *amiddleward* the brain.
>*Metrical Romance of the Seven Wise Masters.*

Amort, dejected, depressed, dis-spirited; at death's door.

>How fares my Kate? What, sweeting! all *amort?*
>*The Taming of the Shrew.*

Anan, an interrogative, applied by an inferior to a superior, to express that he has not caught the meaning of something said to him. It saves a long periphrasis, such as, '*I beg your pardon, I did not hear what you said.*'

Anent, } relating to, concerning. The first of these forms
Anempst, } is retained in Scotland, the north of England, and America; the second, which was more commonly used in the south and west of England, has become obsolete.

>'We will speak *anent* this matter.'

Anent—*continued.*

'And we humbly beseech your Highness we may knowe your Grace's pleasure, how we shall order ourselves *anempst* your Grace's sayd citie and castell.'—*State Papers, Vol. II., quoted by Halliwell.*

Anywhen, at any time. This word is in common use among the peasants in the south of England; but has not yet been admitted to the honors of the Dictionary. 'I will talk it over with you, *anywhere* and *anywhen*,' said a carter, at Leatherhead, in Surrey. The word seems quite as well entitled to a literary position as anyhow, anywhere, anywhither, or anywise,—all of which are recognised English.

Arl,
Arles,
Erl,
Earles,
Yearles, } in Scotland, and the north of England, the arl, or erl-penny, is a deposit paid down in confirmation of a bargain; an earnest of whatever kind; a pledge of full possession.

> Here tak' this gowd and never want,
> Enough to gar you drink and rant,
> And this is but an *arle* penny
> To what I afterwards design ye.—*Allan Ramsay.*
>
> This was but *erlys* for to tell
> Of infortune that after fell.—*Wyntown.*

"This word," says Jamieson, "is evidently from the Latin arrhabo, which the Romans abbreviated into *arrha.* It denoted an earnest—a pledge in general. It was very often given to signify the earnest which a man gave to the woman he espoused, for the confirmation of the pledge between them."

The French have the word *arrhes,*—also signifying a deposit of money on a bargain.

Arval, probably a corruption of earthal; or putting to earth. A funeral.

Arval-supper, a supper given after a funeral.

Arval-cake,
Arval-bread, } funeral-baked meats.

Asper, (French, âpre,) rough.

Asperly, roughly.

Athattens, in that manner.

Athissens, in this manner.

Averoyne, the herb Southernwood.

Backstand, resistance.

Backword, a contradiction, or answer, to put off an engagement.

Bade, preterite of bid. This useful word is fast perishing. Not only in conversation, but in writing, persons who ought to know good English from bad use such an inelegancy as, ' I *bid* you do it yesterday.'

Bale, sorrow, hurt, damage, mischief, misery ; whence *baleful*, mischievous, and *balefulness*.

> Now full of blisse and now of *bale*.—*Gower : Confessio Amantis.*

> Amid my *bale*, I bathe in blisse,
> I swim in heaven, I sink in hell.—*Gascoigne : Strange Passion.*

> But make you ready your stiff bats and clubs,
> Rome and her rats are at the point of battle ;
> The one side must have *bale*.—*Shakespeare : Coriolanus.*

Bangle, to waste by little and little, to dissipate an estate by thoughtlessness and bad management.

> We *bangle* away our days—befool our time.
> *Burton's Anatomy of Melancholy.*

> He *bangled* all his father's money,

a Lancashire phrase, applied to a man who has allowed his inheritance to slip out of his hands.

Bangled, beaten down by the wind, like corn or long grass. ' A *bangle*-eared dog,' signifies a dog like a spaniel, with hanging ears.

Barm, yeast. Derived apparently from beer-ream (Germ. Bierrahm), the cream, or fermentation of beer. Dryden speaks of,—

> ' Windy cyder and *barmy* beer,'

and in the ' Cherry and the Sloe,' of Captain Alexander Montgomery, 1590, we find,—

> ' Hope puts that taste into your heads,
> That boils your *barmy* brain.'

In the ' Midsummer Night's Dream,' the Fairy says to Puck,—

Barm—*continued.*

> Are you not he
> That frights the maidens of the villages,
> *   *   *   *   *   *
> And sometimes makes the drink to bear no *barm ?*'

Burns, in his ' Epistle to James Smith,' uses the word in the sense given to it in the ' Cherry and the Sloe,'—

> Just now I've ta'en the fit o' rhyme,
> My *barmy* noddle's workin' prime.

Barn, ⎱ a true English word ; too long consigned, in modern
Bairn, ⎰ times, to the use of the Scottish writers. It is common to all the northern and eastern shires of England and Scotland, and is used in Sussex, Hampshire, and Dorset. Shakespeare, in the ' Winter's Tale,' has,—

> ' Mercy on us, a *barne !* a very pretty *barne !*'

He also quibbles upon bairns and barns, in ' Much Ado about Nothing,' where Beatrice says,—

> Yea, Light-o'-love into your heels :
> Then, if your husband have stables enough,
> You'll see he shall lack no *barns.*

In the ' Pious Ploughman ' the Saviour is called,

> That blessed *Barne* that boughte us on the rode.

Barrel fever, the headache caused by intemperance in ale or beer.

Barth, a shelter for cattle.

Bat, the preterite of *beat ;* whence probably a bat to *beat* with.

Bate, contention, strife; whence make-bate, and breed-bate— a barrator, or breeder and stirrer-up of strife.

Bateful, quarrelsome, contentious.

Batten, All the Dictionaries define this word as meaning ' to fatten, or grow fat.' Mr. Halliwell explains it, ' to thrive, or grow fat ;' and adds that, ' to *batten* in dung, is to lie upon it and beat it close together.' In Sternberg's ' Folk Lore and Glossary of Northamptonshire,' the local phrase is quoted, ' Them pigs *batten* in the sun.' The word, as used by Shakespeare and Milton, does not seem susceptible of the common interpretation. It rather seems to signify, to feed insufficiently—applied to animals only, or to men and women derisively. Thus Shakespeare, to whom we owe the

Batten—*continued.*

literary preservation of the word, makes Hamlet say to his mother, when upbraiding her with her new marriage, and showing her the pictures of her first and second husbands,—

> Have you eyes;
> Could you on this fair mountain leave to feed,
> And *batten* on this moor?

i.e., she fed well on the rich pastures of the mountain, but starved—fed insufficiently, or *battened*—upon the bare herbage of the moorland. In another passage, Shakespeare says,—

> Go and *batten* on cold bits;

in which the use of the word is more consistent with the idea of insufficiency than with that of repletion.

Milton has the line, '*Battening* our flocks with the fresh dews of night,'—a diet which, without fresh grass, as well as dew, would not add much to their plumpness.

A north-country toast at christening-feasts is,—

> The wife a good church-going, and a *battening* to the bairn.
> *Brockett's Glossary of North-Country Words.*

> One with another they would lie and play,
> And in the deep fog *batten* all the day.—*Drayton.*

Bauch, indifferent; insipid.

> Beauty but bounty's but *bauch.—Allan Ramsay's Scotch Proverbs.*

In Cheshire, a pudding made with milk and flour only, without any sweetening or condiment, is called a *baugh.*

Bavin, } a loose faggot of brushwood, bound with one withe.
Baven, } A faggot, says Mr. Halliwell, is bound with two.

> Shallow jesters and rash *bavin* wits,
> Soon kindled: and soon burned.—*Shakespeare: Henry IV.*

Be, as an augmentative of verbs, is more extensively employed by the uneducated than by the educated classes. Bewildered is stronger than ' wildered;' or, ' I am *beteazed* by the children from morning till night,' than 'teazed.' ' I am sore *besmitten* with ailments,' said a farm-labourer in Kent; a more touching and poetical phrase than if he had said, ' I am greatly afflicted with diseases.'

'The tears berain my cheeks.'—*The Earl of Surrey. Temp. Henry VIII.*

An Irishman, in America, speaking of the incessant talk, or jabber, in Congress, said he was almost *bejabbered* out of his senses by it.

Beasel,
Basel, } that part of a ring in which the jewel is set.

Beck, a brook; used in Sussex, in Cumberland, and in Lincoln-shire; and common throughout Holland and Belgium as a termination to the names of villages through which flow small streams,—as Scarbeck, Etterbeck, &c., derived from the German *Bach*—a brook; and bächlein—a little brook.

> The brooks, the *becks*, the rills, the rivulets.—*Drayton's Polyolbion.*

> The tongue, the trainer, the paunch, the neck,
> When they be well washed with water of the *beck*.
> > *Booke of Hunting,* 1586.

> Little John Jiggy Jog
> > Went to Wigan to woo,
> He came to a *beck*
> And broke his neck;
> > Johnny how dost thou now ?—*Nursery Rhymes of England.*

Bedgang, accouchment, lying in; a purely English word, for which there needs no French synonym.

Bedswerver, adulterer.—*Shakespeare.*

Bed-thrall,
Bedral, } a bedridden person; one confined to bed by sick-
Bedrel, } ness.

> His father—who as *Bedrel* lay
> Before his gate—of his life in despair.—*Douglas: Translation of Virgil.*

Beet, } to help, mend, assist the gradual waste of anything;
Bete, } and more especially to add fuel to the fire.

> I will do sacrifice, and fires *bete.*—*Chaucer: The Knight's Tale.*

> A corowne of a grene oak ceriul
> Upon his head was set full faire and mete;
> Two fires on the altar 'gan he *bete.*—*Idem.*

> Whereby the day was dawning well I knew;
> Bad *bete* the fire and the candell alicht.
> > *Gavin Douglas: Translation of Virgil.*

> Picking up peats to *beet* his ingle.
> > *Allan Ramsay: Epistle to Robert Yarde of Devonshire.*

'Bete my bale;' i.e., feed or aliment my sorrow. In Kent, according to Mr. Halliwell, a *beeter* constantly attends the malt-kilns to *beet* the fire,—i.e., to put fresh straw into the mouth of the kiln.

Belive, immediately; by-and-bye.

> If Triamour be alive,
> Hither will he come *belive.*
> God send us grace to speed.—*Metrical Romance of Sir Triamour.*

Belive—*continued.*

> For God's sake, love, hie we *belive,*
> And look whether Ogier be alive.—*Metrical Romance of Sir Otuel.*

> Ours went again *belive,*
> Into the city of Carohaise.—*Metrical Romance of Merlin, Part II.*

> *Belive* the elder bairns come dropping in.
> *Burns: Cotter's Saturday Night.*

Bellbloom, the hedge convolvolus; in some parts of England this name is given to the daffodil.

Bellen, to swell out; a word preferable to the more modern " belly ;" as the *bellying, bellening,* or bulging sail of a ship with a fair wind.

Bell-penny, money laid up by anyone to pay the expenses of his own funeral; or the ringing of the bell for the same.

Bend, a drink.

> Come, gie's the other *bend,*
> We'll drink their health, however it may end.—*Allan Ramsay.*

Bender, a hard drinker.

> Now lend your lungs, ye *benders* fine,
> Wha ken the benefit of wine.—*Allan Ramsay.*

In America, ' to go on the bender,' is a common expression,—to go on the *spree,* or on a drinking bout.

Bendsome, pliable; yielding.

Benison, a blessing ; a benediction

> And when his leave of me he took,
> The tears they wat mine e'e ;
> I gied him sic a parting look,—
> My *benison* gang wi' thee.—*Ballad of Gilderoy.*

Benothinged, annihilated.

Bent, the open field—where the long grass grows.

Benty, overgrown with long coarse grass.

> ' Lay the *bent* to the bonny broom.'—*Old English Song.*

Besmirch, besmear.

Betterness, something better than goodness; a meaning not to be expressed by the imperfect synonyme, ' amelioration.'

Bevel, out of the level; crooked.

> I may be straight, though they themselves be *bevel.*
> *Shakespeare's Sonnets.*

Bever, a drink between meals.

> ' Thirty meals a day, and ten *bevers,* a small trifle to suffice nature.'
> *Marlowe: Dr. Faustus.*

Bide, abide, remain, dwell.

> For some days she did with him *bide.—John Thomson and the Turk.*

Bield, a shelter. This word occurs in the Morte Arthur, and is pure English, though long since consigned to the exclusive use of Scottish writers.

> Then peeping, half sleeping,
>   Frae forth my rural *bield,*
> It easit me and pleasit me,
>   To see and smell the field.—*Allan Ramsay : The Vision.*

> Every man bows to the tree he gets *bield* from.

> Better a wee bush than nae *bield.*
>   (Adopted by Robert Burns as his motto.)

> There's *bield* beneath an auld man's beard.

> As the wind blows seek your *bield.*
> > *Allan Ramsay's Scotch Proverbs.*

> The sun blinks kindly in the *biel,*
> Where blythe I turn my spinning wheel.
> > *Burns : Bess and her Spinning-wheel.*

> The flaunting flowers our garden yield,
> High sheltering woods and wa's maun shield,
> But thou beneath the random *bield* of clod or stone,
> Adorn the histie (dry) stubble field.—*Burns : To a Daisy.*

Bilk, to defraud; cheat; run away without payment. This word has in modern days degenerated into slang : having in its proper use, been, unnecessarily, superseded by *balk.* Dryden uses the one form, and Pope the other, to express the same meaning.

> What comedy, what farce, can more delight
> Than grinning hunger, and the pleasing sight
> Of your *bilk'd* hopes ?—*Dryden.*

> An unknown country girl was delivered of him under a tree ; where she *bilked* him : he was found by a sexton-priest of the church.—*Spenser : Secret History of the House of Medici,* 1689.

> Is there a variance ? enter but his door,
> *Balked* are the courts ; and contest is no more.—*Pope.*

> *Balked* of his prey, the yelling monster cries.—*Pope.*

Bilk seems worthy of restoration to the honourable place given it by Dryden and Spenser in the foregoing extracts, because it expresses an idea of which balk is not the equivalent. To *balk* a wild animal of its prey, a thief of his plunder, or the courts of justice of a suit, is a rightful act, and

Bilk—*continued.*

the word suggests no wrong or injustice. But to *bilk*, is to defraud another of that which is his due,—as a mother who *bilks* her helpless child of the protection she owes it; or as a passenger, who *bilks* a coach-driver or cabman, by running off without payment of his debt.

Bike, ⎫ a crowd.
Byke, ⎭ a nest of wild bees, or wasps.

> A *byke* of waspes bred in his nose.—*MS. Cott. Calig. (quoted by Halliwell.)*

> As bees bizz out wi' angry fyke *(fret)*,
> When plundering herds assail their *byke.*—*Burns : Tam o' Shanter.*

> I am a bard of no regard,
> Wi' gentle folk and a' that,
> But Homer-like the glowrin' *byke,*
> Frae town to town, I draw that.—*Burns : The Jolly Beggars.*

Bir, force; manliness,—from the Latin *vir.* Used in Scotland, and on the English border; and stated in Grose's Provincial Glossary to be current in Cheshire.

Birl, ⎫ to pour out wine or liquor; whence *purl*; as a stream.
Byrl, ⎭

> Oh, she has *birled* these mery yong men
> With the ale but and the wine,
> Until they were as deadly drunk,
> As any wild wood swine.
>   *Scott's Border Minstrelsy : Ballad of Fause Foodrage.*

> There were three lords *birling* at the wine,
> On the dowie dens o' Yarrow,
> They made a compact them between,
> They would go fecht to-morrow.
>   *Motherwell's Ancient Minstrelsy.*

> On the playne grene was buylded a fountain ; gylte with fine golde ; engrayled with antique workes, the olde god of wine called Baccus, *birling* the wine."—*Hall : Henry VIII.*

Birl, to turn round.

> He keepit close the house and *birled* at the wheel.·—*Hector Macneill.*

Birler, a butler, or pourer out of liquor.

In Cumberland, according to Mr. Halliwell, *birler* signifies a master of the revels at a wedding ; one of his duties being to superintend the refreshments for the party. In some districts, ' birl ' means a rattling noise ; and the becks, or mountain streams, in Westmoreland and Cumberland are said to come *birling* down.

Birs, the thick hairs on the spine of the boar; whence the diminutive (*birstle* or *bristle*).

> The souter (cobbler) gave the sow a kiss—
> 'Humph,' quo' she, 'it's for my *birs*.'—*Northern Proverb.*

Bladd, a leaf; a blade; or a flat piece of anything.

Blae, of a pale blue colour; a sickly blue.

> The morning *blae* and wan.
> > *Douglas : Translation of Virgil.*

> Diseases, heaviness, and spleen,
> With visage dull and *blae*.—*Allan Ramsay : The Fair Assembly.*

Be in dread, oh, sirs! Some of you will stand with a *blae* countenance before the tribunal of God!—*Bruce's Soul's Confirmation.*

Blare, ⎫ to roar; to bellow.
Blore, ⎭ to cry out, as with the brassy sound of a trumpet. A blast of wind is called a *blore* in the northern counties and, in Scotland.

> The terrible trumpets *blare*.—*Barry Cornwell.*

Blashy, thin, poor, weak, small; applied to drink,—as 'blashy beer—very small beer;' or 'blashy tea.'

Blate, cold; insipid; bashful; modest; shy.

> And Eve, without her loving mate,
> Had thought the garden wondrous *blate*.—*Collins's Miscellanies*, 1762.

> Says Lord Mark Kerr, 'ye are na *blate*
> To bring us the news o' yourn ain defeat—
> > Get out o' my sight this morning.'
> > > *Jacobite Ballad : Johnnie Cope.*

A *blate* cat makes a proud mouse.—*Allan Ramsay's Scottish Proverbs.*

> The youngster's artless head o'erflows with joy,
> And *blate* and laithfu' scarce can well behave.
> > *Burns : Cotter's Saturday Night.*

Blaver, the blue corn-flower, or the corn blue-bottle. In the Ballad of the Gardener Lad, Vol. ii. of Buchan's Collection of Ancient Ballads and Songs of the North of Scotland, occurs the passage,—

> Your gloves shall be o' the green clover
> Come lockerin' to your hand
> Well dropped o'er wi' blue *blavers*,
> That grow amang white land.

Blee, colour; appearance; complexion.

> A cloth of silke, she wonde hin,
> That was of swithe (very) fair *ble.—Legend : Cathol.*

> The ladies that were fair and free,
> And one that brighter was of *blee,*
> Weeped sore and handes wrung.—*Morte Arthur.*

> And pale pale grew her rosy cheek,
>   That was so bright of *blee,*
> And she seemed to be as surely dead
>   As any one could be.—*The Gay Goss Hawk, Border Minstrelsy.*

Blether, } to talk nonsense in a loud manner ; to be full of
Blather, } wind as a *bladder.*

This is a common word in Scotland, and on the English border; as well as in Yorkshire and Lincolnshire.

> There's nothing gained by being witty : fame
> Gathers but wind to *blather* up a name.—*Beaumont and Fletcher.*

> When Phœbus' head turns light as cork,
> And Neptune leans upon his fork,
> And limping Vulcan *blethers.—Allan Ramsay : The Vision.*

> But I shall scribble down some *blether,*
> Just clear aff loof (off hand.)—*Burns : Epistle to Lapraik.*

> Then in we go to see the show,
>   On every side they're gatherin',
> Some carrying deals, some chairs and stools,
>   And some are busy *bletherin'*
>   Right loud this day.—*Burns : The Holy Fair.*

> All in this moisty misty clime,
> I backward mused on wasted time,
> How I had spent my youthful prime,
>   And done nae thing,
> But stringing *blethers* up in rhyme,
>   For fools to sing.—*Burns : The Vision.*

Bleary, confused; cloudy; misty.

> Oh give me back my native hills,
> If bleak or *bleary,* grim or gray.—*Cumberland Ballad.*

Blear-eyed, with dull, cloudy eyes.

Blin, }
Blynn, } to stop ; to cease.

> They shall be blenked ere they *blinn.*
>   *Ritson's Ancient Songs and Ballads,* Vol. I. p. 49.

> Withouten *blin,* (without ceasing.)—*Ben Jonson.*

Bloach, } to variegate.
Blotch, } to spot.

"The *bloached* holly."

Blob, } a drop of water or of dew; from whence *blebster* and
Bleb, } *blister*,—drops of water formed under the skin.

Sir Thomas More, in his 'Consolations of the Soul,' says we look on 'this troubled passing stream of the generations of men, to as little purpose almost as idle boys do on dancing *blebs* or bubbles in the water.'

Blob, the northern and Scottish form of the word.

> She kisses the lips o' her bonnie red rose,
> Wet wi' the *blobs* o' dew.
> *Bonnie Lady Ann, by Allan Cunningham, in Cromwell's Remains of Nithsdale and Galloway Song.*

Oh sweet upon the gowan tap the dew *blobs* fa'.—*The Bridal Sark, ib.*

Her e'en the clearest *blob* o' dew outshining.—*Allan Ramsay.*

Blooth, a blossom; useful as a rhyme to youth, truth, &c.

Blonk } a large, powerful horse.
Blonke }

—— his burlike (burly) *blonke.*—*Morte Arthur.*

Blote, to dry in smoke; whence the modern bloater, a Yarmouth bloater.

Blurt, to cry out suddenly, and without premeditation; whence, 'to blurt out a secret.'

Bode, a message.

> Assembled ben his answer for to here,
> And afterwards this knight was *bode* appere.
> *Chaucer : The wife of Bathe's Tale.*

The owle that of death the *bode* bringeth.—*Chaucer.*

Ye may hae was (worse) *bodes* ere Beltan (May Day.)
Allan Ramsay's Scottish Proverbs.

> Tell down your money, said Willie Wallace,
> Tell down your money if it be good,
> I'm sure I have it in my power,
> And never had a better *bode.*
> *William Wallace : Motherwell's Ancient Minstrelsy.*

Bole, the trunk of a tree.

> View well this tree, the queen of all the grove,
> How vast her bole.—*Dryden.*

Bolt, an arrow; from whence, the phrases, *bolt*-upright, straight up as an arrow; and *bolt* on end, perpendicular. The word thunderbolt thus means the arrow, or weapon, that falls to the earth, after being discharged from the bow of the thunder-clouds. The vulgarism, to *bolt*—to run away—is derived from this root,—to go straight off, and out of sight—like an arrow.

> Mincing she was, as is a jolly colt,
> Long as a mast, and upright as a *bolt.—Chaucer: The Miller's Tale.*
> '.Wide!' quoth Bolton, when his *bolt* flew backward.
> *Proverb quoted by Halliwell.*
> Yet marked I where the *bolt* of Cupid fell.—*Shakespeare.*
> 'I have shot my *bolt.*'—*Letter from Mr. E. Horsman, M.P. to the Right Hon. W. E. Gladstone:—Times, May 3rd,* 1861.

Bolter, } a round mass of conglomerate sand is called a *balter* in
Balter, } Northamptonshire. The word is also used as a verb. In Bedfordshire, hasty-pudding is said to be *boltered*, when much of the flour remains in lumps.—*Sternberg's Northamptonshire Glossary.*

The word is used in Shakespeare, when Macbeth speaks of 'blood-*boltered* Banquo.'

In Webster's and Worcester's Dictionary, *bolter* is said to mean *besmear*, and in the latter this passage is quoted as signifying blood-*smeared* Banquo; but *clotted*, or covered with gory lumps, seems to be the real signification.

Bonny, } this word holds a place midway between *pretty* and
Bonnie, } *beautiful*, signifying the possession of more loveliness and grace than the one, and of less dignity and majesty than the other. To say of one that she is a bonnie lass, is a higher compliment than to say that she is a pretty girl, for bonnieness implies health as well as loveliness. The word, though considered Scottish in consequence of its more frequent use by Ramsay, Burns, and the song writers and novelists of Scotland, than by those of England, is as English as Shakespeare and his contemporaries can make it.

> And every little grass
> Broad itself spreadeth;
> Proud that this *bonny* lass,
> Upon it treadeth.— *Drayton's Shepherd's Sirena.*
> So blythe and *bonnie* now the lads and lassies are.
> *Drayton's Polyolbion.*

Bonny—*continued*.

> We say that Shore's wife hath a pretty foot,
> A cherry lip, a *bonny* eye, a passing-pleasing tongue.
>> *Shakspeare: Richard III.*

> As the *bonny* lass passed by,
> She roved at me with glancing eye.
>> *Spenser: Shepherd's Calendar.*

> Broom, broom, the *bonny* broom,
>   Come buy my birchen broom;
> In the wars we've no more room,
>   Buy all my *bonny* broom.—*Beaumont and Fletcher.*

> Bow to the sun, to our queen and the fair one,
>   Come to behold our sports,
> Each *bonny* lass is here counted a rare one.—*John Ford*, 1623.

> The *bonny* broome, the well favoured broome,
>   The broome blows fair on hill,
>> *Poor Corydon: Ballad in the Pepys Collection.*

> There was a lady in the North Country,
>   Lay the bent to the *bonnie* broom,
> And she had lovely daughters three,
>   Fa, la, la, la, la, la, lee.—*Durfy's Pills to purge Melancholy.*

> Oh where is the boatman? my *bonny* lass,
>   Oh where is the boatman? bring him to me;
> To ferry me over the Tyne to my love,
>   And I will remember the boatman and thee.
>> *Song: The Water of Tyne, Newcastle.*

> Who's like my Johnny,
> So leish, so blithe, so *bonny*,
> He's foremost 'mong the many,
> Lads o' coaly Tyne.—*Song: The Keel Row.*

With these examples to prove its English use, it may well be asked why so beautiful and much needed a word, should be considered local, and left to the Scottish song writers?

Boon, a bonus, from 'bon,' good; a day's work given gratuitously to help a man to build his house, or plough his field. *Boon* companions, drank together afterwards; and hence the modern meaning of the adjective, as signifying jovial and merry, as well as good. In Lincolnshire to *boon*, according to Halliwell, means to work at the reparation of the public roads; as in Yorkshire, *boons* are higher rates, and the surveyor a *boon* master.

Bord, } a joke. This word survives in Scottish poetry, and in
Bourd, } the wit and philosophy of ancient proverbs, but has disappeared from English literature; in which, from the

Bord—*continued.*

days of Chaucer to those of Spencer and Shakespeare, it was ever a frequent ornament.

The early author of 'Lay Le Fraine,' commences his poem by observing that lays and songs to be accompanied by the harp, were composed on all sorts of subjects :—

> Some of war and some of woe,
> And some of joy and mirth also,
> And some of treachery and guile,
> Of old adventures that fell erewhile,
> And some of *bourds :* &c.,
> * * * * * *
> But most of love forsooth there be.

> You should not in a strange land,
> Mock, nor yet be over *bourdened* ;
> But if ye will with *bourdings* deck,
> Right clearly then ye should them veil.
> > *Sir Eger, Sir Graham, and Sir Gray Steel.*

> 'Fool !' he said, ' thou *bourdest* grete,
> With my spear I shall thee beat.'
> > *Metrical Romance : The Life of Ipomydon.*

> With sugered words she woo'd and spared no speed,
> But *bourded* him with many a pleasant tale.—*Turberville.*

> They all agreed : so turning all to game
> And pleasant *bord,* they past forth on their way.
> > *Spenser : Faerie Queene.*

> The wizard could no longer bear her *bord,*
> But bursting forth in laughter to her said.—*Idem.*

> Gramercy Borril for the company,
> For all thy jests and all thy merry *bourds.*
> > *Drayton's Pastorals.*

' I'll tell the *bourd,* but nae the body,' *i.e.* the joke, but not the person it was made upon. ' A sooth *bourd* is nae *bourd,*' *i.e.* a true jest is no jest.

Bourd na with Bawtie (the watch dog) lest he bite you.

They that *bourd* with cats may count upon scarts (scratches).

Bouse, to revel, drink, carouse.

Burns, in his paraphrase from Solomon's Proverbs, says :

> Then let us *bouse* and deep carouse,
> With bumpers flowing o'er.

And in Tam o' Shanter :

> While we sit *bousing* at the nappy,
> An' getting fou and unco' happy.

Bouse—*continued.*

> Venison! oh, generous food,
> Drest as though bold Robin Hood,
> Would with his maid Marian,
> Sup and *bouse* from horn and can.
>   *Keats : The Mermaid Tavern.*

Bottle-thrall, a confirmed drunkard, a slave to the bottle.

Bowboy, a scarecrow.

Bower, a lady's chamber.

Bowermaid, a chambermaid.

Brabble, *v.* to quarrel.

Brabble,
Brabblement, } *n.* a quarrel.

This pretty *brabble* will undo us all.—*Shakespeare ; Titus Andronicus.*

Brag, the best, foremost, and most flourishing.

> Your Charlie Cochran was the sprout of an aik,
> Bonnie, and blooming, and straight was its make ;
> The sun took delight to shine for its sake,
> And it will be the *brag* o' the forest yet.
>   *Lady Mary Ann : Border Ballad.*

Braird, the first sprouting of the corn.—*Scottish and Northern.*

Brander, a gridiron.

Brant,
Brent, } steep high, precipitous.   Roger Ascham says :

> The grapes grew on the *brant* rocks ;

and Gawin Douglas in the translation of the Æneid :

> His blythe brow is *brent*.

In the song of John Anderson my Joe, the good wife says to her husband :

> When we were first acquent,
> Your locks were like the raven,
> Your bonnie brow was *brent ;*

a high compliment both to his personal graces and his intellect.

The same phrase occurs in the Ballad of Lady Elspet, (Jamieson's Popular Ballads, vol. ii.)

> How *brent's* your brow my Lady Elspet,
> How gouden yellow is your hair.

In Allan Ramsay's Pastoral on the death of the Countess of Wigton, he says :

Brant—*continued.*
> Her fair *brent* brow, smooth as the unwrinkled deep.

In Yorkshire there is a proverb that 'It is good to set a stout heart to a stiff *brant.*' The same proverb is current in Scotland, in phraseology, encumbered with fewer consonants. 'Set a stout heart to a stey brae.'

> A *brant* hill—as *brant* as the ridge of a house.
> *Ray's North Country Words.*
> The excellent Prince, Thomas Howard Duke of Norfolk, with bowmen of England, slew King James with many a noble Scot, even *brant* against Flodden Hill.—*Ascham's Toxophilus.*

The word *brunt*, in the sense of bearing the 'brunt' of battle, of strife, or of difficulty, has been derived by all the lexicographers, from Johnson to Worcester, from burned or burnt, and *brunt;* and Archbishop Trench says that the *brunt* of the battle is the heat of the battle, where it burns the most fiercely; but *brent, brant,* and *brunt* are all forms of the same word, and in the sense of steep, difficult to surmount, hard of access, *brant* seems the more obvious and more natural derivation.

Brangle, *v.* to dispute, quarrel, derived from be-wrangle. In Lincolnshire, according to Mr. Halliwell, *brangled* means confused, intricate, tangled.

> Here I conceive that flesh and blood will *brangle,*
> And murmuring Reason, with the Almighty wrangle.—*Du Bartas.*

Branglesome, quarrelsome.

Brash, clippings of hedges, or wind-scattered boughs and branches of trees.

Brath, fierce.

Brathly, fiercely.

> Bears to Sir Berill and *brathly* him hittes, [hits him fiercely.]—
> *Morte Arthur.*

Brattle, a confused noise or clatter of feet.

Breme,
Brim, } vigorous, lively, lusty, strong, sharp.
Bryme

> When *brim* blastis of the northern art,
> O'erwhelmit had Neptunus in his cart.
> *Garvin Douglas : Translation of the Æneis.*

Breme—*continued.*

> They are bold and *breme* as bare.—*MS. Harleian, quoted by Halliwell.*
>
> The *breme* winter.—*Spenser.*

In Milton's line—

> By dimpled brook and fountain *brim,*

brim is probably not the rim or edge of the fountain, as commonly supposed, but the adjective *brim*, lively, as distinguished from the gentler epithet of *dimpling*, applied to the brook. The brimming glasses may have originally meant glasses filled with lusty, vigorous, *brim* liquor; and if this supposition be correct, brimful, as now used, is a corruption of rim-full, full up to the rim or edge. But the corruption, if such it be, has been sanctified by Shakespeare, Dryden, Addison, and Pope, and by the general usage of nearly three centuries; and will keep possession in spite of philology, even should philology not happen to be wrong in the derivation.

Breezeblossom, the wild anemone.

Brightsome, shiny.

Brinch, to drink in answer to a pledge.—*Halliwell.*

Brisken, to make brisk,—such verbs as *freshen* and *gladden* are recognized English—but *brisken* has not yet recovered its lost place, and is partially if not entirely deprived by its less elegant synonyme to ' *brisk up.*'

Brust, }
Birst, } the thick hair on a hog's spine; the same as *birs.*

> Roland lough (laughed) and said,
> No is worth the *brust* of a swine.
>
> *Romance of Roland.*

> The bearded buck clamb up the brae,
> With *brissy* bears and brocks (badgers).
>
> *The Cherry and the Sloe,* 1590.

Buck, the breast; whence, 'buck,' a-dandy or one that walks proudly, with his breast stuck out.

Buck, to wash; whence bucket, a washing pail. Falstaff's misadventure in the *buck*-basket, among the dirty linen, keeps the word in remembrance.

Burly, portly; a man rather *round* than tall.

Burdy-bud, } the flower of the burr-thistle, or burdock.
Buddy-bud, }

Bub, any liquor that froths or bubbles. The Ballad of the
'Brewer,' in Durfey's Pills to purge Melancholy, ends by
calling upon the guests to leave off singing and drink
off their *bub.*

Matthew Prior says of one of his heroes :

> He loves cheap port and double *bub,*

or what, in the present day, would be called ' double X.'

In one of the satirical effusions in that excellent collection,
the ' Convivial Songster,' London, 1782, a priest is described
as one who would ' cant out any nonsense,' to please the
' illiterate crowd,' if he could thereby get

> Good victuals and *bub.*

In the same collection occurs the following description of the emotions excited in the breast of a country lass,
by the arrival of a regiment of soldiers in a dull country
town :

> Dear mother, I'm quite transported,
>   To think of the boon comrades ;
> They say we shall all be courted,
>   Wives, widows, and buxom maids.
> Oh, this will be joyful news, girls,
>   We'll dress up our houses with holly,
> We'll broach a tub of humming *bub,*
>   To treat those who come with a rub-a-dub-dub,
> Dear mother ! they'll make us jolly !

' My *grub* and *bub,*' is a phrase often employed by the
peasantry, and an ale-bubber is as common an expression
as a wine-bibber.

One of the finest passages in which the word occurs is in
Spenser—

> Rude Acheron a loathsome lake, to tell,
> That boils and *bubs* with swelth as black as hell ;

Bummel, an idle fellow, a drone.

Burdalane, } the last child surviving in a family ; the lonely
Burdalone, } bird.

> And Newton Gordon, *birdalone,*
>   And Dalgatie both stout and keen,
> And gallant Veitch upon the field,
>   A braver face was never seen.
>   *Minstrelsy of the Scottish Border.*

Burn, brook, or small stream. This word was once common in English poetry, as *bourne*; and survives in the names of such streams and places as Ravensbourne, Holborn, Kilburn, Sittingbourne, Blackburn, &c. A song quoted in King Lear has

> Come o'er the *bourn*, Bessy, to me.

In Drayton's Polyolbion we find:

> The *bourns*, the brooks, the becks, the rills, the rivulets.

In the Fairie Queene:

> My little boat can safely pass this perilous *bourne*.

and in Browne's Pastorals:

> The muttering *bourns* and pretty rills.

In Stow's Annals, under the reign of Henry III. A.D. 1217, he says that ' divers *bournes* suddenly brake out of the hollow places of the earth, and overflowed a great part of the city of Canterbury.'

Bourne also signifies a boundary:

> The undiscovered regions, from whose *bourne*,
> No traveller returns.

It has been supposed, with reason, that the word in this passage was derived from the fact, that in early ages, as is often the case now, streams were the obvious (as they were the natural) boundary lines of landed property.

In the form of *burn* and *burnie*—familiar to all the readers of Scottish poetry and romance—the word has of late years been making its way into English composition, to which it strictly and rightfully belongs. In his Epistle to William Simpson, of Ochiltree, Burns (happily omened name for such a subject) complains of the neglect by poets of the streams and *burnies* of his native country; and prophesies the fame that he will give them by his verse:

> The 'Ilyssus, Tiber, Thames, and Seine,
> Glide sweet in many a tuneful line,
> But Willie, set your foot to mine,
>   And cock your crest;
> We'll gar our streams and *burnies* shine,
>   Up wi' the best.

Burn—*continued.*

The prediction has been verified; and the banks of every stream which he has celebrated have become classic-ground to the fancy and memory of the English-speaking race in two hemispheres.

Busk, to make ready, to dress, to adorn. The Scottish proverb says that ' a bonnie bride is soon *buskit.*'

The lines:

> *Busk* ye! *busk* ye! my bonnie, bonnie bride;
> *Busk* ye! *busk* ye! my winsome marrow,

in William Hamilton's, of Bangour, beautiful ballad of ' The Braes o' Yarrow,' and its constant use in Scottish romantic and legendary poetry, have rendered the word familiar to all readers of taste. It well deserves to be reinstated in the place in English literature to which it formerly belonged. In a MS. in the Harleian library, quoted by Halliwell, we find :

> Bade them *busk* and make them yare,
> All that stiffe were on steed.

Nares, who says the word is Scotch, quotes Fairfax's Translation of Tasso, and thus proves it to be English also :

> The noble Barn with his courage hot,
> And *busked* him boldly to the dreadful fight.

In the Romance of Guy of Warwick, the word occurs :

> The Danishmen *busked* them yare
> Into the battle forth to fare.

It is found also in Sir Triamour :

> When Triamour was whole and sound,
> And well healed of his wound,
> He *busked* him forth to fare.

But, } out of doors and indoors ; the front and back rooms of
Ben, } a cottage. These words, abbreviations of ' be out,' and ' be in,' belong to a once numerous class, of which the poetical phrases, *doff*, or ' do off,' and *don*, or ' do on,' and *dout*, or ' do out,' are the best known remnants. They have the merit of greater comprehensiveness and beauty than their paraphrastic synonymes.

Caller, fresh, cool.   The word fresh seems to have been derived
in all of its various forms in Anglo-Saxon, German, and
French, from the Latin *frigidus*, cold.   The beautiful word
caller, so common in Scotland, comes in the same manner
from cauld or cold.   'The *caller* air,' the fresh air.   '*Caller*
herrings,' fresh herrings; the well known cry of the New-
haven fishwomen in the streets of Edinburgh, and the name
of a very beautiful melody composed by Neil Gow.   The popular song, 'There's nae luck about the house,' which Burns calls
the finest love song in our language, and written originally by
William Julius Mickle, the author of the Lusiad, contains a
stanza, afterwards added by Dr. James Beattie, the author
of the 'Minstrel;' in which the word is beautifully introduced.

> Sae sweet his voice, sae smooth his tongue,
>   His breath's like *caller* air;
> His very foot has music in't,
>   As he goes up the stair.

In Newcastle, according to Brockett's Glossary, '*caller*
herrings,' '*caller* cockles,' and '*caller* ripe grosets' (gooseberries), were formerly common street cries.

Callet, a vulgar, scolding, ill-tempered, unchaste woman; an
ancient word, in common use, though perishing from literature.

> A *callet* of boundless tongue who late hat beath her husband.
> > *Winter's Tale.*
> A beggar in his drink could not have laid such terms upon his *callet*.
> > *Othello.*

Can } to be able.
Canning } being able.
'I can do it, if I like,' said a man who did not fancy a
particular job to which he was set.   'What's the use of *canning*, if you don't work,' was the master's rejoinder.

Canakin } a small can or drinking cup.
Canikin }

> Let the *canikin* clink.—*Old Song.*

Cannie,) a word that has no synonyme in this language, and
Canny,) is common even in the north of England and in Scotland. ' *Canny* Newcastle,' and a ' *canny* Scotchman,' are both provincial phrases. It means wise, prudent, cunning, gentle; Brockett's Glossary affirms it to imply beauty of form as well as of manners and of morals; but in Scotland it has a more extended signification. A *canny* man is a kindly man, but not so overkindly and simple as to be over-reached in business, or otherwise deceived. The word also implies dexterity and ability; as in the proverb : ' They have need of a *canny* cook who have but one egg for their dinner.'

> Bonny lass, *cannie* lass, wilta be mine ?
> Thou'st neither wash dishes, nor sarrup* the swine ;
> Thou sall sit on a cushion and sew up a seam,
> And thou sall eat strawberries, sugar, and cream.
> *Cumberland Courtship : Nursery Rhymes of England.*

Cantie,) cheerful, derived by some from the Latin *cantare* to
Canty,) sing ; a man so cheerful as to sing at his work, or on his way.

Though the word is now used only in Scotland and in the English Border Countries; it occurs in Langtoft's Chronicle, and is more likely derived from the Anglo-Saxon, ' *kanne* ' or ' *can*,' than from *cantare*, and is suggestive of power and ability. A *cantie* man is not only a strong man, but a man who is cheerfully strong.

> I wot she was a *cantie* queen.—*Roy's Wife of Aldivalloch.*

> Contented wi' little, and *cantie* wi' mair.—*Burns.*

> The clashan yill (ale) had made me *canty*,
> I was na' foo but just had plenty.
> *Burns : Death and Dr. Hornbook.*

> Some cannie wee bodie may be me lot,
> And aw'll be *cantie* in thinking o't.
> *Newcastle Song : Quoted in Brockett's North Country Glossary.*

Cark, to be fretfully anxious ; the present participle or adjective ; ' *carking*' conjoined with care, as ' *carking* care,' is used by Milton.

> I *carke*—I care—*je me chagrine.*—*Palsgrave : quoted by Halliwell.*

Carle,) Chaucer has *carle* a hardy country fellow, a word
Carline,) which has been diverted from its original meaning,

* Serve or wait upon.

Carle, Carline—*continued.*

and degenerated into churl, a rude, rough, ill-natured fellow.
'Carle' as distinguished from 'churl,' deserves to be restored
to a place among the honest words of the language ; in the
sense in which Chaucer uses it :—

> The miller was a stout *carle* for the nones,
> Full big he was of braun, and eke of bones :

a fine picture, in which churlishness has no place. The
Germans use the word in its original sense of a fellow or
man, and speak of '*ein guter kerl*,' or '*ein dummer kerl*,' as
the case may be. 'Carline,' the feminine of fellow, is a word
much needed, but which has never yet been naturalized
in English literature. Burns employs it with great effect
when describing what Tam o' Shanter saw in the Dance of
Witches :—

> The piper loud and louder blew,
> The dancers quick and quicker flew,
> They reel'd, they set, they cross'd, they cleekit,
> Till ilka *carline* swat and reekit.

And in his epistle to James Smith,

> That auld capricious *carline* Nature
> Has turned you off, a human creatu
> On her first plan,
> And in her freaks, on every feature
> She's written—MAN.

And again in the Jolly Beggars.

> And next outspoke a rauchle *carline.*

The Northumberland and Scotch Proverb says that 'cats
and *carlines* love to sit in the sun.' And another advises no
man to 'let his hens crow, or the carline wear the breeks.'
'Crooked carlin ! said the cripple to his wife,' is a Scottish
proverb quoted by Allan Ramsay, that conveys the same idea
as the English proverb of the pot that accused the kettle of
being black.

The phrase, 'a drucken carline,' can only be rendered in
English—'a drunken woman,' which is not the exact meaning, for a duchess if she drank, would be a drunken woman,
not a *carline.*

In the north of England and south of Scotland, a *tom*
cat, is popularly known as a '*carle*-cat; a jack-daw,' is also
called a '*carle*-daw.'

Carpe, to argue ; whence the modern carping, argumentation, but in an ill humour.

> For my profit and my health,
> *Carpe* I would with contrition.—*Piers Ploughman.*

Chaffer, to haggle,

Chancely, accidentally.

Chancy, fortunate.

Chang, the humming noise of the conversation of a great number of persons, or the singing of a great number of birds.

> Then doubly sweet the laverock sang,
> Wi' smiling sweets the cowslips sprang,
> And all the grove in gladsome *chang,*
> Their joy confessed.—*John Stagg: Cumberland Ballads.*

Char,) to work by the day. The vulgar saying that 'job is
Char,) jobbed,' was formerly, as we learn from Ray's Proverbs, ' that char is chared, as the good wife said when she hanged her husband.'

> And drew his sworde prively,
> That the childe were not war,
> As he hadde done that *char.*
> *Cursor Mundi MS., Trinity College, Cambridge, quoted by Halliwell.*

Chare, a day's work.

> But e'en a woman and commanded,
> By such poor passions as the maid that milks.
> And does the meanest *chares.*
> *Shakespeare : Anthony and Cleopatra.*

> I have no time up town to roam,
> There is odd *chares* for me to do at home.
> *Praise of Yorkshire Ale,* 1697.

In some parts 'of England the word is pronounced *chores.*

Chares, odd jobs, piece work, day work; whence a ' charewoman.'

Chatsome, full of gossip, chatty.

Chide-ster, a scolding woman, a female chider, a scolder; whence, perhaps, the American word ' *shyster.*'

> Men must enquire (this is mine assent),
> Whade she be wise and sober, or drunkelewe,
> Or proude, or elles otherways a shrewe,
> A *chidester*—or a waster of the food.
> *Chaucer : The Marchant's Tale.*

Chiel, } a knight, a fellow. The word has long disappeared
Childe, } from English literature, though Byron made a gallant
attempt to revive it in Childe Harold.

> Lord Ingram and *chiel* Wyett,
> Were both born in one bower,
> Laid both their hearts in one lady,
> The less was their bonheur.
> *The North Countrie Garland.*

> *Childe* Harold was he hight; but whence his name,
> And lineage long it suits me not to say.—*Byron.*

> Scotland whom never a land surpasses,
> For buirdly *chiels* and clever hizzies.—*Burns.*

Child, } to bear or bring forth a child.
Childe, }

Childing, child-bearing.

> Which the goddess of *childing* is,
> And clepid was by name Isis.
> *Gower MS., quoted by Halliwell.*

Chimble, } to crumble into very small fragments; to gnaw
Chumble, } like a mouse or rat.

Chimbled, } the preterite of chimble and chumble.
Chumbled, }

> Where hips and haws for food suffice,
> That *chumbled* lie about his hole.
> *Clare's Shepherd's Calendar.*

Chirming, the low, melancholy, confused twittering and murmuring of birds, that huddle in the trees before a storm.

> *Chyrme,* or chur as birds do.—*Huloet,* 1552.

> Small birds,[a]
> With *chirming* and with cheping changed their song.
> *Gavin Douglas : Æneis.*

Chit, *v.,* to germinate, whence *chits,* children ; *chitty faced,*
baby faced ; *chitterling,* a very young child, a very new blossom ; *chitling,* a small, early apple ; and *chits,* the first
sprouts of corn from the seed.

Chode, preterite of chide, to reprove, scold, admonish.

Choile, to over-reach.

Chuckie, a hen.

Chuckie stone, a stone about the size of a hen's egg.

Chuff, a a term of contempt or reproach, applied to a fat, avaricious citizen. Thus Shakespeare in the first part of Henry IV., Act II., scene ii.

> Are ye undone? No, ye fat *chuffs*, I would your store were here.

And in the Honest Whore we find,

> Troth, sister, I thought you were married to a very rich *chuff*.

Nash, in Pierce Penniless, 1592, has ' *chuff* headed burgomasters.'

Burns in the 'Author's Earnest Cry and Prayer to the Scotch Representatives in the House of Commons,' speaks of ' a blackguard smuggler,' cheek and jowl, with a ' *chuffy* vintner.'

Clamberscull, strong drink that clambers up to the skull; a *heady* liquor.

Clam, ⎱ *v.* to famish, or starve with hunger. The word starve
Clem, ⎰ originally meant to die; and we still say that a person *starves* or dies with cold; as well as with hunger.

> Hard is the choice when the valiant must eat their arms, or *clem*.
> > *Ben Jonson : Every Man out of Humour.*

> I cannot ̄eat stones and turf. What will he *clem* me and my followers? Ask him, an he will *clem* me.—*Ben Jonson : The Poetaster.*

> My entrails were *clamm'd* with keeping a perpetual fast.
> > *Massinger : The Roman Actor.*

In Lancashire, Yorkshire, and the Eastern Countries, and in the Eastern Counties, the labouring man of independent spirit still uses the expression, and says, ' I would rather *clam* than go into the workhouse.'

Clash, an idle tale, or rumour of the day.

Claw, to flatter, to praise. The Scotch proverb says, ' Claw me, and I'll claw you ;' *i.e.* ' praise and flatter me, and I'll praise and flatter you ;' and not ' scratch me and I'll scratch you ;' as some have mistranslated it : To ' clap and *claw*,' is to caress and fondle, like lovers.

> Sleep when I am drowsy and tend on no man's business; laugh when I am merry, and *claw* no man in his humour.
> > *Shakespeare : Much Ado about Nothing.*

Cleave, to split.

Clove, ⎱ split.
Cleft, ⎰

Cloven, split.

'Cloven' foot, is used as a scriptural phrase; but the words cleft and cloven, are dropping out of the language. 'We split it into two;' instead of 'we clove it into two,' and 'it was split into two;' instead of it 'was cloven into two.'

Cleave, to adhere to.

Clave, adhered.

> Moral vulgarity *cleaved* unto him like an hereditary error.
> > *Felix Holt, the Radical, Vol. I. page* 212.

> The ground *clave* asunder.—*Numbers* xvi. 31.

Clepe, to call or name.

> The compagnie of comfort,
> Men *cleped* it some time.—*Vision of Piers Ploughman.*

> They *clept* us drunkards.—*Shakespeare.*

> To the Gods I *clepe.*—*Shakespeare.*

> The Pope *clepeth* himself servant of the servants of God.
> > *Chaucer : The Persone's Tale.*

> As hounds and greyhounds, mongrels, spaniels, curs,
> Though water-rugs, and demi-wolves are *clep'd*
> All by the name of dogs.—*Macbeth.*

> He *clepeth* a calf, cauf.—*Love's Labour Lost.*

> The miser threw himself as an offal,
> Straight at his foot in base humilitie,
> And *cleped* him liege.—*Spenser's Faerie Queen.*

'Some other shipbuilder may *christen* a new venture after the lost vessel and have better luck.'—*Morning Star,* July 12th, 1866. (Article on the shipwreck of the 'Monarch of the Seas.') If *clepe* cannot be revived, it would be more correct to use the word 'name,' instead of '*christen*' in such a case as this. There may be christened and Christian people on board of a ship, but the ship itself can scarcely be either christened or a Christian.

'The engagement at Custozza, or Villafranca, 'for I know not by what name the battle may be *baptized.*'— *Daily Telegraph,* July 5th, 1866. Here again the word 'clepe' would be appropriate. The phrase, to *baptize* a battle is both incorrect and nonsensical. And if 'clepe' be inadmissible, would not the expression : 'I know not how the battle may be named,' have answered the purpose.

Y-clept.

The only form in which the past participle of 'clepe' is used in modern days, is *y-clept*, applied solely in mock heroics, or in derision; or by people unaccustomed to literary composition, by whom it has been degraded into slang.

Clevel, a grain of corn.

Cleven, the cliffs.

Clip, to embrace, to fondle.

> Oh that I had my lady at this bay,
> To kiss and *clip* me till I run away.—*Shakespeare.*

> Oh let me *clip* ye
> In arms as round as when I woo'd.
> > *Shakespeare: Coriolanus.*

Then embraces his son-in-law; then again worries he his daughter with *clipping* her.—*Shakspeare: Winter's Tale.*

> The lusty vine not jealous of the ivy,
> Because she *clips* the elm.—*Beaumont and Fletcher.*

> Worse than Tantalus is her annoy,
> To *clip* Elysium and lack her joy.
> > *Shakespeare: Venus and Adonis.*

The preterite of 'clip' was formerly 'clap,' to embrace. This is lost as a verb, but survives as a substantive, and sometimes as the infinitive of a verb, with an offensive meaning.

Clointer, to tread heavily.

Clomb, preterite of climb.

> So *clomb* this first grand thief into God's fold.—*Paradise Lost.*

> The moon had *clomb* the highest hill.—*Burns.*

Clout, to patch, to mend;—a patch, a rag; whence dish-clout, a dish-rag.

> And cast on my clothes,
> Y-*clouted* and whole.—*Piers Ploughman.*

Thereon lay a little childe lapped in *cloutes*.—*Pierce Ploughman.*

From the following line in Love's Labour Lost,

> Indeed and must shoot nearer, or he'll ne'er hit the *clout,*

it would appear that a rag—probably a white one—was placed in the middle of a target as a mark.

> *Clout* the auld, the new are dear,
> My Jo. Janet.—*Scotch Song.*

Clout—*continued.*

> As he went for the weel faur'd maid,
>   A beggar bold, I wat met he,
> Was covered in 'a *clouted* cloak.
>   *Willie Wallace, Johnson's Museum.*

> Better a *clout* in, than a hole out.

> An old sack craves muckle *clouting.*

> Money is welcome in the dirtiest *clout.*

> Never find fault with my shoon, unless ye'll pay the *clouter.*
>   *Allan Ramsay's Scotch Proverbs.*

>   I thought he slept ; and put
> My *clouted* brogues from off my feet, whose rudeness
> Answered my steps too loud.—*Shakspeare : Cymbeline.*

Many sentences of one meaning, *clouted* up together.—*Roger Ascham.*

Clouter, a cobbler, in the north of England, and midland counties of Scotland.

Clouterly, clumsily, in a cobbler's manner.

Clump, to walk heavily and awkwardly ; whence clumsy.

Clunch, close grained ; applied to stone or wood ; and metaphorically to the temper or disposition.

Clyte ; this useful word is employed in Scotland to express the confusion of an orator, who for want of a word or an idea, suddenly stops in his speech ; and sits down. When a bird of prey pounces down from the clouds upon a small bird, he is said to ' clyte ' upon it ; and in like manner the lark, when it suddenly ceases its song, and drops like a stone to the ground, ' clytes.' In the Dutch and Flemish languages, that have so many words in common with the English, *kluyt*, from whence the English 'clod,' signifies the green sward ; and hence the word *clyte* may possibly be derived from the action of dropping or falling from a height upon the *clyte,* clod, or grass. ' I could na find words to finish my speech,' said a Glasgow Bailie, ' so I *clyted.*' In Allan Ramsay's poems the word is spelled *cloit.*

> I fairly *cloited,*
> On the cauld eard.
>   *William Hamilton of Gilbertfield, to Allan Ramsay.*

Clyte—*continued.*

In Grose's Provincial Glossary, *clyte* is stated to be a Kentish word for clay or mire.

Clythe, the herb ' burdock,' or burr-thistle.

Cod, a pillow, bag, or cushion. In Scottish phrase a ' down-cod,' signifies a pillow of down.

> Fair *cod* of silke,
> Chalk white as the milke.
>
> *MS., Lincoln, quoted by Halliwell.*

Cod also signifies a bag or receptacle, as in the modern word, peas-cod, the bag in which the peas rest.

Cog, to entice, to swindle, to lie, to cheat, to load dice. Thus the Perian in Love's Labour Lost:—

> Sweet adieu,
> Since you can *cog*, I'll play no more with you.

Richard III. says to Lord Grey :

> Because I cannot flatter and speak fair,
> Smile in men's faces, smooth, deceive and *cog*.

Falstaff is called in like manner a *cogging* knave.

Fox's Book of Martyrs says, ' Lo, here good reader, another manifest example of the unhonest dealing and false *cogging* of those men."

> Quality ! as quality in fashion,
> Drinking, lying, *cogging*, eating, &c., &c.
>
> *Ford : The Sun's Darling.*

> He heard there was a club of cheats,
> Who had contrived a thousand feats ;
> Could change the stock, or *cog* a dye,
> And thus deceive the sharpest eye.
>
> *Swift.*

> When lazy queens have nought to do,
> But study how to *cog* and lie,
> To make debate and mischief too,
> 'Twixt one another secretly.
>
> *Robin Goodfellow : Percy's Reliques.*

Coil, a din ; a confusion. The word *coil* in Hamlet's soliloquy :

> When we have shuffled off this mortal *coil,*

has not this meaning, but apparently refers to the bondage of life ; from coil, a twisted mass of rope.

Coil—*continued.*

> To see them about nothing, keeping such a *coil*.
>> *Sir John Suckling.*

> This bubble shall not henceforth trouble me,
> Here is a *coil* with protestation.
>> *Two Gentlemen of Verona.*

> You mistress, all this *coil* is coy of you.
>> *Midsummer Night's Dream.*

> The wedding being there to-morrow, there is a great *coil* to-night.
>> *Much Ado about Nothing.*

Coost, preterite of cast, to throw.

> And they *coost* kevils them amang,
> Who should to the greenwood gang.
>> *Border Minstrelsy.*

Covine, a deceitful contrivance between two or more persons to get the better of, or injure another; also, to contrive deceitfully.

Crambles, boughs and branches of trees, broken off by the wind.

Creel, from the French *creil*, a wicker or fish basket.

> The boatie rows, the boatie rows,
> The boatie rows fu' weel,
> And muckle luck attend the boat,
> The merlin and the *creel*.
>> *Scotch Song.*

Couth,
Couthie, } kindly, graceful, familiar, affectionate, smooth, agreeable. The common word *un*couth expresses the absence of these qualities, with the addition of strangeness, oddity. Couth originally meant ' known,' and uncouth ' unknown.' From uncouth come the Scottish 'unco,' or very. *Couth*, known, has gradually come to signify familiar, and therefore pleasant.

> My ain *couthie* dame.—*Archibald Mackay's Ingle-side Lilts.*

Coy, quiet.

> Tenes vous *coi.—J'appellerai ma mère.*
> Keep it *coy.—The Evergreen, by Allan Ramsay.*

Cozie, snug, warm, pleasant, more than comfortable.

The French have borrowed the word comfortable from the English; and the English language that borrows from every source might well adopt *cozie*, expressive as it is of an idea, not to be otherwise conveyed, except by a periphrasis.

Craft, a trade, art, business, strength, whence handicraft, craftsman, and crafty. In Anglo-Saxon, crafty, signified skilfully made. Astronomy, was star-craft ; surgery, leech-craft, and a ship skilfully put together was, and is still called a good ' craft.'

Of all *crafts*, says an ancient English proverb, ' an honest man is the master *craft*.' This aphorism recurs in fewer words in Allan Ramsay's Scottish proverbs : ' Honesty is the best *craft ;*' or, in more modern phrase : the best policy.

' Craft and cunning,' originally meant skill and ability. It speaks well for the virtue of our Anglo-Saxon ancestors, that they had so great a paucity of words to express the refinements of wickedness, and to depict the shady side of human nature. It is a pity, however, that increasing civilization has not been able to coin words of its own, to convey the new meanings, that a more artificial state of society renders necessary ; and that the sturdy old words are perverted from their original signification, without any necessity.

Crank, a twist, a turn, a bend ; whence the modern vulgarism ' cranky,' applied to one who has a twist in his intellect ; also a turn of words, as in Milton :

> Quips and *cranks* and wanton wiles.

In Shakespere's Venus and Adonis, we have

> *Cranks* and crosses with a thousand doubles.

Crants, from the German '*kranz ;*' a wreath, a coronal of flowers·

> Yet here she is allowed her virgin *crants*.
> *Shakespeare : Hamlet, act* v. *scene* 2.

Crine, to shrink, or become less by drying up, whence the diminutive crinkle.

Crink, a very small shrunken child.

Crisple, a curl, a lovelock.

Crone, preterite of crine, to shrink, whence *crone*, a diminutive, shrunken old woman.

Croodle, to creep close ; the diminutive of crowd, to fiddle, and signifying the low faint music of birds, as well as the humming of a tune. In Scotland ' a *croodlin* doo,' or dove, is a term of peculiar endearment to a timid child.

Croodle—*continued.*

> There's ae thing keeps my heart right, |
>   Whate'er the world may do,
> A wee thing, mine ain thing,
>   Wi e'en o' sparkling blue
> A wee thing, mine ain thing,
>   A pledge o' love most true,
> A bonnie, bonnie, bonnie, bonnie
>   Wee *croodlin doo.*—*Old Song.*

> Far ben thy dark green plantin' shade,
> The cushat *croodles* amorously.—*Tunnihill.*

Crooken, to crook, to bend.

> Knightes croukett (*crooken*) him to.—*Piers Ploughman.*

Crool, defined in Phillips' World of Words, 1678; as an old word, meaning to *mutter.*

Croon, to hum over a tune to one's self; to try, or prelude a melody.

> The sisters gray, before this day,
> Did *croon* within their cloister.
> > *Allan Ramsay : The Evergreen.*

> Whiles holding fast his guid blue bonnet,
> Whiles *crooning* o'er some auld Scots sonnet.
> > *Burns : Tam o' Shanter.*

> Wi hand on hauch and upward e'e,
> He *croon'd* his gamut, one, two, three.
> > *Burns : The Jolly Beggars.*

Crope, preterite of creep.

Crouse, merry, brisk, lively. A Scotch and Border word; apparently derived from the same source as *carouse.*

Drayton uses it in a somewhat different sense: meaning bold, and excited.

> And now of late Duke Humphrey's old allies,
> Which banished Eleanor's accomplices,
> Attending their revenge grow wondrous *crouse,*
> And threaten death and vengeance to our house.

Dr. Jamieson thinks the word is derived from the Dutch *croes,* or the German *kraus,* crisp, and curly; while Mr. Halliwell thinks it connected with *crus ;* or cross, angry; as in the following passage from *Cursor Mundi, MS., Trinity College, Cambridge*:

> Against him was he kene and *crous,*
> And said, goth out of my Fadir hous.

Crouse—*continued.*

In Scottish poetry the word has invariably a signification of liveliness and jovialty : more suggestive of its French, than of its supposed German and Dutch origin.

Crowd, *n.,* from the Welsh *crwde,* a fiddle, violin.

Crowd, } to play the violin, or other similar instrument ; to
Crood, } sing.

Crowder, a fiddler ; or public singer.

> A lackey that can warble upon a *crowd* a little.—*Ben Jonson.*

> I never heard the old song of Percy and Douglas, that I found not my heart moved more than with a trumpet ; and yet it is but sung by some blind *crowder.*—*Sir Philip Sidney.*

Culver, a pigeon, or dove.

> Like as the *culver* on the bared baugh,
> Sits mourning for the absence of her mate.—*Spenser.*

Culverhouse, a dove-cot.

Culverwort, the herb columbine.

Cumber, an encumbrance.

Cumberworld, a man or woman so old as to be helpless ; or a person so idle, dissolute, or deformed as to be a burthen to his friends and to society.

Cumberground, anything utterly worthless and in people's way, something that ought to be destroyed or buried out of sight.

Cushat, the wood-pigeon.

Dab, dexterous, clever.

Dabster, a proficient.

Daff, to befool or make game of; whence dafft, or *daft*, foolish, or crazy; still current in Scotland and the English border counties.

Dag, } a hanging shred, or rag; *daglet*, an icicle; *daggle*, to
Dagge, } trail one's rags on the ground or in the mire. The sharp projecting stump of a tree or branch, is in Dorsetshire and Devonshire called a *dag ;* and in Kent, *dag wool* means the shreds of wool, torn by thorns, brushwood, or hedges from the backs of the sheep.

Daggled, wet.

Daggly, showery.

Bedaggled, wet, wetted.

> Good morrow to the day so fare,
> Good morrow, sir, to you,
> Good morrow to my own brown hair,
> *Bedaggled* with the dew.—*The Mad Maid's Song.*

Daggle-tail, } a slovenly woman, whose skirts draggle in the
Draggle-tail, } wet.

Damerel, } an effeminate man, over-fond of the society of
Dammerel, } women, and disinclined to that of his own sex.

Darg. Upon the principle that one word which expresses a meaning not otherwise to be conveyed except in two or more, *darg*, a day's work, ought to be reinstated in the language with all the honour to which it is entitled. The most recent dictionaries pass it over, and both Dr. Trench and Dean Hoare in their interesting treatises upon ancient English Words, omit all mention of it. Worcester's Dictionary (1860), cites and mis-spells the word, as *dargue*, and describes it, on the authority of the Farmer's Encyclopædia, to mean the quantity of peat one man can cut, and two can wheel in one day; but the true meaning is a day's work, whether at peat-cutting, or any other occupation. Mr. Halliwell gives the Cumberland pronunciation of the word as darrack. 'I'll do my *darg* before I arg,' (i.e., argue), is a proverb current in the eastern counties, and one much to be commended. Another well known on both sides of the Border, tells us truly 'that the man never did a good *darg* who went grumbling about it;' while a third says 'You will spoil the *darg*, if you stop the plough to slay a mouse.'

Luath, the poor man's dog in Burns' poem, tells his friend Cesar, that his master has himself, his wife, and a 'smytrie o' wee duddie weans,' (i.e., a host of little ragged children,) to keep out of nothing, but his 'hand-*darg*,' or the day's work of his hands. And the Auld Farmer in his New Year's salutation to his auld mare Maggie, says to her:

> Mony a sair *darg* we twa hae wrought,
> An' wi' the weary world fought.

Dash, a knot, a bow in a ribbon; whence *chin-bow-dash*, a cravat under the chin; and berdash, or beard-dash, the knot or cravat tied under the beard. *Dashing,* in the sense of gay and lively, and adorned with finery, is perhaps from the same root; 'a *dashing* girl;' 'a *dashing* white serjeant.'

Daunch, fastidious, dainty, overnice, squeamish.

Daunt, } to subdue, tame, or terrify; hence the ancient word
Daunton, } 'horse-daunter,' a man whose business it was to break or tame horses.

> And though his subtile wittes,
> He *daunted* down.—*Piers Ploughman.*

> To *daunt* thy heart.—*Chaucer: Romance of the Rose.*

> If a man will not *daunt* sensualitie when he may, therefore is he worthy to have shame.—*Chaucer: The Purser's Tale.*

Dauntless, and undaunted, derived from this root, are used by the best writers and speakers. In Scotland the verb is current under the form of daunton:

> To *daunton* me, to *daunton* me,
> And me king Charles's eldest son.—*Jacobite Ballad.*

Daw-cock, a Jackdaw.

Dawks, a woman who wears very fine clothes, but puts them on slovenly, so that they do not become her.

Dave, to thaw.

Daver, to droop.

Daysmath, a day's mowing.

Daze,
Daize, } to stupefy, whence dazzle, or blind the eyes with
Daise, } excess of light; to benumb, to congeal with cold.

> For in good faith thy visage is full pale,
> Thine eyes *dasen*, soothly as me thinketh.
> *Chaucer: The Maniciple's Prologue.*

> My *daisit* held,
> I raised up half in one lethargie.—*Police of Honour.*

> Gin he likes drink 'twad alter soon the case,
> It son wad gar his love to me turn cauld,
> And mak him *dazed* and doited ere half auld.—*Shirref.*

Deal, } from the German *Theil*, a portion. A great deal is
Dealth, } still a common phrase. The opposite, ' a small deal,'
has dropped out of use.

> All the ground that they had, a man might have bought with a small
> *deal* of money.—*Roger Ascham, quoted by Nares.*

> Where Fortune has bestowed her largest *dealth.*—*Nares.*

Dearworth, precious.—*Chaucer.*

Deave, to deafen, stun, or perplex one with much noise.

> The jargon of the jangling jays,
> The croaking craws and kackling kayes,
> They *deaved* me with their din.—*The Cherry and the Sloe*, 1590.

> Last May a braw wooer came down the lang glen,
> And sair wi' his love he did *deave* me.—*Burns.*

> She has an e'e, she has but ane,
>   The cat has two the very colour,
> Five rusty teeth, forbye a stump,
>   A clapper tongue wad *deave* a miller.
> *Burns: Sic a Wife as Willie had.*

> If mair they *deave* us with their din,
> Of patronage intrusion.—*Burns : The Ordination.*

A north country proverb says: 'I would not be *deaved*
with your cackling for all your eggs.'

Deft, dexterous, neat, clever, handy.

> He said I were a *deft* lass.—*Brown's Northern Lass.*

> A laughter never left,
> Shook all the blessed deities, to see the lame so *deft,*
> At that cup service.—*Chapman's Homer.*

> A clear nymph, from Shefford sallying on,
> Comes *deftly* dancing.—*Drayton's Polyolbion.*

> They dance*deftly*, and sing sweet.
> *Spenser : Shepherd's Calendar.*

Deftster, one who is deft, a proficient in his art or craft ; corrupted into *dabster.*

Delightsome, Delightful.

> Then deck them with thy loose *delightsome* breath,
> And on thy wings bring delicate perfumes.
> > *Peele.*
>
> Laughed *delightsomely.*
> > *Chapman's Homer.*

Delve,
Dolve, } to dig, to bury. This word is still in common use
Dolven, among the peasantry; but the past preterite and the participle, have long since disappeared.

> When Adam *delved,* and Eve span,
> Who was then the gentleman?

was a distich popular during Wat Tyler's rebellion; and written by John Ball, the priest; hanged and beheaded at St. Albans.

In the Romance of Merlin, we find the past participle *dolven.*

> All *quick* he should *dolven* be.

Dene,
Den, } a woody valley of small extent; such as Deepdene, near Dorking; Hawthornden, near Edinburgh, the seat of the poet Drummond; and many other places of less note in various parts of this island.

> The dowie *dens* of Yarrow.

Dere, to injure.

> Shall never devil him *dere.—Piers Ploughman.*
> No dint shall him *dere.—Ibid.*
> May no death him *dere.—Ibid.*

Derne,
Dernely, } secret.
secretly.

A word in use among the English before their language was diluted by unnecessary admixture from the French and Latin; and still current in the northern counties.

> Her eggs fall *derne,*
> In mareys and moores.—*Piers Ploughman.*

Derne, eager, earnest, sharp.

> By many a *derne* and painful perch.—*Pericles.*
>
> By *derne* love of the dear loving lord.
> > *Spiritual Sonnets,* 1595.

Dew-cup,
Dew-drink, } the first allowance of beer to harvest labourers.

Dight, to prepare, dress, get ready.

> The lady looked out of her pavilion,
> And saw him *dight* the venison.
>> *Metrical Romance: The Life of Ipomydon.*

> The lady lay in a high tower,
> And saw between them all the stour;
> But she wist na which for her did fight,
> For they in like weed were *dight*.   *Ibid.*

> Soon was the lady *dight*
> In arms, as if it were a knight,
> He gave her spear and shield.
>> *Metrical Romance of Sir Isumbras.*

> Against even the king did *dight*,
> A bate for that gentle knight,
> That was of herbes good,
> Sir Eglamour therein lay,
> Till it was light of day.—*Romance of Sir Eglamour.*

> Then forth the stranger knight he came,
>   In his black armour *dight*;
> The lady sighed a gentle sigh,
>   That this were my true knight!
>> *Sir Caulyne : Percy's Reliques.*

> Come, Colin, *dight* your cheeks and banish care;
> Our lady's happy.—*Allan Ramsay: On the Death of the Countess of Wigton.*

> The clouds in thousand liveries *dight*.—*Milton's L'Allegro.*

> *Dight* your bonny moŭ!—*Burns.*

> Let me rax (reach) up to *dight* that tear,
> And go wi' me and be my dear.—*Burns : The Jolly Beggars.*

Dill, the aromatic plant, *Anethum gradeolens.*

Dill-water, an anodyne.

Dimmen, to grow dark or dim.

Dimmet, }
Dimming, } the twilight.

Dimpse, the dimming of the daylight.

Ding, } overturn, beat, knock down.
Dang, } preterite of ding.
Dung, } past participle of ding.

> That wolde defend me the doore.
> *Dyng* I never so late.—*Piers Ploughman.*
> But *Do Well* shall *dyngen* him adown.—*Ibid.*

Ding—*continued.*

> His head he struck, his hands he wrang,
> And each hand on another *dang.* — *Romance of Sir Eger, Sir*
> *Grahame, and his Gray Steel.*

> This stone wall I shall down *ding.*
> *MS. Cantab., quoted by Halliwell.*

> Now let us sing our cares to *ding,*
> And make a gladsome sound.
> *Advice to be Liberal and Blythe ; The Evergreen, edited*
> *by Allan Ramsay.*

> Facts are chiels that winna *ding.—Burns.*

> Jenny *dang* the weaver.—*Sir Alex. Boswell.*

> He's sairest *dung* that's paid wi' his own wand.

> Its a sair *dung* bairn that may na greet.

> Ye may drive the devil into a wife, but ye'll no *ding* him out
> of her.—*Allan Ramsay.*

'To *ding* it into' a child, means in Shropshire, says Mr.
Halliwell, to teach it; i.e., to *beat* instruction into it.

And in Shropshire as well as in the north, according to
Mr. Halliwell, ' dung,' is a word still current, meaning
beaten, or overcome.

Dung is a common word among the English working
classes, to signify a man who consents to work for a master,
when his fellows are out on strike; he is one who is *dung,*
i.e., subdued, beaten down, or conquered by his employer.

' Dang it, Bill, don't say so,' is, according to Mr. Sternberg, a contraction of ' God hang it ;' but is more probably
derived from ' ding it,' or ' dang it,' i.e., knock it down.

> The goat gives a good milking but *dings* it down with her feet.
> *Ramsay's Scotch Proverb.*

> Let one devil *ding* another.—*Northern Proverb.*

> But alas ! my ain wand *dings* me now.
> *Ballad of the Marchioness of Douglas.*

> The carline she was stark and sture,
> She off the hinges *dang* the door.
> *Ballad of Cospatrick, Motherwell's Collection.*

The common phrase, ' *ding* it into one's ears,' i.e., *beat* it
into one's ears by incessant repetition, is the only form in

Ding—*continued.*

which this useful word has held its place to the present day in England and America.

In the common phrase ' *ding, dong,* bell,' the word survives, with a variation of the preterite, dong, instead of dang.

Dingthrift, a prodigal; i.e., a person who *dings* or strikes at and beats down the thrift, or savings of his ancestors.

Dirl, to vibrate and shake from the effects of a heavy blow, or of a loud noise. In Yorkshire, according to Mr. Halliwell, *dirl* means to move briskly; and a *dirler* is an active person. In Scottish poetry the word is highly expressive. Thus, in Death and Dr. Hornbook, when Death complains that he threw a dart that ought to have killed a man; and with less than which he had slain hundreds; Hornbook had so fortified the part; that the arrow point played *dirl* upon the bone; and was so blunt afterwards that he could not have pierced a cabbage stalk with it.

And in Tam o' Shanter the devil plays the bag-pipes so loudly that ' the roof and rafters a' did *dirl.*'

> The raptures *dirl* through every part.
> *John Staggs : The Blind Bard of Cumberland.*

Dither, to shake, to tremble.

Dodder, to tremble in the wind, to nod and shake, as in palsy or decrepitude.

In some parts of England the word is pronounced *ditter.* ' Totter,' is evidently the same word, but tottering suggests the idea of falling to pieces; as in Pope's line:

> Troy's torrents *totter* on the rocking plain.

Whereas, dodder, as applied to trembling grass; and an old man shaking with palsy, or to the mast of a vessel as in the following lines, suggests bending without breaking.

> Rocked by the blast and cabined in the storm,
> The sailor hugs them to the *doddering* mast,
> Of shipwreck negligence, while thou art kind.
> *Thompson's Seasons.*

> There vexit, perplexit,
> I leant me down to weep,
> In brief there, with grief there,
> I *doddered* owre in sleep.—*Allan Ramsay : The Vision.*

Dodder-grass, quaking grass, that trembles in the wind.

Dodderil or **Dotteril**, a very old tree; one that has lost its head, and shakes to every storm.

Doff, do off.

> *Doff* that lion's hide,
> And hang a calf-skin, a recreant limb.—*Shakespeare.*

Doit, to stupefy.

Doited, stupid.

> Thou (drink) clears the head o' *doited* lear.—*Burns : Scotch Drink.*

Dole, preterite of *deal.*

> He *dole* it out.

Dole, (substantive), a lot.

> Happy may be his *dole.*

Doly, mournful, melancholy, doleful.

Don, to do on.

Dorty, conceited, proud.

Dout, to do out, or extinguish.

> I have a speech of fire that fain would blaze,
> But that this folly *douts* it.—*Shakespeare : Hamlet.*

Dout the glim : i.e., extinguish the light, nautical phrase.

Douter, an extinguisher.

> He's *douted*, a vulgarism, for he is dead, done for, extinguished.—*Halliwell.*

Dow, to be able, to thrive, to prosper. 'A mispronunciation as well as a misconception of this word, which has never attained to English literary honours, though current among the rural population in most parts of England and throughout Scotland, has produced the common salutation by which an Englishman is known all over the world:

'How do you *do* ?'

The phrase means how do you *dow ?* i.e., how is your power, strength, or ability ? Are you strong ? From this root comes *dought*, the power of doing anything, used in the Romance of Sir Tristem, and other old ballads; and *doughty*, powerful, puissant, mighty, brave, valiant.

Dow—*continued.*

> Long maist thou live an thrive and *dow !*

writes William Hamilton, of Gilbertfield, to his friend Allan Ramsay.

Grose quotes a Northumbrian saying, applied to a man who is long ill and does not mend, 'he neither dies nor *dows.*'

Burns used the word frequently, and with much greater force and beauty than its quasi synonyme, *can.* Thus, in a noble dedication to Gavin Hamilton, he says of himself:

> When I *dow*na yoke a naig,
> The Lord be thankit, I can beg.

Of Gavin Hamilton himself, he says:

> He *downa* see a poor man want.

In his second epistle to Lapraik, he says, though fortune that has so often played him tricks, should reduce him to beggary, and grey hair he 'll still keep up his heart:

> I'll laugh and sing and shake my leg,
> As lang's I *dow.*

And in a phrase that has become proverbial, he asserts the dignity of facts:

> 'Tis very true my sovereign king,
> My skill may weel be doubted,
> But facts are chiels that winna ding,
> And *downa* be disputed.

In this passage the *downa* is infinitely more suggestive of stubbornness and unyieldingness than *canna* would have been.

> Do as well as you *dow;* i.e., do as well as you can.
> *Cumberland Proverb.*

Downcome, a stroke of adversity.

Dowff, dispirited, weary, dejected.

Dowie, forlorn, weary, worn out.

> Sore and long may their sorrow last,
> Binnorie, oh Binnorie,
> That wrought them sic a *dowie* cast,
> By the bonnie mill dams o' Binnorie.
> *Minstrelsy of the Scottish Border.*

Dowie—*continued.*

> Sir, I am standing here she says,
> This *dowie* death to die,
> One kiss o' your comelie mouth,
> I'm sure would comfort me.—*Motherwell's Scottish Ballads.*

> Stay at home, my lord, she said
> For that will breed much sorrow,
> For my true brethren will them slay,
> On the *dowie* dens o' Yarrow.
> 　　　　*Minstrelsy of the Scottish Border.*

> The hardest heart would hae blew to hear,
> It moaned wi' sie a *dowie* cheer.
> 　　　　*Minstrelsy of the Scottish Border.*

Drab, to follow drabs, or loose women of the lowest class.

> Drinking, fencing, swearing, quarrelling,
> *Drabbing*, you may go.—*Shakespeare: Hamlet.*

> The miserable rogue must steal no more, nor drink nor *drab.*
> 　　　　*Massenger : Renegade.*

Drabble, dirty people, drabs, scullions.

> Rabble and *drabble.*

One is said to *drabble* his clothes, who slobbers his vest or other attire in eating.—*Jamieson's Dictionary.*

Drad, preterite of dread.

> But what I *drad* did me, poor wretch, betide
> 　　　　*Robert Greene : Mamillia,* 1593.

> In his haubeck Guy him clad,
> He *drad* no stroke while he it had.—*Guy of Warwick.*

Dree, to suffer, to endure.

> Another dule ye *dree.*—*Percy's Reliques.*

> Pride in a poor man's breast has muckle to *dree.*
> 　　　　*Northern Proverb.*

Droil, } *n.* a drudge, drudgery.
Droil, } *v.* to drudge.

> Then I begin to rave at my star's bitterness,
> To see how many muckhills placed above me,
> Peasants and *droils.*
> 　　　　*Beaumont and Fletcher.*

> 'Tis I do all the *droil,* the dirt work.
> 　　　　*Shirley : Gentleman of Venice.*

> Oh who would *droil,*
> Or delve in such a soil,
> Where gain's uncertain, and the pain the more ?
> 　　　　*Quarles' Emblems.*

Droil—*continued.*

> Let such vile vassals, born to base vocation,
> Drudge in the world and for their living *droil,*
> Which have no wit to live withouten toil.
>
> *Spenser : Fairie Queen.*

Left the dull and *droiling* carcase to plod on in the old road and drudging trade of controversy.—*Milton : Of Reform.*

Drouk,
Drook, } to soak, or wet.

Droukit,
Drookit, } soaked.

> My *drookit* sark sleeve as ye ken.—*Robert Burns.*

Drouth, thirst, or dryness.

Drouthy, thirsty, or dry.

These words are rarely employed in English literature, or met with in conversation, but *drowth* is found in Carew's poems.

> Now noise prevails and he is taxed for *drowth*
> Of wit.

In Hudibras Redivivus, we find :

> So that I now began to think,
> Being *drouthy* on a little drink.

And in Granger's Sugar Cane :

> Then comes the feverish fiend with fiery eyes,
> Whom *drouth*, convulsions and death surround.

It is evidently derived from the same root as the modern *drought* ; formerly, says Johnson, written *drouth,* and in still older time *drythe.*

An old proverb says :

> Drink and *drouth*, and *drouth* and drink do not always come together.

Another proverb puts into English the Latin, ' in vino veritas.' ' He speaks in his drink, what he thought in his *drouth ;*' while a third aphorism thinks it hard that a neighbour should ' speak of a man's drinking, without giving a thought about his *drouth.*'

In the old Scotch song of ' My Kimmer and I,' the gudeman says :

Drouthy—*continued.*

> The well o' life is dribbling dry,
> And *drouthie, drouthie*'s my kimmer and I.

Burns in Tam o' Shanter uses the expression twice:

> When Chapman Willies leave the street
> And *drouthy* neighbours, neighbours meet.

> *   *   *   *   *   *

> And at his elbow souter Johny,
> His ancient, trusty, *drouthy* crony.

Shakespeare in Pericles has:

> The blither for their *drouth.*

Drowse, to slumber, or to be sleepy. ' The old man *drowses* by the fire.' The word survives in the adjective *drowsy*, and the substantive *drowsiness.*

> All their shape,
> Spangled with eyes more numerous than those
> Of Argus, and more wakeful than to *drowse.*
> > *Milton.*

> There gentle sleep
> First found me, and with soft oppression seized
> My *drowsed* sense.
> > *Paradise Lost.*

Drossel, }
Drazel, } a dirty girl or woman; a draggle-tailed slut.

Drumly, *a.* In the South-western shires of England *droum* signifies *mud.* In the North of England and in Scotland, this root is not found as a substantive, but the adjective *drumly*, meaning thick or muddy, is common both in literature and conversation.

Cesar says to Luath in Burn's 'Twa Dogs;' that the rich man drinks

> —— *drumly* German water,
> To make himself look fair and fatter.

And in one of his best known songs, the poet prays for clear streams in his native district:

> Ye banks and braes and streams around
> The Castle o' Montgomery;
> Green be your woods and fair your flowers,
> Your waters never *drumly.*

This word is much wanted in English literature, and is far more poetical than either of its synonymes *turbid* or

Drumly—*continued.*

muddy. It is used with fine effect in the ballad of the
' Demon Lover,' communicated to Sir Walter Scott's ' Minstrelsy of the Scottish Border,' by his friend and amanu-
ensis, William Laidlaw : The Demon's eye in his anger, no
longer clear as before, grows dark :

> They had na sailed a league, a league,
> A league, but barely three,
> When dismal grew his countenance,
> And *drumlie* grew his e'e.

No other word in the language could so admirably convey
the meaning.   Allan Ramsay uses it with equal power and
beauty in the following passage, descriptive of a time of
plague.

> When blue diseases fill the *drumly* air.
> > *Masque on the Nuptials of the Duke of Hamilton.*
>
> Draw me some water out of this spring,
> Madam, it is all foul, it is all *drumly*, black, muddy !
> > *French and English Grammar,* 1623.
>
> Oh, boatman, haste, put off your boat !
> Put off your boat for golden money,
> I cross the *drumlie* stream to-night,
> Or never more I meet my honey.
> > *Minstrelsy of the Scottish Border.*

Drumble, to go about any thing in a confused and awkward
manner, as if not understanding, or heeding what is to be
done.

> What, John ! Robert ! John ! So take up these clothes here quickly !
> Where's the cowl staff?   Look—how you *drumble* !
> > *Merry Wives of Windsor.*

Drunk-wort, tobacco ; or the intoxicating herb.

Drury, gallantry, courtship.

Dub, a puddle, a goose or a duck pond ; a dirty pool ; a common provincial word in England and Scotland.

> The young men knew the country well,
> So soon where he would be,
> And they have ta'en another way,
> Was nearer by miles three,
> They rudely ran with all their might,
> Spared neither *dub* nor mire.
> > *Robin Hood and the Beggar.   Gutch's Collection.*

Dub—*continued.*

> Through dirt and *dub* for life I'll paddle.
>> *The Inventory, by Burns.*

> Give me a spark o' Nature's fire,
> That's a' the learning I desire,
> Then though I drudge through *dub* and mire,
>> At plough or cart,
> My muse though homely in attire,
>> May touch the heart.
>> *Burns : Epistle to Lapraik.*

> Standing *dubs* gather dirt.

> There never was a good town but there was a *dub* at the end of it.
>> *Ramsay's Scotch Proverbs.*

The Goose *Dubs* is the name of a street in Glasgow.

Dud, a rag.

Duddy, a little rag.

Duds, old clothes.

Duddle, to tatter.

Duddy, ragged.

Dudman, a rag man, or a man of rags ; i.e., a scarecrow made of old garments, set up in a garden or field to scare the birds.

From this ancient English word, it is suggested by Nares in his Glossary, that the name of the *Duddery* was formerly given to one of the booths in Stourbridge Fair near Cambridge, where old clothes were sold, as mentioned in Defoe's Tour of Great Britain. In the *Newest Academy of Compliments* occurs the passage.

> Come off with your *duds*, and so pack away,
> And likewise your ribbons, your gloves, and your hair,
> For naked you came, and out you go bare.

Johnson recognizes the word *dud* signifying clothes as used in the West of England, but neither it, nor any of its derivations have found a place in Richardson. In Webster, *dud* is said to be a vulgar word, signifying an old garment. But if Webster had studied Scottish poetry from the days of James I., a contemporary of Chaucer, to those of Burns, he might have found reason to qualify his verdict as to its vulgarity ; and to admit its vigor and usefulness. In the

Dudman—*continued.*

joyous ballad : ' We'll gang nae mair a roving,' attributed
to the Royal author of the ' King's Quair,' the stanza descriptive of the action, by which the king, after his successful wooing of the farmer's daughter, throws off his
disguise, introduces the word with much effect :—

> Then he took out his little knife,
> Let a' his *duddies* fa'
> And he was the brawest gentlemen
> That stood among them a'.

And in Tam o' Shanter, the Witches in Alloway Kirk, in
order to dance with the less restraint, cast off ' their *duddies*
to the wark.'

Dudgeon, the box-wood handle of a knife or dagger.   To take
a thing ' in dudgeon,' meant, to take a thing so angrily, as
to be impelled to touch one's weapon, whether it were sword
or dagger.

> I see thee still,
> And on thy blade and *dudgeon* gouts of blood.
> > *Macbeth.*

Dule, ⎫ grief, sorrow, lamentation.   This word apparently
Doole, ⎭ derived from the French *deuil,* has been to a great
extent superseded by its synonyme *dole,* derived directly
from the Latin ; but is still current in this form in the English Border counties and, in Scotland : but dule is worthy of
revival, if it were only to avoid identity of orthography,
with a word of totally different origin and meaning ; meaning a lot, share, division or portion.   Chaucer writes the
word ' dole,' but the Earl of Surrey in his translation of
Virgil, and Spenser in the *Faerie Queene* have *doole* and
dooleful.

> Time of thy *doole,* thy spouse now dead, I grant,
> None might thee move.—*Surrey.*

> Now twenty days (by which the sons of men,
> Divide their works) have past through heaven sheen,
> Since I was brought into this *dooleful* den.
> > *Spenser.*

In its forms of dulsome, dulesome, and dolesome, the word
is current in most parts of England.

Dumble, very stupid.

Dump, to throw down a heavy weight. To unload, to shoot rubbish.

Dumping-ground, a place where rubbish may be shot or ' dumped.' This phrase is common in America.

Dumps,
Dumpish, } melancholy.

> As one in doleful *dumps.—Battle of Chevy Chase.*
>
> Mr. Fearing the pilgrim was *dumpish* at the House Beautiful.
> *Pilgrim's Progress.*

Dunt, a hard blow.

> Let now stand *dunt* for *dunt.*
> *Metrical Romance of Sir Otuel.*
>
> I have a wife o' my ain ;
> I'll take *dunts* frae naebody.
> *Burns.*
>
> Why draw the dagger when a *dunt* will do the business ?
> *Allan Ramsay's Scotch Proverbs.*

Dunt, preterite of *dint,* to deal so strong a blow as to leave an impression on the thing struck, whence *dunt,* a deep mark.

Durst, preterite of dare. ' I told him he *dare* not do it ;' instead of ' he *durst* not do it ;' is a common error both in print and conversation.

Dare was originally *durre* (see ' Dictionary of the oldest words in the English Language,' by Herbert Coleridge. London, J. C. Hotten, 1862).

Specimens of the confusion too common in the use of the verb *dare,* its preterite *durst,* and its past participle *dared,* will be found in the following quotation :—

> Thus we find that a meeting was held in the park after all on the Monday evening respecting which the now celebrated ' misunderstanding' prevailed ; and the Government which dare [durst] not consent to its being held dared [durst] not prevent it. We applaud their caution. We think them wise in allowing the people quietly to establish by use a right which, once so established, no court of law will ever disturb ; but no one can feel anything but contempt for the Government which meanly attempts to gain a cheap reputation for firmness by fulminations which it dare [dares] not carry out, and by prohibiting meetings which it dare [dares] not prevent and cannot punish.—*Morning Star,* July 31, 1866. On the Hyde Park Riots.
>
> Neither her maidens nor the priest *dare* speak to her for half an hour.—*Hereward the Wake, by the Rev. C. Kingsley,* vol. i. p. 45.

Dwale, the Deadly Nightshade; a sleeping potion. In heraldry, a black colour.

> For well I know by thy tale,
> That thou hast dronken of the *dwale.*
>
> *Gower: MS. Soc. Antiq.*

> 'Arise!' quoth she, 'what have you drunken *dwale?*
> Why sleep you?'
>
> *Chaucer: The Court of Love.*

> Needeth him no *dwale,*
> This miller hath so wisely bibbed ale,
> That as an horse he snorteth in his sleep.
>
> *Chaucer: The Reeve's Tale.*

'He's in a *dwale,*' a dead sleep; a common expression in the North of England.

Dwine, to pine, or waste away slowly; from whence the diminutive, *dwindle.*

> Dethe on me hath sette his mark,
> As grass in meadows I dry and *dwine.*
>
> *MS. Cantab., quoted by Halliwell.*

> Thus *dwineth* he till he be dead,
> In minding of his own estate.
>
> *Gower: MS. Soc. Antiq.*

> All woxen was her body unveiled,
> And dry and *dwined* all for eild.
>
> *Chaucer: Romance of the Rose.*

> Kindly he'd laugh when thus he saw me *dwine,*
> And talk of happiness like a divine.
>
> *Allan Ramsay: On the Death of Addison.*

> Bacchus hates repining,
> Venus loves nae *dwining.*
>
> *The Toast, Allan Ramsay.*

In Kent a weakly child is called a *dwine* or a *dwindle.*

Ear, to plough, from the Sanscrit 'ar;' whence Ear-eth, the Earth, that which can be ploughed.

Ear-fest, harvest, the festival of earing, or gathering the crops.

Earth-fast, } firm in the earth, and difficult to be removed;
Yird-fast, } of the same derivation as steadfast, fast in stead, or place, and metaphorically, to a purpose. Thus a tree that rocks to and fro in the wind, is not so much steadfast, as earth-fast; and a rock, or stone in the river, as in the following example, is properly called *earth-fast.*

> About the middle o' Clyde water,
> There was a *yird-fast* stane.
> > *Ballad of Burd Helen.*

Earth-tilth, agriculture.

Eath, }
Eith, } easy.

> When ease abounds it's *eath* to do amiss.
> > *Spenser : Fairie Queene.*

> *Uneath* may she endure the flinty streets.
> > *Shakspeare : King Henry VI.*

> The Miller sat *unethes* (uneasily) upon his horse.
> > *Chaucer : The Knight's Tale.*

> Who thinks him most secure is *eathest* shamed.
> > *Fairfax : Tasso.*

> A scald head is *eath* to bleed.

> An unlucky man's cart is *eath* tumbled.

> It's *eath* keeping a castle that's no besieged.

> *Eath* earned, soon forgotten.

> It's *eath* finding a stick to beat a dog.
> > *Allan Ramsay : Scotch Proverbs.*

Eft, again, quick, soon.

> And in three days after,
> Edifie it *eft* anew.—*Piers Ploughman.*
> Yea marry that's the *eftest* way.
> > *Much Ado about Nothing.*

Eftsoons, soon, presently, by and bye.

> Hold off! Unhand me, grayhead loon,
> *Eftsoons* his head dropped he.
> > *Coleridge.*

Egg, to instigate, incite, provoke to action. It is now thought a vulgarism to say 'that a man was egged on to do anything;' but the word is pure Anglo-Saxon, from *eggian* to excite; and of the same family as *eager.*

> Through *egging* of his wife.
> > *Chaucer : The Marchant's Tale.*

> Mother, quod she, and maiden bright Mariè,
> Sooth is it that through woman's *eggement.*
> > *Chaucer : The Man of Lawe's Tale.*

They that *egge* a consente to the sinne, bin partners of the sinne, and of the damnation of the sinner.
> > *Chaucer : The Parson's Tale.*

Whom ardour of inclination *eggs* forward and carrieth through every obstacle.—*Denham.*

> Adam and Eve he *egged* to do ill.
> > *Piers Ploughman.*

> How curst an *egging* with a sting of lust.
> > *Cleaveland.*

Eke, *v.* to increase, augment, or add to.

Eke, *n.* an augmentation.

This word has gradually lost its original meaning. Spenser uses it in its ancient sense, when he says in the 'Shepherd's Kalendar:'

> Then *ekes* his speed and faces it again.

But Shakspeare mostly uses it with the addition of the particle 'out,' to eke out, to lengthen, to protract, to make the most of existing materials, rather than to add anything to them. In its almost obsolete form of '*eke*,' also—

> A train band captain *eke* was he,

its derivation from the Teutonic, *auch*, is apparent. The substantive an *eke* still exists in common parlance in Scotland : and signifies the last tumbler of toddy, made after all the guests have had sufficient; the parting cup, before retiring to rest. 'I hate intemperance,' said a worthy magistrate and distiller ; 'what I like to see is the douce honest

Eke—*continued.*

man, takin' his acht (eight) tumblers and an *eke* every night, in the bosom of his family; but intemperance is my abomination.'

Eld,) old age. This word survives in poetical composition,
Eild,) but is banished from the bar, the pulpit and the senate.

Palsied *eld.*—*Shakspeare.*

Well you know,
The superstitious, idle-headed *Eld*,
Received and did deliver to our age.
This tale of Herne the Hunter, for a truth.
Merry Wives of Windsor.

Childless *eld.*—*Milton.*

Though *eild* has crooked me down.
Jacobite Song, When the King comes o'er the water.

Rule youth well,
Eild will rule itsell.

Better eat gray bread in youth than in *eild*.

We can tell your *eild* by the wrunkles (wrinkles) of your horn.

Truth and *eild* never sowder well (solder well) together.
Allan Ramsay: Scotch Proverbs.

Elden, to grow old, to advance in years.

The good wife is *eldening*, poor body.

Eldfather, grandfather, ancestor.

That after his good *eldfather* was called Robert.
Barbour, quoted in Jamieson's Dictionary.

Our king—Dawy by name, was *eldfather* to King William.
Wyntoun.

Eldmother, grandmother, ancestress.

Eldritch, haunted by evil spirits, unearthly, ghastly, horrible.

On the *eldrich* hill there grows a thorn.
Sir Carline, Percy's Reliques.

So Maggie runs—the witches follow,
Wi many an *eldritch* scream and hollow.
Burns: Tam o' Shanter.

Eldritch—*continued.*

> I've heard my reverend grannie say,
> In lonely glens ye like to stray,
> Or where auld ruined castles gray
> Nod to the moon,
> You fright the nightly wandering way
> Wi' *eldritch* croon.
>> *Burns : Address to the Deil.*

Elf, to twist and entangle the hair.

It was supposed to be a spiteful amusement of Queen Mab and her subjects [the Elves] to twist the hair of human creatures, or tie the manes and tails of horses into hard knots, which it was not fortunate to untangle.—*Nares.*

> My face I'll grime with filth,
> Blanket my loins, *elf* all my hair in knots.—*Lear.*

Elf-locks, tangled hair.

> This is that very Mab,
> That plaits the manes of horses in the night,
> And cakes the *elf-locks* in foul sluttish hairs.
>> *Romeo and Juliet.*

Elmen, made of elm ; as an ' *elmen* coffin,' an ' *elmen* grove.'

This is as legitimate an adjective as oaken, ashen, birchen, and other epithets derived from the names of trees ; or as golden, brazen, from the names of metals.

Embrangle, to perplex.

Embranglement, perplexity.

Evenhood, equality.

Eme,
Yeme, } from the German *oheim,* an uncle.

> Think on thine *eme,* King Arthur,
> Knight that is of most valour.
>> *Metrical Romance of Merlin,* part ii.

> In good faith, *Eme,* quoth she, that liketh me.
>> *Chaucer : Troilus and Cressida.*

> While they were young, Cassibelan their *eme,*
> Was by the people chosen in their stead.
>> *Spenser : Fairie Queene.*

> Mony aunts, mony *eems,*
> Mony kin, few friends.
>> *Ramsay's Scottish Proverbs.*

Etayne,⎫ a giant; a word in use in ancient ballads and ro-
Etyn,⎬ mances, prior to the introduction of the French
Eyttyn,⎭ word *geant*.

'The most common word for a giant in the Eddas,' says Mr.
G. W. Dasent, in the Introduction to his Norse Tales,
(London, 1859,) 'was Jotunn,' (Anglo Saxon, Eoten,)
'which, strange to say, survives in the Scotch *etin*.' But
etin is not Scotch only, but ancient English.

> Fy! he said, thou foule! thou *Etayne!*
> Alle my knightes thou gart be slaine.
>
> *MS. Lincoln, quoted by Halliwell.*

An *Etyn* in a fight.—*Sir Tristram.*

> They say the King of Portugal cannot sit at his meat, but the giants and *Etyns* will come and snatch it from him.
>
> *Beaumont and Fletcher : Burning Pestle.*

In Hynde Etyn; or the Gentle Giant, in Kinloch's
Ancient Scottish Ballads, May Margaret goes to the Mul-
berry Woods ; and has an adventure.

> She had na pu'd a nut, a nut,
> A nut but barely ane ;
> When up started the Hynde *Etyn*,
> Says, 'lady, let these alane.'

The *Etyn* threatens her life, but afterwards marries her,
and carries her away, and some years afterwards when hunt-
ing with his eldest son, the latter asks why his mother's
cheeks are so often wet, and so seldom dry ; and the Etyn
replies :

> Na wonder, na wonder, my eldest son,
> That she should brast and die ;
> For your mother was an Earl's daughter,
> Of noble birth and fame,
> And now she's wife o' Hynde *Etyn*,
> Wha ne'er got Christen name.

Ettle, to try, to attempt, to endeavour.

> I looked the traitor in the face,
> Drew out my brand and *ettled* at him.
>
> *Lochmaben Gate, Jacobite Ballad.*

Everly, constantly, continually.

Evil-willing, malevolent.

Evil-willingness, malevolence.

Faa, } a gipsy. Faa, Fa, or Fae, supposed to be derived from
Fae, } Fata (Fate) was long the patronymic of the Gipsy
chiefs in England, calling themselves, or called by others,
Kings of the Gipsies. 'Johnnie Faa, or the Gipsy Laddie,'
is the title of a well known ballad which describes the elope-
ment of a Countess of Cassilis, with the Gipsy King. In
the reign of James I., of Scotland, there came one Faa or
Fae, a gipsy, into his dominions, who called himself Duke of
Italy, and is supposed to be the hero of the adventure:

Fae-gang, a gang of gipsies.

Fadge, to fit, to suit, to be agreeable to.

> If this *fadge* not.—*Love's Labour Lost.*

This word is still in common use, and finds a place in the
'Slang Dictionary,' where it ought not to be. 'Fad,' a
hobby; something that suits or fits a person's humour, is
probably an abbreviation of this word.

Faith-fast, true to one's faith or pledge.

Fall, autumn. This word is not only common, but almost universal in America; and ought to be re-adopted in England.
The names of the other three seasons are pure Saxon;
and either 'Fall,' the fall of the leaf, or 'Harvest,' a word
much used by the English peasantry, should be admitted to
synonymity with the foreign word, which has taken too strong
a hold of the language to be entirely superseded.

> A honey tongue, a heart of gall
> Is Fancy's Spring, but Sorrow's *Fall.*— *Sir W. Raleigh.*

> What crowds of patients the town doctor kills,
> Or how last *Fall,* he raised the weekly bills.—*Dryden.*

Fang, to lay hold of; whence the *fangs* of a wild animal.

Fangle, a toy, trifle, or other article, laid hold of by the fashion,
whence new-*fangled*, or newly fashioned, or laid hold of.

> The synne God hateth that on him hangeth,
> And Goddes hatred helle it *fangeth.*
>> *MS. Harleian, quoted by Halliwell.*

> What fairies haunt this ground?   A Book?   Oh, rare one!
> Be not as our *fangled* world, a garment,
> Nobler than that it covers.—*Shakspeare, Cymbeline.*

Farrand, from fare, to journey, to travel. *Ald* or *auld, farrand*, in Scottish and Border dialect signifies wise, sagacious, as one who travels in the old ruts of experience, or who stands in the ancient ways. The Scotch say of a very wary man that ' he's owre *auld farran*' to be fleyed wie bogles :' i.e., too knowing to be frightened by ghosts.

In Robert de Brunne's ' Chronicles of England,' written in the fourteenth century, we find the phrase, ' well *farrand ;*' in the sense of suitable or becoming, applied to the dress of Rowena, on her first interview with Vortigern :

> Before the king in hall she went,
> A cup with wine she had in hand,
> And her attire was *well-farrand.*

Ill-farrand, means unsuitable, or out of fashion, and *farrantly*, signifies orderly, neat, comely, respectable.

In Northamptonshire, according to Sternberg's Glossary, ' a farrantly body,' means a respectable man. The word when applied to animals, means, that they are strong, and shapely, and fit for labour.

Farthel, the fourth part of anything. Mr. Halliwell has '*farrel*, the *fourth part* of a circular oat cake, the division being made by a cross.' From the same source comes farthing; the fourth part of a penny.

Fastles, } fastenings.
Fassles, }

Feather-heeled, nimble, agile, sprightly ; (apparently derived from the image of Mercury, with feathers or wings at his heels).

Featly, dexterous.

Feck, } power, activity.
Feckful, } powerful.
Feckless, } powerless.

Worcester in his Dictionary, the most complete that has yet been compiled either in England or America ; makes no mention of ' feck,' a common word in Yorkshire, the Border Counties, and Scotland, for power and activity, but inserts the adjective *feckless*, which he supposes to be a corruption of ' effectless.'

Feck—*continued.*

> For as we see a mischief grow
> Oft of a *feckless* thing.
> > *Montgomery : The Cherry and the Sloe.*

> They are mair faschious nor of *feck*.
> > *Cherry and Sloe.*

> Mony a *feckful* chiel that day was slain.
> > *Halton's Wallace.*

> Breathless and *feckless* there she sits her down.
> > *Ross's Helenora.*

> *Feckless* fouk are aye fain of ane another.
> > *Allan Ramsay's Scotch Proverbs.*

Felth, the power of feeling in the fingers. Thus ' a blind man has greater *felth* than one who can see.' ' The tailor's finger would lose its *felth* but for his thimble.'

Fend, to strive, to struggle, to fight for.

> God bless him that *fends* for his living,
> And holds up his head through it a'.
> > *Waugh's Lancashire Songs.*

Fettle, to arrange, mend, prepare, put in order. This word is common throughout the northern English and Scottish Border counties. Its derivation from feat, a deed, job, performance, or arrangement, seems to have escaped notice.

' I'll fettle it,' a common expression in Lancashire, meaning ' I will make a good little job, or *feat* of it.

> We'll *fettle* up ourselves.—*Cumberland Ballads.*

> I'll *fettle* it.—*Lancashire.*

' *Fettled* ale,' ale warmed, spiced, and sugared.

'I homewards *fettled* off ;' i.e., prepared myself to go home. *Cumberland Ballads.*

' The dinner's ill-*fettled* ; i.e., badly cooked or prepared ; ' *Fettle* the horse and cart,' &c.

> When the sheriff saw little John bend his bow,
> He *fettled* him to be gone.
> > *Percy's Reliques.*

> Thank me no thanking, nor proud me no proud,
> But *fettle* your five joints 'gainst Thursday next,
> To go into Paris and Saint Peter's Church,
> Or I will drag thee on a hurdle thither.
> > *Shakspeare : Romeo and Juliet.*

When your master is most busy in company, come in and pretend to *fettle* about the room.—*Swift.*

Ferlie, *v.* to wonder, and when used as an adjective, wonderful, strange, or curious.

Ferlie, *n.* a wonder, a miracle.

> A *ferlie* strife then fell between,
> As they went by the way.
> > *MS. Trin. Col. Cam.*

> Little *ferly* I have.—*Piers Ploughman.*

> On Malvern Hills,
> Me befel a *ferly.*—*Piers Ploughman.*

> Poor fay ! he said a *ferlie* case,
> Either I am of wine drunk,
> Either the firmament is sunk,
> Either woxen is the ground.
> > *Metrical Romance of the Seven Wise Masters.*

> The wheel was *ferly* rich and round,
> In world was never none half so high.
> > *Morte Arthur.*

> Alein the clerk that herd this melodie,
> He poketh John, and sayeth 'Slepest thou,
> Herdest thou ever slike a song ere now ?'

> *　　　*　　　*　　　*　　　*

> Who harkened ever slike a *ferly* thing ?
> > *Chaucer : The Pere's Tale.*

> Light down, light down, now True Thomas,
> And lean your head upon my knee,
> Abide and rest a little space,
> And I will show you *ferlies* three.
> > *Thomas of Ercildoune.*

> Never break out of kind and make your friends *ferly* at you.

> The longer we live the more *ferlies* we see.
> > *Northern Proverbs.*

Ferne, afar.

Ferne-ago, very long ago.

Fey, bewitched, fated to die, in the power of the fates, doomed.

> ' We'll turn again,' said good Lord John,
> ' But no,' said Rothiemay,
> My steed's trapann'd, my bridle's broke,
> I fear this day I'm *fey.*
> > *Ballad of the Fire of Frendranght.*

Fey—*continued.*

> The Romaynes for sadness ruschte to the erthe,
>   *   *   *   as they *fey* were.
> *Morte Arthur: MS. Lincoln, quoted by Halliwell.*

> Let the fate fall upon the *feyest.*

> There is *fey* blood in your veins.

> Take care of the man that God has marked for he's no *fey.*
> *Allan Ramsay's Scottish Proverbs.*

Fibster, a teller of petty lies.

Fire-flaught, sudden sparks of fire.

> The *fire-flaughts* darting from his e'e.
> *Richard Gall to Hector McNeill.*

Fire-flinger, an incendiary.

Flanch, a projection in a building.

Flang, preterite of fling; very unnecessarily superseded by 'flung.'

Flath, filth, dirt, ordure : (*Halliwell*).

> The rhymes to 'wrath,' and 'path,' are few, and this might be admitted to increase the number.

Flathers, rubbish.

Flaunts, finery, gew-gaws, ribbons.

Flaucht, a flash of lightning.

> The thunder crack'd and *flauchts* did rift,
> Frae the black vizzard of the lift.
> *The Vision, by Allan Ramsay.*

Flaun, a pancake.

> With green cheese, clouted cream, with *flauns* and custards stor'd.
> *Drayton.*

Fleck, to spot.

> *Flecked* darkness.—*Romeo and Juliet.*

> We'll *fleck* our white steeds in your christian blood.
> *Four Apprentices.*

Fleer, to mock, to flirt, to sneer, to grin.

> And mark the *fleers,* the gibes, and notable scorns.
> *Shakspeare.*

> Democritus, thou ancient *fleerer,*
> How I miss thy laugh.—*Beaumont and Fletcher.*

Flothery, showy, but vulgar; overdressed, and in ill-taste.—*Halliwell.*

Fleme, a brook, a small river.

> The *fleme* Jordan.—*MS. Cantab. quoted by Halliwell.*

Fleme, to banish.

> Right forth thy Lord will thee reprove,
> And *fleme* thee far out of his sight.
> > *Ritson's Ancient Songs,* vol. i., p. **78.**
>
> Now help thou meek and blissful faire maid,
> Me *flemed* wretch in this desert of galle.
> > *Chaucer: The Second Nun's Tale.*
>
> *Flemer* of fiends, (Banisher of demons).
> > *The Man of Lawes Tale.*

Fley, to frighten, or alarm one person, or animal; as distinguished from ' scare ' to frighten a multitude ; though sometimes used in the same sense as ' scare.'

Flinders, fragments, small pieces, splinters.

> The moon was clear, the day drew near,
> The spears in *flinders* flew,
> And many a gallant Englishman,
> Ere day the Scotsmen slew.
> > *The Battle of Otterbourne.*

Flirt, to move rapidly about from place to place, like a bee or a butterfly, from flower to flower, whence, metaphorically, a ' flirt,' a girl who jumps from admirer to admirer, or lover to lover, and cares for none.

Flit, to remove from one dwelling place to another. From this source come flitter and flutter, applied to small creatures or objects that move rapidly.

> So sore it sticked when I was hit,
> That by no craft I might it *flit.*
> > *Chaucer: Romance of the Rose.*
>
> Better rue sit, than rue *flit ;* (i.e., better remain uncomfortable in an old house than become still more uncomfortable in a new one.)
> > *Allan Ramsay's Scotch Proverbs.*
>
> Two *flittings* are as bad as a fire.
> > *Northern Proverb.*

Flite, to scold.

Flitter, to fly like a fledgling.

Flittermouse, }
Fluttermouse, } a bat.

The bat has been called the winged, or flittering mouse ; and the owl, its enemy, the winged cat.

Flosh, to spill, to splash.

Flottery, slovenly, but attempting to be fine and showy.

Flouren, ⎱ made of flour ; *flouren* cakes, *flouren* bread ; in the
Fluren, ⎰ same meaning as *wheaten* bread, or *oaten* cakes.

Flurch, a great abundance ; ' there is a *flurch* of strawberries
this year.' ' *Flush* of money,' seems to be a corruption of a
' *flurch* of money.'

Flurn, to think little of, to disparage, used in a sense somewhat
less invidious than scorn or sneer. The word occurs in the
preface to Fletcher's Poems, as quoted by Nares, wherein
he says of some of his earlier compositions, ' the abortive
birth slipped from my brain, which can carry neither worth
nor weight in this pregnant age, so fraught and furnished
with a variety of gallant pieces and performances of the
choicest of writers ; give me leave to *flurn* at them, as the
poor excrescences of nature,' &c. Neither the two great
English lexicographers, Johnson and Richardson, nor the
two great Americans, Webster and Worcester, seem to have
been cognizant of the word. Halliwell cites it as a Lincolnshire word, meaning to *sneer* at, or despise.

Fluttersome, quick, agile, restless.

Foison, abundance.

> So may he finden, gode *foison*,
> Of the remnant needeth not to enquire.
> > *Chaucer : The Miller's Prologue.*

> With loaves five and fishes two to feed,
> God sent his *foison* at the greatest neede.
> > *Chaucer : The Man of Lawes Tale.*

> As blossoming time,
> That for the seedness the bare fallow brings,
> To teeming *foison.—Measure for Measure.*

> All *foison*, all abundance,
> To feed my innocent people.
> > *Shakspeare : The Tempest.*

> Earth's increase and *foison* plenty,
> Barns and garners never empty.
> > *The Blessing of Juno and Ceres, The Tempest.*

Foison—*continued.*

In Suffolk, says Mr. Halliwell, the word means, 'the natural juice or moisture of the grass or other herbs; the heart and strength of it.

Fool-happy,) imbecile) so great and hopeless as to be
Fool-happiness,) imbecility) utterly unconscious of sorrow or pain.

Fond,   ) to tempt, whence, probably, the adjective *fond,*
Fonden,) tempting to enjoyment.

> And then *fondeth* the fiend.—*Piers Ploughman.*

> And *fondede* me to mete him.—*Idem.*

Foot-lock, now corrupted into fet-lock, the lock of hair behind the pastern joint of a horse's foot.

For. This syllable as a prefix to a verb, in the same manner as *ver,* in German, serves as an augmentative, or strengthening of the meaning, In some instances, such as *forbear, forbid, forget, forgive,* and *forsake,* it gives the original verb an entirely new signification. The ancient preterite, lorn or lost, with the prefit *for* becomes forlorn, or utterly and entirely lost; as in the following stanza from the ballad of Lady Maisry:

> Ye maun gie up your English lord,
> When your young babe is born,
> For gin ye keep him an hour longer,
> Your life shall be *forlorn ;*

that is, not that you shall live a forlorn life, but that you shall die utterly and without reprieve.

Foranent, right opposite to.

Forbears, ancestors.

Forechosen, predestined.

Fordeme, from 'deme,' to judge; to judge beforehand; and without evidence.

Fordo, to ruin, to destroy, to exhaust.

> This is the night,
> That either makes me or *fordoes* me quite.
>   *Shakspeare : Othello.*

Fordo—*continued.*

> Wilt thou not go further to see where thou hast left
> Thy father Anchisis, *fordone* with age?
>
> > *Earl of Surry.*

> Now the hungry lion roars,
> And the wolf behowls the moon,
> While the heavy ploughman snores,
> All with weary task *fordone.*
>
> > *Shakspeare : Midsummer Night's Dream.*

Fordrunken, dead drunk.

> The miller that *fordrunken* was.
> > *Chaucer : The Knight's Tale.*

Forfend, to prohibit, forbid, ward off.

Fore-elders, ancestors.

Forefighter, a champion. This is almost the only word applicable to battles, hosts, armies, and the military life and profession which remained in the Saxon-English language for any length of time after the Norman conquest. Even the words 'war' and 'peace' are from the Norman French, and rapidly superseded the original *Krieg* and *Friede.* The words soldier, corporal, sergeant, lieutenant, captain, major, colonel, general, are all from the Norman French, and have utterly dispossessed the ancient names. *Here*, an army, was current as late only as the fourteenth century.

Forewent, preterite of forego, to renounce.

Writers and speakers still say :—' I forego the pleasure or the advantage;' but will use a roundabout form of expression rather than say: 'I fore*went* the pleasure,' &c. And why? Forewent is as good a word as forego, and should not to be allowed to perish.

Forewit, anticipation.

Forfoughten, worn out in the struggle of life, exhausted in battle.

Forgab, to mock.

> For who so *forgabbed* a frere,
> Yfounden at his stews.—*Piers Ploughman.*

Forgather, to meet, to encounter.

> I there wi' something did *forgather*.
> > *Burns.*

Forgrown, covered and overgrown with vegetation.

> The path
> *Forgrown* was with grass and weed.
> *Chaucer.*

Forshrunken, utterly shrunk up.

Forspent, wearied, worn out.

Fortrodden, utterly trodden down.

> Virtue is not only without meedes, but it is cast downe and eke *fortrodden* under the feet.—*Chaucer.*

Forswat, worn with the sweat of extreme toil.

Forswink, overtoil, to wear one self out with hard labor.

Forswunk, utterly worn out with *swink,* or hard labor.

> She is my goddess plain,
> And I her shepherd swain,
> Albeit *forswunk* and forswat I am.
> *Spenser: Shepherd's Calendar.*

Forthright, straightforward, in the right direction; a straight path. An excellent word, and the necessary complement of *upright* and *downright.*

> Through *forthright* and meanders.
> *Shakspeare: Tempest, act iii. scene 3.*

> If you give way,
> Or hedge aside from the direct *forthright.*
> *Shakspeare: Troilus and Cressida, act iii. scene 3.*

Forwandered, utterly lost, and strayed out of the way.

Forwasted, utterly wasted.

> *Forwasted* all their land.
> *Spenser: Faerie Queene.*

Forwearied, tired out.

> Some of his diet do from him withdraw,
> For I find him to be too proudly fed,
> Give him more labor and with straiter law,
> That he with work may be *forwearied.*
> *Spenser: Faerie Queene.*

> Your king, whom labored spirits
> *Forwearied* in the action of swift speed,
> Craves harborage within your city walls.
> *Shakspeare: King John.*

Forword, a preface, or introduction to a book.

> The translator wishes to say that he has felt no hesitation in placing the *foreword* to the Edda also, with the afterword to Gylfi's Mocking. *Preface to the Younger Edda, translated by G. W. Dasent, Stockholm,* 1842.

Forworn, worn out.

Foulsome, from foul, unclean; corrupted into fulsome, disgusting.

Fouth, from full, and full-eth, plenty.

> I took a *fouth* of sweetest kisses from her glowing mouth.
>> *Allan Ramsay: The Gentle Shepherd.*

> Let *fouth* of tears dreep like May dew.
>> *Allan Ramsay: Elegy on Maggy Johnston.*

> He had a *fouth* o' auld knick knackits,
> Rusty iron caps and jingling jackets.
>> *Burns: Elegy on Captain Grose.*

Foor,) preterite of fare, to travel. 'They *fure* forth,' i.e.,
Fure,) they travelled forth.

> As o'er the moor, they lightly *foor.*
>> *Burns: There was a lass, they ca'd her Meg.*

Foust, stale dirt, whence *fusty.*

Franch, to crunch with the teeth.

Fratch, to quarrel.

Fratchy, quarrelsome.

> And aye cracked his thumb for a bit of a *fratch.*
>> *Anderson's Cumberland Ballads.*

> O, Donald, ye are just the man,
> Who when he gets a wife,
> Begins to *fratch.*
>> *Miss Blamire: Cumberland Songs.*

Frayne, to ask, enquire.

> Then I *frayned* at Faith.—*Piers Ploughman.*

> And *frayned* full often of folke that I met.
>> *Idem.*

Fret, to devour, or eat, from the German *fressen.* ' A moth *fretting* a garment,' means, a moth eating a garment ; and *fretted* with care, is consumed or eaten with care.

> Like as it were a moth *fretting* a garment.
> *Psalm* xxxix.

Freet, preterite of *fret.*

> Adam *freet* of that fruit,
> And forsook
> The love of our Lord.—*Piers Ploughman.*

Fretten, past participle of fret.

> He has *fretten* of folk mo' than five hundred.
> *Morte Arthur, quoted by Halliwell.*

Freet, a proverb.

> He was the youngest of seven successive sons, a circumstance of which he used jocularly to boast, as conferring on him, according to the old *freet,* supernatural powers of some sort or other.
> *Whistle Binkie, Memoir of John Ireland.*

Fremd, ⎱ strange, unacquainted, unrelated, opposed to *sib,* of
Fremit, ⎰ kin.

> The sext commandment forbids us to synne with any womane, sybbe, or *fremde,* wedde, or unwedde.
> *MS. Lincoln, quoted by Halliwell.*

> Make friends of *fremit* folk ; (i.e., not of your kinspeople and relatives.)
> ———
> Better my friend think me *fremit* than fashious (quarrelsome).
> *Allan Ramsay : Scotch Proverbs.*

Frim, vigorous, healthy, thriving ; as ' a *frim* tree,' a ' *frim* lass.'

Frike, fresh, liberal, hearty.

Frith, ⎱ a free place in the forest, land not enclosed.
Firth, ⎰

> In the chill winter cauld,
> Quhen frostes dois owr flete baith *firth* and fauld.
> *Gavin Douglas : Translation of Virgil.*

> He'll hang thy merry men, pair by pair,
> In any *frith* where he may them find.
> *Border Minstrelsy.*

Frostling, any fruit, flower, or leaf, injured by the frost.

Frory, frosty.

Frounce, a wrinkle; from the French 'froncer le sourcil,' to frown; whence also 'frown,' to *wrinkle* the brow; but formerly employed in the more extended sense of to twist, to curl.

> With she that *frounceth* up the brow
> This covenant I will allow.— *Gower.*

> Some *frounce* their curled hair in courtly guise.
> *Spenser.*

> Dressing, braiding, *frouncing,* flowering.
> *Drayton.*

> Not tricked and *frounced* as she was wont
> With the Attic boy to hunt.
> *Milton, Il Penseroso.*

Frush, to bruise, disturb.

> I like thy armour well,
> I'll *frush* it.— *Chaucer : Troilus and Cressida.*

Fud, a tail, still applied to the tail of a hare or rabbit.

> We'll whack their hydes and fyle their *fuds ;* i.e., drag their tails
> through defilement, or through dirt and mire.
> *Jacobite Ballads, The auld Stuarts back again.*

Gab, the mouth; whence, to gossip, to talk idly, or loudly, to prate.

'*Gabbe*' and '*gabbing*,' appear in the late Herbert Coleridge's 'Dictionary of the Oldest Words in the English Language.' In Gaelic, according to MacIntyre's Dictionary, '*gabb*,' signifies a mouth which is never at rest;' whence, *gabbach,* garrulous. '*Gap*,' an opening, and '*gape*,' to yawn, are from the same root.

The gift of the gab; i.e., the gift of oratory, elocution, or speech-making; is a common expression in England and America. A wealthy citizen, of Philadelphia, was asked to subscribe to a fund for the endowment of a chair of Elocution, in his native state; but indignantly refused. 'I hold,' said he, 'the pernicious "gift of the *gab*," to be the curse of the Republic; and decline to contribute a cent to its extension.'

> Ne though I say't,
> I am not lefe to *gabbe*.
> > *Chaucer: The Miller's Tale.*

> And certes in the same boke I rede,
> Right in the next chapitre after this,
> I *gabbe* not, so have I joy and bliss.
> > *Chaucer: The Nounes Preestes Tale.*

> He is a japer and a *gabber*.
> > *Chaucer: The Parson's Tale.*

Gaed, the ancient preterite of go; the modern preterite 'went,' being derived from wend to turn. 'He wends on his way,' i.e., he turns on his way. From this lost preterite, proceeds, probably, the common expression, 'to *gad*,' or to '*gad* about.'

> I *gae'd* a waeful gate yestreen.
> > *Burns.*

Gainage, profit.

> I trow the *gainage* of the ground.
> > *Piers Ploughman.*

Gainbite, biting back again; i.e., remorse. This word is still current in some parts of England; the original form was *ayerbyte,* or again bite. Mr. Halliwell quotes in his Archaic Dictionary; the '*Ayerbyte* of Inwit,' or 'Remorse of Conscience.'

Gainly, shapely, elegant, whence, ungainly (still used).

Gainstrive, to strive against, to contend.

Gainstrife, contention.

Gainstand, to stand against, to resist, to withstand.

> In all this realm, o'er all this land,
> Is none so wight dare him *gainstand,*
> So wisely can Sir Penny work.
> > *Sir Penny : Lord Haile's version, Hyndford MSS.*

Gale, *n.* a voice, a sound, a cry.

Gale, *v.* to sound, to sing.

This word is from the same root as *call;* and appears with more or less modifications in most of the languages derivable from the Sanscrit.

> And when he heard the Frere *gale.*
> > *Chaucer : The Wife of Bath's Prologue.*

> Gan he crie and *gale,*
> My lippis open, Lord of Love, I crie.
> > *Chaucer : The Court of Love.*

> Then *galed* the gowk; i.e., then sang the cuckoo.)
> > *Morte Arthur.*

Bearing this origin of the word in mind, we find that nightin*gale* means the song of the night; and madri*gal,* the voice, or song of the mother. On the same principle of derivation, a loud sounding wind, becomes a '*gale,*' or singing wind.

Gall, a sore place; the rose-gall, the excrescence on the leaf of the rose when pricked and injured by an insect.

Gall, to fret, make sore, or excoriate.

> Let the *galled* jade wince.—*Shakspeare.*

Gallow, to frighten.

> The wrathful skies,
> *Gallow* the very wanderers of the dark,
> And make them keep their caves.
> > *Shakspeare : King Lear.*

Gant, merry, frolicsome.

Ganty, lusty, hearty, in good health.

Gar, to cause a thing to be done, to force or compel a person to do anything ; the quasi-synonym of which is 'make.' He *gars* me do it: i.e., he makes me do it; but as 'make' is required in another sense, that of construct or build, or shape, and as cause or compel are not only Latinisms but express a different shade of meaning, the word ' gar,' no longer allowed in English, is a clear loss to the language. And that it was once good English, its use by Chaucer and the author of Piers Ploughman, is sufficient evidence.

> Then was folk fain and fed hunger with the best,
> With good ale, as glutton taught, and *gar* hunger sleep.
> > *Piers Ploughman.*

> But specially I pray thee, hoste dere,
> *Gar* us have mete and drinke, and make us chere.
> > *Chaucer : The Reve's Tale.*

In Scottish literature the word is of constant occurrence.

> Bid her do weel to my young son,
> And give him nurses three,
> For gin he live to be a man,
> King James will *gar* him die.
> > *Buchan's Ancient Ballads.*

> She had na pu'd a nut a nut,
> Nor broken a branch but three,
> Till by it came, kind, young Cukin,
> And *gar'd* her let them be.
> > *Buchan's Ancient Ballads and Songs.*

> *Gar* saddle me my bonnie black,
> *Gar* saddle soon and mak' him ready,
> And I will down the Gate Hope slack,
> And a' to see my bonnie ladie.
> > *Minstrelsy of the Scottish Border.*

Gar—*continued.*

> If this be Johnnie o' Breadislee,
> We soon shall *gar* him die.
>> *Border Minstrelsy.*

> And the first kirk that ye come to,
> Ye's *gar* the mass be sung,
> And the nearest kirk that ye come to,
> Ye's *gar* the bells be rung.
>> *The Gay Goss Hawk.*

One man may lead a horse to the water, but four and twenty canna *gar* him drink.—*North Country Proverb.*

Gart, preterite of gar, to make.

> The boy was clad in robes of green,
> Sweet as the infant spring,
> And like the mavis on the bush,
> He *gart* the vallies ring.
>> *Percy's Reliques: Gil Morice.*

> Till Gregory *gart* clerkes go here and preche.
>> *Piers Ploughman.*

Garth, an inclosure, a yard, a garden, whence, kail-garth, a cabbage-garden; kirk-garth, the churchyard; apple-garth, an orchard; and *Hogarth,* a well known surname; meaning the garden, yard, or place of the Hogs.

> In serk and mantle after her I went,
> Into this *garth* most dulce and redolent.
>> *Dunbar: The Thistle and the Rose.*

Gast, to frighten, whence, *aghast* with terror.

> *Gasted* by the noise I made,
> Full suddenly he fled.
>> *Shakspeare: King Lear.*

Gavel, a sheaf of corn before it is tied up.

Gear, in the North of England and Scotland signifies money; wealth, property, belongings, possessions. The word is used by Chaucer and Spenser, in the sense of *graith* or appliance, furniture, accoutrement, and apparel.

> Arrayed herself in her most gorgeous *gear.*
>> *Spenser.*

> Some harmless villager,
> Whom thrift keeps up about his country's *gear.*
>> *Milton.*

Gear—*continued.*

> Little said is soon mended,
> Little *gear* is soon spent.
> > *Allan Ramsay's Scotch Proverbs.*

> I hae been blyth with comrades dear,
> > I hae been merry drinkin',
> I hae been joyful gatherin' *gear*,
> > I hae been happy thinkin'.—*Burns.*

Geason, scarce, rare.

> It was frosty winter's season,
> And Fair Flora's wealth was *geason.*
> > *Robert Greene: Philomela*, 1594.

> Death that took away a man so *geason.*
> > *Robert Greene: Maiden's Dream*, 1591.

> Hard to obtain, once gotten, not *geason*,
> Jewel of jeopardy, that peril doth assail.
> > *Earl of Surry: The Frailty and Hurtfulness of Beauty.*

> Let not thy tongue speak thy will,
> Laughing and speech in the mouth be *geason.*
> > *MS. Cantab.* (*Halliwell.*)

Geck, scorn, derision ; a person scorned.

> Gude man, Gramercy, for your *geck*,
> > Quod Hope, and lowly louts,
> Gif we were sent for, we suspect,
> > Because the doctor douts.
> > > *The Cherry and the Sloe, Montgomery*, 1590.

> And made the most notorious *geck* and gull,
> That e'er inventive played on.
> > *Shakspeare : Twelfth Night.*

> Why did you suffer Jachimo,
> > *   *   *   *
> To become the *geck* and scorn,
> Of the whole village ?
> > *Shakspeare : Cymbeline.*

Geck, to scorn, to mock, to deride.

> Bauldy that drives the car,
> But *gecks* at me and says I smell of tar.
> > *Allan Ramsay : The Gentle Shepherd.*

> You *geck* at me because I'm poor.
> > *Burns : Tibbie I hae seen the day.*

Gilver, to ache, to throb; (a provincialism in the Eastern Counties.

Rhymers sometimes complain of the want of a rhyme to silver; this word might be useful to them.

Gird, a bitter jest or sarcasm, also used as a verb.

Mr. Halliwell defines it to mean, ' to strike with a weapon, to push,' and thence, metaphorically, to deal sarcastic thrusts.

> I thank thee for that *gird*, good Tranio.
> *Shakspeare : Taming of the Shrew.*

> He is still *girding* at the age's vanity.
> *Earl's Microcosmographie.*

The word is common in Scotland and the North of England.

> The poet took notice of this *gird* as is surmised.
> *Shakspeare's Sonnets, by Gerald Massey,* 1866.

Girdlestead, the waist, or place of the girdle.—*Chaucer.*

Girn, to laugh with rage ; as distinguished from ' grin,' to laugh with merriment.

> The Deil sits *girning* in the neuk,
> Riving sticks to roast the Duke.
> *Highland Laddie, Jacobite Ballad.*

Gith, the corn-cockle.

Glamour, ⎱ fascination by the power of the eye, or of enchant-
Glamourie, ⎰ ment.

> She came tripping down the stair,
>   And all her maids before her,
> As soon as they saw her weel-faur'd face,
>   They cast their *glamourie* o'er her.
> *Johnnie Faa : The Gypsy Laddie, Border Minstrelsy.*

Glaver, to flatter, to lear, to ogle.

> To glose or to *glaver*,
> I will for no maiden.
> *Ritson's Ancient Songs, Tye thy mare, Tam, boy.*

> Then shall you see those slaves aloof that stood,
> And would have let him starved like spaniels to him crouch,
> And with their *glavering* lips his very feet to toad.
> *Drayton's Polyolbion.*

> These *glaverers* gone ; myself to rest I laid,
> And doubting nothing, soundly fell asleep.
> *Mirror for Magistrates.*

> A slavish *glavering*, flattering, parasite.
> *South's Sermons.*

Glaver—*continued.*

> Oh *glavering* flattery,
> How potent art thou!—*Marston's What you Will.*

> Bear not a flattering tongue to *glaver* any.
> > *Antonio and Mellida.*

> *Glavering* upon a man to do him harm
> > *Holland's Ammianus Marcellinus,* 1609.

> And by such subtle *glavering* means,
> Prevent distrust of their designs.
> > *Hudibras Redivivus,* 1708.

> Mary Beatson with the *glavering* mirth about her mouth.
Athenæum, April 21, 1866. Notice of the National Portrait Exhibition.

Glaverer, a flatterer.

> These *glaverers* gone, myself to rest I laid.
> > *Mirror for Magistrates.*

Glee, music. Before our Anglo-Saxon and Scandinavian ancestors had learned to borrow from the Norman French or from the Latin, new and strange words to express old and familiar meanings, they had, necessarily, a word for the art of music. That word was *glee* ; which by the progress of change and corruption, has come to signify that state of mind which music is so calculated to produce : joyfulness and pleasure. A glee-man was originally a musician. At a later period, when the word Minstrel superseded that of Glee-man, we find the word *glee*, still in use to signify music, as in a passage from ' *The Life of Alexander,*' by Adam Davie, translated from the French in the reign of Edward II. : ' Orgnes, chymbes, each manner of *glee*,' i.e., organs, cymbals, and all manner of music.

The same idea of music and joyousness, pervaded the European languages in the Middle Ages, and music was the ' gay science' in the speech of Germany, England, France, Italy, and Spain. The word '*glee*,' as representing that particular description of music and song, in which English musicians have excelled from the very earliest times to our own still remains ; though a ' glee ' is not necessarily joyous, but may be plaintive, or even melancholy.

Gleed, }
Glede, } a bright, burning coal.

> As sparkles glide off the *glede.*
> > *Romance of Sir Isambras.*

Glede—*continued.*

> I saw Troy fall doun in burning *gledes*.
> > *Earl of Surry, Translation of the Æneid.*

> The cruel ire, red as any *glede*.
> > *Chaucer : The Knight's Tale.*

> My eyes with tears against the fire striving,
> Whose scorching *gleed* my heart to cinders turneth.
> > *Drayton : Idem.*

> Quick sparkes and glowing furious *gleed*.
> > *Romeo and Juliet, Supplement to Shakspeare.*

> Fair Ilium fell in burning red *gleed* down.
> > *Mirror for Magistrates.*

> My destiny to behold her doth me lead.
> And yet I know I run into the *gleed*.—*Sir Thomas Wyatt.*

> For when we see the sun go to *gleed*, we say to-morrow shall be faire
> weather.—*Udal, Matthew.*

> His een glittering for anger like a fiery *gleed*.
> > *The Fray of Suport, Border Minstrelsy.*

> And as glowing *gledes*,
> Gladdeth not those workmen.—*Piers Ploughman.*

> The sparks and *gledes* that flew out of Muspelheim.
> > *Gylfi's Mocking, translated by G. W. Dasent, Stockholm,* 1842.

Gleek, *v.*, to scoff, to jest at.

> Nay, I can *gleek* upon occasion,
> Titania, thou art as wise as thou art beautiful.
> > *Shakspeare : Midsummer Night's Dream, act* iii. *scene* 1.

> I have seen you *gleeking* and galling upon this gentleman twice or
> thrice.—*Henry* V., *act* v. *scene* i.

> Here, Juno, here : but stay, I do espy
> A pretty *gleek* coming from Pallas's eye.
> > *Beaumont and Fletcher.*

> The more that I get her, the more she doth *gleek* at me.
> > *Tom Tyler and his Wife,* 1598.

Glent,
Glint, } to flash, to glare, to shine.

In Morte Arthur, when Sir Bediver casts the magic
sword, Excalibur, into the lake, in obedience to the command
of the king,

> There came a band withouten rest,
> Out of the water and fain it hent,
> And brandished it, as it should brest,
> And anon as gleme away it *glent*.

i.e., glided away like a flash of lightning.

Glint—*continued.*

> The sun beams are *glintin'* far over the sea.
> > *Fisher's Newcastle Garland.*

> The rising sun owre Galston muir,
> Wi' glorious light was *glintin.*
> > *Burns : The Holy Fair.*

> Cauld blew the bitter, biting North,
> Upon thy early humble birth,
> Yet cheerfully thou *glinted* forth,
> > Amid the storm.
> > *Burns : To a Mountain Daisy.*

Glincy, smooth and shining, mirror like. ' The *glincy* water.'

Glime, ⎫ to shine brightly and steadfastly ; whence *glim,* a
Glyme, ⎭ small light : and glimmer, to shine fitfully.

Gloaming, twilight ; from gloom to darken ; a word common in Scotland and the North of England, as well as in America.

> Give me the hour o' *gloaming* grey,
> > It makes my heart sae cheery o'
> To meet thee on the lae-rig,
> My ain kind dearie O !
> > *Robert Burns.*

> Twixt the *gloaming* and the mirk,
> When the kye come hame.
> > *The Ettrick Shepherd.*

Glode, preterite of glide.

> Through Guy's shield it *glode.*
> > *Guy of Warwick.*

> His goode stede he all bestrode,
> And forth upon his way he *glode,*
> > As sparkle out of brand.
> > *Chaucer.*

To **gloom**, to look angry.

> It is of love, as of fortune,
> Which whilom will on folke smile,
> And *gloom* on them another while.
> > *Chaucer : Romance of the Rose.*

> Why use the taws (the rod) when a *gloom* will do it ?
> > *Allan Ramsay.*

Glose, to flatter for an evil purpose.

Grome, the snout of a boar.

Groundstalworth, strongly and firmly fixed in the ground, like a vigorous tree or a well-built edifice.

Groundwall, the foundation.

Guest-meal, a dinner-party.

Gutter-slush, a term applied metaphorically to an ill-behaved, coarse, vulgar, dirty woman, of the lowest class.

Glow, to stare with amazement, a common word in Cornwall and Devonshire.

Glower, to gaze, to stare stupidly.

> Ye *glowered* at the moon and fell on the midden.
> > *Allan Ramsay.*
>
> Poor gaping *glowering* superstition.
> > *Burns: To John Gowdie of Kilmarnock.*
>
> Satan *glowered* and fidged fu' fain.
> > *Burns: Tam o' Shanter.*
>
> Phœbus gi'es a short-lived *glower,*
> Far south the lift.—*Burns: A Winter Night.*

Glouse, a strong gleam of heat.—*Halliwell.*

Glout, to look sulky.

Glumpse, sullenness; whence the common colloquialism, ' glumpy,' ill-tempered, morose, out of humour.

Glunch, to frown.

Gome, the old Anglo-Saxon for a man, a fellow, a companion.

> The first *gome* Adam.—*Piers Ploughman.*
>
> For I will go with this *gome,*
> If God will give me grace.—*Piers Ploughman.*

Gomeril, a lout, a stupid man.

Gotten, past participle of get.

> We knew we were *gotten* far enough out of their reach.
> > *Robinson Crusoe.*

Gowk, a cuckoo; metaphorically a fool; whence *gawk* and *gawky,* a tall, ungainly, awkward, and stupid person; from whence also, *gawk-a-mouth,* used in Dorset and Devon, signifying a gaping, wide-mouthed fool, male or female.

> You breed of the *gowk,* you have never a song but one.
> > *Allan Ramsay's Scotch Proverbs.*
>
> Sae young the *gowk* tries to appear,
> And fain would mock ilk wrinkle liar.
> > *Miss Blamire : Cumberland Songs.*

Gowl, to weep in anger, more than in sorrow, sulkily, and vin-
dictively, rather than in penitence.

> *Gowlin'* and whinglin' sae muckle.
> > *Lover in Cumberland.*
>
> A child born fully,
> Beginnes to *gowle* and cry.
> > *Halliwell's Archaic Dictionary.*

Gown. This word, once so common, is in our day, almost superseded by ' dress,' which correctly interpreted, would mean
the whole costume, upper and under, from the crown of the
head to the sole of the foot. Thus a man's ' dress,' would
include all his garments ; while in modern phrase, a woman's dress, is only part of her dress.

Graith, an excellent and convenient word, meaning all things
necessary for preparation or readiness ; the trappings,
caparison, or gear, needed in any pursuit, vocation, business,
or play. Thus the *graith* of a sportsman would be the
costume, gun, powder, shot, and other trappings ; the graith
of a fisherman, or angler, the things that should be ready
for the pursuit of his business or sport. The verb, to
graithe or *greithe*, signifies to prepare or make ready.

Thus Chaucer in the Reve's Tale :

> Unto the Jews such a hate had he,
> That he bade *greithe* (make ready) his chair full hastilie.

> Go warn me Perthshire and Angus baith,
> And *graith* my horse.—*Song of the Outlaw Murray.*

The Scottish proverb says :

> He that rides ere be he ready, is sure to want some of his *graith.*

A critic in the ' Literary Gazette,' of the 30th of March,
1861, calls a poet to account for using such an unallowable
word as *graith*, of which he (the critic) declares his utter
ignorance.

In Scottish and Border poetry the word is frequent. Burns
in the Holy Fair speaks of sensible farmers in

> their riding *graith.*

And in Scotch Drink, of the time,

> When Vulcan gi'es his bellows breath,
> And ploughmen gather wi' their *graith.*

Graith—*continued.*

Again in Tam Samson's Elegy, when he supposes the sportsman to be saying, he says:

> That woeful moon be ever mourned,
> Saw him in shooting *graith* adorned,
> While pointers round impatient burned,
> Frae couples freed.

Grayle, fine particles of gravel.

Greet,
Grat, } to weep.
Grutten,

> And then gar Gloton *greet.*—*Piers Ploughman.*

> Better bairns should *greet* than bearded men.
> *Allan Ramsay's Proverbs.*

> The bridgroom *grat* when the sun gaed down.
> *Old Song.*

> O I hae *grutten* mony a day.
> For one that's banished far away.
> *Jacobite Songs,* '*Somebody*,' page 128, Griffin's Edition.

An old Scotchwoman in describing her favourite preacher, said he was one 'who spat, and swat, and *grat*, over his sermon.'

Grieve, a bailiff, overseer, or magistrate; from the German graf, and Anglo-Saxon ge-refa, a lord or earl.

> Too many *grieves* hinder the work.
> *Allan Ramsay's Scotch Proverbs.*

Grip, to seize, to lay fast hold of. It is said of Scotchmen in America, that they have greater grip of purpose, knowledge, and business, than Englishmen or Germans. In London a man would say, 'he caught hold of me by the arm,' or 'he seized or took my hand and shook it warmly.' In Scotland and the Border counties, and in old English, the expression would be, 'he *gripped* or grippet me by the arm or hand,' &c.

> The masons' mystic word and *grip.*
> *Burns : Address to the Deil.*

> But when you feel your honor *grip.*
> *Idem : Epistle to a Young Friend.*

Grisly, terrible, the 'grisly bear.'

> So spake the *grisly* terror.—*Paradise Lost.*

Grith, peace, (Anglo-Saxon.)

Grithserjeant, a constable or peace officer.

Grub, this word as applied to food is a modern vulgarism; but nevertheless can be traced to a pure English root, being the preterite of grab, to dig, whence also *grave*, a hole in the ground. Grub, therefore, signifies something dug out of the ground, as potatoes, or other edible roots.

Grue, *v.* to pain or grieve, used in this sense in Lincolnshire.

Gruesome, fearful, ugly, disagreeable.

> Death, that *gruesome* carle.—*Burns.*

Grythe, to tremble; whence earth·*grythe*, an earthquake; '*Dictionary of the Oldest Words in the English Language.*' *J. C. Hotten,* 1862.

Gurl, to growl.

Gurly, growly, savage.

> The lift grew dark and the wind blew loud,
> And *gurly* grew the sea.
>> *Ballad of Sir Patrick Spens.*

> When northern blasts the ocean *smurl*,
> And gan the heights and houses look *gurl*.
>> *Allan Ramsay.*

> Waesome wailed the snow-white sprites,
> Upon the *gurly* sea.
>> *Ballad of the Demon Lover.*

> Iberius with a *gurly* nod,
> Cried Hogan! yes, we ken your god,
> 'Tis herrings you adore.
>> *Allan Ramsay: The Vision.*

Hain, to save, to preserve with care, to spare, to keep without use.

> To ' hain' a pasture is to exclude cattle from it; so that the grass may grow for hay.

> > The weel *hained* kebbuck; (The well-preserved cheese.)
> > > *Burns : Cotter's Saturday Night.*

> > Chiels wha their characters winna *hain*,
> > But tune their lays.
> > > *Burns : To William Simpson.*

> > Long fasting *hains* no meat.—*Northern Proverb.*

Hale, as contradistinguished from sick. As in the phrase, *hale* and hearty.

Halfendele,
Halfendeal, } a moiety.

Hap, to enwrap, to swathe, to swaddle, to cover up or in warm clothing, or coverlets.

> > He should be better *hapt*, or covered from the cold.
> > > *More's Utopia.*

> > *Hap* well your backs, and well your bellies fill.
> > > *Poor Robin.*

> > I digged a grave and laid him in,
> > And *happed* him with the sod so green.
> > > *Lament of the Border Widow, Minstrelsy of the Scottish Border.*

> > *Hap* and lowe ; *hap* and rowe,
> > *Hap* and rowe the feetie o't.—*Burns.*

Hap, fate, fortune ; also as a verb, to befall, happen, come to pass.

> > No man can make his ain *hap.*
> > > *Allan Ramsay.*

Haps, travelling rugs, or great coats.

> > Never travel in Scotland, without *haps.* If ye dinna want them for the cauld, ye'll need them for the rain.
> > > *Scott.*

Hardel, the back of the hand.

Hearten, to encourage, or inspire with heart.

Hedge-bell, the wild convolvulus.

Helve, a handle.

> Throw the helve after the hatchet.—*Proverb.*

Hend,
Hende, } gentle, courteous, polite.
Hynde,

> Chaucer in the Frere's prologue, says:
>> Tho' spake our host; ah sire ye should been *hende,*
>> And courteous as a man of your estate.

> In the Morte Arthur we find,
>> Lancelot spoke with hearte free,
>> For to comfort that lady *hende.*

> and in the same romance:
>> Lordes they were and ladies *hend.*

> In Bevis of Hampton:
>> Whereto should I that maid deceive,
>> She was the fairest thing on live,
>> She was so *hend* and so well taught.

> Mr. Halliwell quotes from a MS. at Cambridge:
>> *Hende* he was and mild of mood,
>> All men spoke of him great good.

> And from another MS. with different spelling:
>> She was both courteous and *hynde,*
>> Every man was her frynde.

It may not unreasonably be concluded from these examples, that *hende* is the root of the modern *handsome.* The proverb, 'handsome is that handsome does;' means that he who does a gentle and a courteous action, is himself gentle and courteous, or *hende.*

Hent, to hold, or seize; also a hold, an opportunity, a purpose.

> The steward by the throte he *hente.*
>> *MS. quoted by Halliwell.*
> Up sword, and know thou a more horrid *hent.*
>> *Hamlet.*

Henter, a thief, a holder, or seizer of that which does not belong to him.—*Lydgate.*

Het, preterite of hit, to strike.

> He buffeted me so about the mouth,
> That out my teeth he *hette.*—*Piers Ploughman.*

Hext, highest. Nigh, nigher, and next, are the three recognized and common degrees of comparison, of the adjective nigh or near. The adjective high formerly underwent similar changes; but the superlative *hext,* useful as a rhyme if for no other purpose, has become obsolete. Chaucer in his 'Dreame,' speaks of

> The first apple and the *hext,*
> Which ygrowth unto you next;
> Yhath three virtues notable,
> And keepeth youth aye durable.

Mr. Halliwell quotes but one example of the word from a MS. in the Library of Trinity College:

> The Archbishope of Canterburye,
> In Engelande that is *hext.*

Hickery, ill-natured.

Hidel, a hiding-place.

Hie, } to haste. This word is nearly obsolete, but survives
Hye, } in heroic and mock heroic verse; as, '*hie* thee hence,' make haste to away: '*he *hied* him home,' he made the best of his way home.

Hind, a peasant, or farm labourer.

> One morning early a farmer you'll find,
> Was walking along when he met with a *hind,*
> A poor honest fellow upon the highway.
> *The Farmer and the Hind; Notes and Queries,* April 21, 1866.

Hinderling, a marplot, an obstructive, a wet blanket.

Hindersome, }
Hindrous, } retarding, preventing.

Hirple, to limp, to halt.

> The hares were *hirplin'* down the furze.
> *Burns: The Holy Fair.*

Hirtle, }
Hurtle, } to clash, to meet together with violence.

> They drew out their swords and *hurtled* together.
> *History of Prince Arthur.*

> And he him *hurtleth* with his horse adown.
> *Chaucer: The Knight's Tale.*

> That heaven hastilie and erth should *hurtel* together.
> *William and the Werwolf.*

> Iron sleet of arrowy shower
> *Hurtled* in the darkened air.—*Gray's Bard.*

Hithercome, arrival.

Hoils, the beards of barley.

Holme, a meadow near a river; in some parts of the country called a botham or bottom.

Holp, helped, preterite of help.

Holpen, helped. 'I have *holpen* him in extremity.'

And blind men *holpen.—Piers Ploughman.*

Holyrood, the holy cross.

Holystead, a holy place.

Holt, a small patch of forest.

About the rivers, valleys, *holts*, and drags,
Among the oziers and the waving flags.
Browne : Britannia's Pastorals.

Home-come, arrival at home.

Hoo, she.

When I put little Sallie to bed,
Hoo cried that her father warnt there.
Waugh's Lancashire Songs.

Hore, the preterite of hire, whence whore, a corruption of *hore*, one who does for hire or pay, that which should be done for love and duty alone. From the same root comes hireling, one who is *paid* to do a particular work. A *soldier* is a hireling, but there is no word in the English language, to express his status. Soldier, from solde pay, and *soldat*, paid, is the only English synonyme remaining in the language. In the original sense of the word *hire*, and its preterite *hore*, a barrister, a physician, or in a lower rank, anyone receiving pay, or wages for service rendered, is a *hore*.

Hotfoot, in such haste that the foot is hot with running the errand.

House-carle, a male domestic servant.

Rebuking, as every child has heard, her *house-carle's* flattery.
Rereward the Wake, by the Rev. Charles Kingsley, vol. i. p. 9.

He is a *house-carle* of mine, Lord King.
Ibid. page 63.

Hove, preterite of heave, to hoist; and preferable to the modern and weaker preterite *heaved*. 'The ship *hove* in sight;' is still a correct nautical phrase.

Howk, to dig, or scrape up the earth like an animal, or without tools.

> He's *howket* a grave by the light o' the moon.
>> *Cumberland Ballads, The Sun shines fair on Carlisle wa'.*
>
> She has *howked* a hole both deep and wide,
> And put them in both, side by side.
>> *The Cruel Mother.*

Huly,
Hooly, } softly, fairly, comfortably.

> When he was on the other side,
> Then fair and *hulie* could he ride.
>> *Romance of Sir Eger, Sir Graham and Sir Gray Steel.*
>
> 'Friend! *huly!* haste not half so fast,
> Lest,' quoth Experience, 'at the last,
> Ye buy my doctrine dear.'
>> *The Cherry and the Sloe*, 1590.
>
> *Hooly* and fairly go far in a day.
>> *Northern Proverb.*
>
> Oh *hooly, hooly*, ran she up,
> To the place where he was lying,
> And when she drew the curtain, said
> 'Young man I think you're dying.'
>> *Barbara Allan, Percy's Reliques.*
>
> Oh gin my wife would drink *hooly* and fairly.
>> *Burns.*

Humoursome, capricious, full of odd conceits, crotchets and *humours*.

Hurkle, to shrug the shoulders.

Hurly, a noise, whence *hurly burly*, a confused noise.

Imp, to lengthen, or shoot out, to *imp* the wings for flight.

> That pretty Cupid, God of love,
> Whom *imped* wings with speckled plumes are dight.
>> *Drayton Pastorals.*

> *Imp* out our drooping country's broken wings.
>> *Shakspeare.*

Imp, from the Anglo-Saxon impa, to engraft, emplant; or from the German empfangen, to receive, to conceive, to become pregnant; or from impfen, to graft, or inoculate; from whence *imp,* a child, a bud, a shoot. In German, impfling is a child that has been vaccinated.

> He took upon him to protect him from them all, and not to suffer so goodly an *imp* (Alcibiades) to lose the good fruit of his youth.
>> *North's Plutarch.*

> Of feeble trees there cometh wretched *impes.*
>> *Chaucer.*

> Ye sacred *imps* that in Parnassus dwell.
>> *Spenser.*

> And thou most dreaded *imp* of highest Jove,
> Fair Venus' son.
>> *Spenser : Fairie Queene.*

> A lad of life, an *imp* of fame.
>> *Shakspeare : Henry V.*

> *Ympe* it in our thoughts, (i.e., engraft it in our minds).
>> *MS. Digby, (Halliwell).*

The word like so many others derived from the Anglo-Saxon, has been gradually perverted from its original meaning; and *imp* now signifies a young demon; or is applied in wrath or contempt, to a very wicked or disagreeable child.

> But as the devil owes all his *imps* a shame,
> He chose the apostate as his proper theme.
>> *Dryden : Absalom and Achitophel.*

> The serpent, fittest *imp* of fraud.
>> *Milton.*

Impleach, interweave.

> With twisted metal amorously *impleached*.
> > *Shakspeare: A Lover's Complaint.*

Ingle, a fire-place, or fire-side. The original meaning of the word seems to have been a favourite or dear friend; as in the phrase quoted by Nares from the 'Honest Whore,' 'Call me your love, your *ingle*, your cousin, or so; but sister, at no hand.' Or in 'Donne's Elegies:

> Thy little brethren, which like fairy sprites,
> Oft skipt into our chamber those sweet nights,
> And kiss'd and *ingled* on thy father's knee.

From this idea, probably, the fire-side, or place most comfortable and sought after in the house, came to be called the *ingle*, or the favourite; the place of honor reserved for age, or for the evening assemblage of the family. A proverb in Allan Ramsay's Collection seems to lend strength to this supposition. It says, 'a good *ingle* makes a room fireside;' as if fireside and ingle were not altogether synonymous.

In the ancient sense the word has utterly disappeared, but, as the name for the blazing hearth and favorite corner, it subsists throughout the North of England and Scotland. Burns, in his 'Cotter's Saturday Night,' has made it familiar to all the lovers of poetry:

> His wee-bit *ingle* blinkin' bonnily;

and it has been used by some of the best modern writers and speakers, both north and south of the Tweed.

> Better a wee *ingle* to warm you, than a muckle fire to burn you.
> > *Scotch Proverb.*

Inwit, conscience; as distinguished from outwit, knowledge, ability, information.

> Who murthereth a good man,
> Methinketh by mine *inwit*,
> He fordeth the livest light,
> That our hand loveth.
> > *Piers Ploughman.*

> With *inwit* and with *outwit*,
> Imaginin' and studie.
> > *Idem.*

Irk, to weary, tire, trouble or distress, derived by some grammarians from work.

> King Edward in his life, albeit, that this dissension between his friends somewhat *irked* him.
> > *Sir Thomas More's Works.*
>
> Now use it *irketh* me,
> That to thy bliss I made this luckless breach.
> > *Spenser.*
>
> Even Christ's easy yoke they *irke* to bear.
> > *Stirling : Domes Day, The Fifth Hour.*

As a verb the word is almost obsolete, but the adjective *irksome* remains fixed in the language.

Jade, to exhaust, or weary. The past participle *jaded*, wearied, remains in common usage. To jade, was a new word in the time of James I., as may be inferred from Lord Bacon, who says :

> It is a dull thing to tire, or as we now say to *jade*, any thing too far.]

Janglesome, quarrelsome.

Jape, to jest, to cheat, to mock, to laugh at. This word and its derivatives, *japer*, a buffoon ; *japery*, buffoonery ; and *japeworthy*, ridiculous ; are of common occurrence in Chaucer, in the prologue to the Rhyme of Sir Topaz :

> Till that our host to *japen* he began.

And in the Knight's Tale :

> Thus hath he *japed* thee for many a year.

So also in the Coke's prologue :

> I will tell you as well as ever I can,
> A little *jape* that fell in our citie.

And in a MS. of Occleve, cited in Halliwell's Dictionary of Archaic and Provincial words :

> Demosthenes his hands once put
> Into a woman's bosom *japingly*.

Jant, cheerful, merry, whence the modern *jaunty.*

Jaunce, to ride hard.

> And yet I bear a burden like an ass,
> Spur-galled and tired by *jauncing* Bolingbroke.
>> *Shakspeare: Richard II.*

' Jaunce,' says Nares, ' was also used for a jaunt.' A jaunting car, would thus be a *jauncing* car, or a car driven swiftly.

Jig, this word that now signifies a dance, formerly signified a song or ballad. The word *ballad* is from *ballare* to dance; so that both jig and ballad, are words that conbine the ideas of singing or dancing. When there were no musical instruments or players available at a festivity, it would seem from their derivatives, that the voice of a singer was used to set the feet of the dancers in motion.

> While here you *jig*,
> How is your ballad titled?
>> *The Fatal Contract.*

> Look to it you booksellers and stationers, and let not your shops be infected with such stinking garbage—as the *jigs* of news mongers.
>> *Pierce Penniless.*

Jimp, dainty, well formed, well-fitting.

> Of all these maidens mild as mead,
> Was nane sae *jimp* as Gillie.
>> *Christ's Kirk on the Green.*

> Oh wha will shoe my fair foot,
> Or wha will glove my hand,
> Or wha will lace my middle *jimp*,
> Wi' a new made London band?
>> *Annie o' Lochroyam.*

> There were pipers playing in every neuk,
> And ladies dancing *jimp* and sma'.
>> *The wee wee man ; Minstrelsy of the Scottish Border.*

Jobbernowle, a thick-headed, dull, heavy person.

> His guts are in his brains, huge *jobbernowle.*
>> *Marston.*

Joss, to crowd or press together; whence the diminutive jostle, to press against in a crowd.

Jow, the swing of a bell.

> And every *jow* that the dead-bell gied,
> Cried woe to Barbara Allan.
>> *Barbara Allan, Border Minstrelsy.*

Jowl, a monotonous sound, as of a bell.

> They drew their swords to the *jowl* o' the bell.
> > *Cumberland Border Ballads.*

Jug-bitten, drunk.

> Nor when any of them are wounded, *pot-shot, jug-bitten,* or *cup-shaken,* so that they have lost all reasonable faculties of the mind.
> > *Taylor's Workes,* 1631, *quoted by Nares.*

July. The original and correct pronunciation of the name of the month, now accentuated on the last syllable. If Jùly be Julỳ, Aùgust should be Augùst, and Àpril Aprìl. Chaucer has *Juil* without the second syllable.

> And lowly *Jùly* in her eyes takes place.
> > *Robert Greene: Perimedes the Blacksmith,* 1588.

Jump, exact, to the point; from *jimp,* elegant and well-fitting.

> And brings him *jump* where he may Cassio find.
> > *Shakspeare: Othello.*

> He said the music best these powers displayed,
> Was *jump* concord betwixt our wit and will.
> > *Pembroke's Arcadia.*

The common phrase, that the ideas of two people jump together, means that they fit together exactly.

> I will not choose what many men desire,
> Because I will not *jump* with common spirits,
> And rank me with the barbarous multitude.
> > *Shakspeare: Merchant of Venice.*

Jumply, suitably, opportunely.

> My meeting so *jumply* with them, makes me abashed with the strangeness of it.—*Pembroke's Arcadia.*

Kail, cabbage ; erroneonsly printed 'kell ' in Nare's Glossary.

Kail-blade, a cabbage leaf.

Kail-runt, a cabbage stalk.

Kam, crooked ; from the Gaelic.

> This is clean *kam.*
> > *Shakspeare : Coriolanus.*
>
> Clean contrary *clam,* quite crooked.
> > *Cotgrave.*

Kane, } tribute, or rent paid in kind.   Mr. Halliwell says the
Kain, } word is current in this sense in the East of England.

> Our laird gets in his racked rents,
> His coals, his *kain.*
> > *Burns : The Twa Dogs.*
>
> I'd hae paid my *kane* seven times to hell,
> Ere you'd been won away.
> > *Ballad of the Young Tamlane ; Motherwell's Collection.*

There is a well known Jacobite song, of which the burthen is, 'They shall pay *kane* to the king the morn.'

A Northern proverb says of a man who has atoned for all his faults by death :

> He has paid the *kane* for all.

Keach, to lade or ladle out water ; or take water out of a well by dipping in a pitcher or other utensil.

Kebars, rafters of a house or other building.

> He ended and the *kebars* shook.
> > *Burns : The Jolly Beggars.*

Keech, a fat round lump, whence also a keg (of butter). Shakspeare uses the word to caricature the personal appearance of Cardinal Wolsey :

> That such a *keech* (as Wolsey) can with his very bulk,
> Take up the rays o' the beneficial sun,
> And keep them from the earth.
> > *Henry VIII.*

Kelf, a fool, Scotticè, a coof or cuif.

> One, Squire Ereas, a great *kelf,*
> Some wandering hangman like himself.
> *Cotton,* 1734.

Kelpie, a water spirit; noted in the superstition of Scotland.

Kemp, a soldier, a champion.

> Till *kemp* Owyne come o'er the sea,
> And borrow you with kisses three.
> *Kemp Owyne, Motherwell's Ancient and Modern Minstrelsy.*

Kemp, to strive with another who shall do most work in a given time; i.e., who shall become the kemp, champion, or foremost man.

> There is no kynge under Christe who can *kemp* with him.
> *Morte Arthur.*

Kempt, preterite and past participle of comb. *Unkempt,* for uncombed, is still used in literary and poetical composition.

> There is nothing valiant or solid to be hoped for from such as are always *kempt,* perfumed, and every day smell of the tailor.
> *Ben Jonson.*

Kep, to catch, to receive; from the same root as 'keep,' to retain, but distinguished from 'keep' by a sensible difference; 'for you may *kep* what you do not keep:' i.e., you may catch what you do not hold; you may receive a hundred pounds and fail to retain them.

> Ilka blade o' grass *keps* its ain drap o' dew.
> *Scotch Proverb.*

> Mourn Spring, the darling of the year,
> Ilk cowslip cup shall *kep* a tear.
> *Burns : Elegy on Captain Maitland Henderson.*

Kern, (whence corn,) the fruit of wheat; and in the form of kernel, or 'little corn,' the edible portion of a nut.

Kern, to turn from blossom to fruit, to set, to granulate.

Kevil,
Kavel,
Gavil, a lot. To cast kevils, or kavels; to draw lots. *Gavel kind,* distribution of an estate by lot, among the children. In 'Thompson's Etymons of English Words,' it is stated that *kavel* or *cavel,* originally meant a stick; and that the father of a family, in Kent, where the law of gavel-kind prevailed, had the names of the different portions of his estate inscribed on pieces of wood, which he enclosed in a box. At his decease, his children drew their lots, and in-

Kevil—*continued.*

herited accordingly. A similar practice was known to the ancient Greeks.

> Happy man, happy *kevil!*

> Let every man be content with his ain *kavel.*
> > *Allan Ramsay.*

> And they cast *kevils* them amang,
> Wha should to the greenwood gang.
> > *Cospatrick : Scott's Border Minstrelsy.*

Kex, dry stalk of hemlock or corn; a rush.

> As doth a *kex* or a candle.
> > *Piers Ploughman.*

> I bring with me a booke as dry as a *kex.*
> > *Skelton.*

Kexy,
Kisky, } juiceless, sapless, dry.

Kilt, to lift up the petticoats or clothes, to avoid wetting them, when going on a journey on foot.

> She has *kilted* her coats of green satin,
> She has *kilted* them up to the knee,
> And is off wi' Lord Ronald McDonald,
> His bride and his darling to be.

From this verb comes kilt, the English or Saxon name for the most conspicuous portion of the Highland garb, called by the Highlanders themselves the fillibeg, or little coat. The participle *kilted* is sometimes used metaphorically to denote language that borders upon indecency; as in the following description of the popular Muse of Scotland.

> If sometimes *high kilted* in her language, her heart is pure. She never jests at virtue, though she often has a fling at hypocrisy. Her laughter is as refreshing as her tears ; and her humour is as exquisite as her tenderness.
> > *Jacobite Songs and Ballads of Scotland,* 1861.

Kime, a silly fellow.

Kinchen, a small child; from the German diminutive of *kind,* a child, *kindchen.* This word is said by Nares to be a ' cant term ;' but is not such by its derivation. Properly it should be kinkin, on the same principle as ' mannikin,' a little man.

Kindle, to inflame. This word is not quite obsolete, either in literature or conversation; but is partially superseded by a less elegant and forcible word, ' to light.' ' To *kindle* a fire,' is better English than to *light* a fire. ' Light the candle,' is correct, because the candle is required for its light; whereas light the fire is not so forcible, because the fire is *kindled*, not for its light, but its heat.

Kindling-wood, fire-wood, wood for kindling fires. This phrase is common in America, but almost obsolete in England.

Kink, { *v.* to twist, entangle.
{ *n.* a curl, a notion.

> May Margaret sits in the Queen's Bower,
> *Kinking* her fingers, one by one.
>> *Ballad of May Margaret : Motherwell's Collection.*

This word is common in America both as noun and verb. A curly headed man is said to have *kinks* in his hair; and a man with odd ideas to have *kinks* in his brain.

Kike,
Keek, } to peep slyly, to look in.

> When the tod (fox) is in the wood, he cares na how many *keek* at his tail.—*Allan Ramsay : Scotch Proverbs.*

> Stars dinna *keek* in,
> And see me wi' Mary.
>> *Burns.*

> The gossip *keekit* in his loop (hand).
> Quo' she, who lives will see the proof,
> This waly boy will be na coof (fool),
> I think we'll ca' him Robin.
>> *Burns.*

> And now the sun *keeks* in the west,
> And I maun rise among the rest.
>> *Burns : Epistle to Lapraik.*

> The Robin came to the wren's nest,
> And *keeked* in.
>> *Nursery Rhymes.*

> This Nicholas sat even gaping upright,
> As he had *keyked* on the new moone.
>> *Chaucer : The Miller's Tale.*

Kirtle, a petticoat, or loose gown.

> What stuff wilt thou have a *kirtle* of?
> > *Shakspeare : Henry IV.*

> All in a *kirtle* of discoloured soy.
> > *Spenser : Faerie Queene.*

Kiss-worthy, deserving of a kiss, inspiring affection.

> Thy most *kiss-worthy* face,
> Anger invests with such lovely grace,
> That Anger's self I needs must kiss again.
> > *Sir Philip Sidney.*

Kith, ⎫ to show, to appear, to make known, from whence the
Kithe, ⎬ preterite *kouth* or *couth*, known ; *sel-couth* used by
Kythe, ⎭ Chaucer, and meaning seldom known ; and the modern
word *uncouth*, which originally meant strange and unknown,
but which has by degrees come to signify, rough, rude, and
unshapely. The modern word *kith*, as distinguished from
kin, in the phrase of 'kith and kin,' means acquaintances, as
distinguished from relatives.

> Take your sport and *kythe* you knights.
> > *Metrical Romance of Sir Ferumbras.*

> Lift up thine hart and sing with gude intent,
> > And in thy notes sweete the treson telle,
> That to thy sister true and innocent,
> > Was *kythet* by her husband false and fell.
> > > *The King's Quair.*

> Their faces blythe, they sweetly *kythe*,
> Hearts leal and warm and true.
> > *Burns : Halloween.*

> If you love me, *kythe* it.

> True love *kythes* in time of need.

> *Kythe* in your ain colours, that folk may know you.
> > *Allan Ramsay : Scotch Proverbs.*

> The deed that thou hast done this night,
> Will *kythe* upon the morrow.
> > *Sweet William and Lady Margaret.*

Kittle, difficult, perilous, ticklish.

'A *kittle* question, one that is not only difficult but in-
convenient to answer ; 'a *kittle* horse,' one troublesome to
manage ; 'a *kittle* subject,' a ticklish subject.

Kittle—*continued.*

> Gude man, quoth he, put up your whittle,
> I'm no designed to try its mettle,
> But if I did ; I wad be *kittle*
>   To be mislear'd.
>
> *Tam o' Shanter.*

The following proverbs from Allan Ramsay's Collection, show some of the various shades of meaning in this word :

> Butter and burn trout are *kittle* meat for maidens.

> It's *kittle* shooting at crows and clergy.

> It's *kittle* to waken sleeping dogs.

> It's *kittle* for the cheeks when a wheelbarrow goes over the nose.

Knab, to take hold of, to bite, or gnaw ; to take the head off ; whence also knib, nib, and nibble.

> I had (could) much rather lie *knabbing* crusts without fear, than be mistress of the world with cares.
>
> *L'Estrange.*

> Oh once I had the best of hay
>   And fodder in the stall,
> But now I'm forced to *knab* the grass
>   That grows beneath the wall.
>   Poor old horse !
>
> *Old Ballad.*

Knabb, }
Knapp, } the top or head of a mountain. This word is common in Westmoreland and Cumberland ; and constantly occurs in topographical nomenclature. *Knabb*-Scaur, opposite Rydal Mount, the former residence of Wordsworth, is frequently mentioned in his poems. Knapdale is also a well-known district. By a corruption of this word we have the slang phrase, ' You'll *nab* it ;' *i.e.* ' You'll have a blow on the head.

Knobbly, }
Nobby, } round, lumpy, like a mountain.

Knoll, }
Knowle, } a round hill.

Knee-bending, a genuflection.

Knee-crooking, obsequious, slavish in homage.

> Many a duteous and *knee-crooking* knave.
>
> *Shakspeare,*

Knell, to ring or toll the bell for a funeral : to sound the *knell*.

Knoll, preterite of *knell*.

Knevel, the moustache. The hair on the upper lip was worn for ages, before the modern, and now the only, name for the thing was borrowed from the Spanish. The word is entirely obsolete, but pure English.

Knit, now used as the infinitive of the verb to knit, was originally the preterite of ' knot,' to tie in a knot, as in Robert Burns' Song of the Ploughman :

> The ploughman he's a bonny lad,
> His mind is ever true jo,
> His garter *knit,* below his knee.

Knoppe, a button or a bud ; a word in common use before the English people began to import their fashions as well as their speech from the continent ; and one form of which still survives as *knob,* the knob or button of a door. The French still say ' les *boutons* de la rose,' i.e., the *buttons,* buds, or *knoppes* of the rose.

> And with a bend of golde tassiled,
> And *knoppes* fine of golde.
> > *Chaucer : Romance of the Rose.*

> About the rede roses springing,
> The stalke was as rushe right,
> And there stoode the *knoppe* upright.
> > *Idem.*

> Take half a pound of rede rose flowers that be gadenyd early whyle the dew lasts, and ben ful sprad, and pulle off the *knoppes* and clyppe hem with a pair sherys.
> > *MS., 15th Century quoted by Halliwell.*

Knurl, sometimes written *nirl,* to shrink up with the cold. A dwarf, or any shrunken object. A common word in the Border Counties of England and Scotland.

> The corn has been *nirled* with the drowth.
> > *Jamieson.*

> A perfect *knurl ;* I've seen as buirdly a chiel in a glass bottle upon a doctor's shelf.—*Reginald Dalton.*

Koister, a rough, ignorant, ill-tempered fellow, a churl, from the French *cuistre.*

Kye, cows, or cattle generally. The plural *kine* is still used in the north of England and Scotland, and in poetic composition.

Kype, a grimace.

Lack, to be in want of: a verb that is fast becoming obsolete. '*Lack*-wit,' '*lack*-penny,' '*lack*-land,' '*lack*-lustre,' '*lack*-love,' '*lack*-beard,' '*lack*-teeth,' '*lack*-brain,' &c. ; were once common expressions, the disuse of which has not been remedied by the modern synonymes and paraphrastic circumlocutions employed to represent them.

Lade, to empty out or to let in water by degrees, whence the diminutive *ladle.*

Lag, *n.* the extreme end, and also as a verb, to remain behind, at the very end or last.

> The *lag* end of my life.
> > *Shakspeare: Henry IV.*
>
> The senators of Athens with the common *lag* of people.
> > *Shakspeare: Timon of Athens.*

Langsyne, a long time ago. This word is commonly supposed to be pure Scottish; but is not so; as it extends not only into Northumberland and Cumberland, but into Yorkshire. Miss Blamire of Thackwood, Cumberland, makes the word the burden of one of her best poems, 'The Traveller's Return:'

> I closed the door and sobbed aloud,
> To think o' *auld langsyne.*

Allan Ramsay and Robert Burns have rendered the word classical.

Langsyner, a person who lived a long while ago, [Northumbrian and Scottish.]

Lanken, } to grow lean and lanky.
Lank, }

> Thy cheek so much as *lank'd* not.
> > *Shakspeare : Antony and Cleopatra.*

Lass-lorn, having lost or been dismissed by a mistress.

> Whose shadow the dismissed bachelor loves,
> Being *lass-lorn.—Shakspeare : The Tempest.*

Lave, the residue ; that which is omitted or left out ; a purely
Saxon word, and much wanted. The Anglo-Saxons called
a widow, a *lafe*, or *lave*, i.e., a relict. In the Ode on Athel-
stane's Victory in 'Ellis's Specimens of Early English Poets,'
the word occurs twice : ' Mid hyra here *leafuna*,' with the
lave or remainder ' of the army ;' and ' Dreorig dare the
laf,' ' dreary there the lave.' In the excellent song of
Burns, ' First when Maggy was my care,' the chorus ' whistle
o'er the *lave* o't ;' could not be rendered by any synonyme,
without the total destruction of the strength and beauty of
the expression. ' Whistle o'er the *rest* of it,' would be tame,
besides being liable to the misinterpretation of rest for re-
pose ; and 'whistle o'er the *remainder* or residue of it,' would
be prosaic.

Laze, to loll, to idle, to lie in the sunshine doing nothing ;
whence the adjective *lazy*.

> Cupid *lazeth* 'mong the fairy lasses.
> *Nares.*

Lea, ⎫ a field. Not obsolete in poetry, but almost obsolete
Lee,   ⎬ in prose. It survives in Scotland and the North of Eng-
Ley,   ⎭ land ; and throughout England as a termination to many
well-known surnames, such as Stan*ley*, the stone-field ; Win-
stan*ley*, the whin-stone field ; Edge*ley*, the field on the edge ;
Endsleigh or Ends*ley*, the field at the end ; Buck*ley*, the
field of the beech tree ; Oak*ley*, the field of the oak ; Far-
ley, the far field ; Fairleigh or Fair*ley*, the fair-field, &c.

Lele, ⎫ loyal, faithful, true ; ' The land o' the leal,' heaven.
Leal, ⎭

> Her love is ever true and *lele*.
> *Cursor Mundi, MS. Trin. Coll. Cantab.*

> But a clere virgin that is *lele*,
> Has yet more than has the angele.
> *MS. Har..*

> Oh stop ! oh stop ! young man, she said,
>   For I in dule am dight,
> Oh stop and win a fair lady's love,
>   If you be a *leal* true knight.
> *Ballad of Sir Roland.*

Lele—*continued.*

> I'm wearing awa, Jean,
> Like snow wreaths in thaw, Jean,
> I'm wearing awa, Jean,
> > To the land o' the *leal.*
> > > *Lady Nairne.*

> *Leal*-heart never lied.

> Lang *leal*, lang poor.

> Spier at Jack Thief if I be a *leal* man.
> > *Allan Ramsay's Scottish Proverbs.*

Leath, cessation or soothing.

> The *leath* of pain in sleep.

Leer, empty.

This word is sufficiently common in every part of Devonshire; a leer stomach, an empty stomach.—*Giffard.*

A leer horse, a horse without a rider (empty), whence the phrase came to signify a led horse.—*Nares.*

Leeze, to approve, to be highly in favour of any thing.

> *Leeze* me on the spinning wheel.
> > *Burns.*

Leman, a lover; originally applied to both sexes, but in progress of time, and in the improvement, or may be corruption of the language, applied solely to the female; and by a still later corruption, to signify a mistress, as distinguished from a wife.

> Many a lovely lady and *leman* of knightes,
> Swoonden and swelten for sorow of death's dints.
> > *Piers Ploughman.*

> Every maiden chose her lover,
> Every knight his *leman.*
> > *Guy of Warwick.*

> Of Ascalot, that maiden free,
> I said you, she was his *leman.*
> > *Morte Arthur.*

Leme,
Leam, } to shine; a light.

> The light of Heaven is a *leme,*
> Brighter than is the sone beme.
> > *MS. Ashmole.*

Leme—*continued.*

> The lawnces with lorayne and *lemande* scheldes.
> > *Morte Arthur.*

> The starres with the *leming* leven,
> Shall sadly falle down from heaven.
> > *Cursor Mundi, MS. Trin. Coll. Cam., quoted by Halliwell.*

> Which causeth folk to dreden in their dremes,
> Of arwes and of fire with rede *lemes.*
> > *Chaucer : The Nonnes Preestes Tale.*

> The bright *leme* of a torch.
> > *Sir T. Elyot.*

> With lily white cheek and *leming* eye,
> She look'd and laughed to him.
> > *The Jolly Goss-Hawk, Border Minstrelsy.*

Lesing, a lie.

> For we lived on the *lesynges.*
> > *Piers Ploughman.*

Lest,⎫ to please. I *lest*, I please ; I *list*, I pleased ; I have
List, ⎬ *lust*, I have pleased ; seem to have been the original
Lust,⎭ forms for the conjugation of this verb ; but at an early period, the present, the preterite, and the past participle, were indiscriminately used as the infinitive. In Chaucer we find *lest* :

> And then our hoste began his horse to reste,
> And saide, lordes ! harkeneth if you *lest.*
> > *The Knighte's Tale.*

In Lord Surrey's Translation of Virgil ; and in the authorized translation of the Bible, it is *list* :

> To whatsoever land
> By sliding seas we *listed* them to lead.
> > *Surrey, Æneis.*

> The wind bloweth where it *listeth.*
> > *John* iii. 8.

The word *lust* had been perverted from its original meaning long before the divines, appointed by James I., had commenced the translation of the Bible ; and had come to signify unlawful or inordinate animal or worldly desire ; as in the saying of Jesus : ' Whoso looketh on a woman to *lust* after her, hath committed adultery with her already in his heart ;' and in St. Paul's first Epistle to the Corinthians : ' We should not *lust* after evil things as they also *lusted.*'

Lest—*continued.*

Lest and *lust*, the preterite and past participle of the verb, were both converted into substantives, signifying delight and pleasure, but not necessarily in an evil sense. Chaucer in the *Knighte's Tale* says,

> Farewell my life, my *luste*, and my gladness,

and in the 'Assemblie of Fowles,' where he speaks of his own love of literature, he says :

> Of usage, what for *lust*, and what for love,
> In bookes rede I oft, as I you told.

Fuller in his worthies, has *list* instead of *lust*, in the same sense :

> Those Irish lords made their *list* the law to such whom they could overpower.

From this root comes the modern word *listless*, without desire of pleasure ; and perhaps the colloquial expression to *list* (afterwards *enlist*) for a soldier, i.e., to please to become a soldier ; to go voluntarily, and not by conscription as in other counties.

Lerd and **lewd**, learned and common people. See Introduction to English Provincial Dialects, by J. O. Halliwell.

Query, does not the Scotch laird, and the English lord, come from lerd, learned, and *lored*, having lore or learning ?

Let, to prevent, impede, or hinder. This word survives in the passports granted to British subjects by the Foreign Office ; in which the Princes and Potentates of Europe, are notified to permit Mr. A. B., or C. D., to travel in their territories ' without *let* or hindrance.'

> Unhand me, gentlemen !
> By heaven ! I'll make a ghost of him that *lets* me !
> *Hamlet.*

Levin, } the lightning. In Mr. Dasent's introduction to
Leven, } 'Popular Tales from the Norse,' he says, ' The trolls cannot bear the glorious face of the sun, Balder's beaming visage, or the bright flash of Thor's *levin* bolt.' Chaucer rhymes the word with heaven. In the ' Wife of Bath's prologue,' he imprecates vengeance on the scorners of women, in a magnificent line in which the word occurs :

Levin—*continued.*

> Thus sayest thou lorel, when thou goest to bed,
> And that no wise man needeth for to wed,
> Ne no man that intendeth unto heaven ;
> *With wild thunder dint and fiery* LEVEN,
> Mote thy welked neck be to be broke !

Gower in a MS. in the possession of the Society of Antiquaries, as quoted by Mr. Halliwell says :

> The thunder with his fiery *leven*,
> So cruel was upon the heaven.

And the Earl of Surrey in his translation of the Æneid :

> Since that the sire of gods, and kings of men,
> Struck me with thunder, and with *levening* blast.

Spenser in the Faery Queen, has ;

> And when the flashing *leven* leaps to light
> Upon two stubborn oaks.

Sir Walter Scott in Marmion, has :

> To him as to the burning *leven*,
> Short, bright, resistless course was given.

Levin-brand, a thunderbolt.

> His burning *levin-brand* in hand he took.
> *Spenser : Faerie Queene.*

Lewdster, an indecent, lewd, obscene person.

> Against such *lewdsters* and their lechery,
> Those that betray them do no treachery.
> *Shakspeare : Merry Wives of Windsor.*

Leuch, preterite of laugh.

> When she had read wise William's letter,
> She smiled and she *leuch*.
> *Ballad of Redisdale and Wise William, Motherwell's Collection.*

Lief, ⎱ derived from the Anglo-Saxon *leof*, and German liebe,
Liever, ⎰ love or inclination ; but displaced in modern liter-
Liefer, ⎰ ature for the less forcible phrases ' as soon as,'
' sooner,' ' rather.' The old forms are still current among
the people all over England and Scotland, though banished
from books.

> Do way ! said Guy, thereof speak nought,
> By him that all this world hath wrought,
> I had *liefer* thou wert a hog.
> *Romance of Sir Guy of Warwick*

Lief—*continued.*

> Alle woman *lievest* would,
> Be sovereign of men's love.
> > *Gower.*

> But be him *lief,* or be him loth,
> Unto the earth forth he go'th.
> > *Idem.*

> And said anon with heavy cheer,
> We had *liefer* than all my kingdom dear,
> That I were fair out of this land.
> > *Romance of Sir Degoré.*

> He wept and said, ' Well away ;
> I had *liever* till Doomesday,
> Have lain in sorrow and woe.
> > *Romance of Ancys and Amytus.*

> I had as *lief* the town crier cried my lives.
> > *Shakspeare : Hamlet.*

> I had as *lief* not be, as live to be,
> In awe of such a thing as I myself.
> > *Shakspeare.*

> Do not injure me so much as suppose I am a lawyer, I had as
> *lief* be a Scotchman.—*Junius.*

> And he that wad *liefer* drink water,
> Shall never be stinted by me.
> > *Waugh's Lancashire Songs.*

Lief, dear.

> Oft have I heard my *lief* Corydon report on a love day.
> > *Robert Greene,* 1590.

> Had my swain been *lief* to me.
> > *Idem.*

Lig, } to lie, to lie down ; from the German *liegen,* a better
Liggen, } word than ' lie,' which has another and wholly different meaning.

> Or *ligge* thus ever lollyng in my lap.
> > *Piers Ploughman.*

Lift, the sky, the air, the atmosphere. This pure Saxon word, though used in the North of England, and by the predecessors and contemporaries of Chaucer, has not yet succeeded in re-establishing itself in modern English literature. In Scottish song it is well known, and for the purposes of poetry is far more expressive and beautiful than any of its synonymes.

Lift—*continued.*

> They had na sailed a league, a league,
> A league, but barely three,
> When the *lift* grew dark, and the wind blew hard.
> > *Ballad of Sir Patrick Spens.*

> It is the moon, I ken her horn,
> That's blinkin' in the *lift* sae hie.
> She smiles so sweet to wile us hame,
> But by my troth she'll wait a wee.
> > *Burns.*

Mr. Halliwell cites two instances of the use of this word from ' Cursor Mundi,' a MS. in the library of Trinity College, Cambridge:

> Some in the earth, some in the *lift*,

and

> Now at the earth, now at the *lift*.

In the 'Land of Cockayne,' quoted in ' Ellis's Specimens of Early English Poetry,' we find:

> N' is there hawk nor foul so swift,
> Better fleeing by the *lift*.

Limber,
Limp, } loose, flexible, pliant.

> And had I lived when song was greet,
> And legs of trees were *limber*.
> > *Tennyson's Amphion.*

In America, *limber* is the most common form that the word assumes; though in New England, *limp* has been transformed into *limpsie*, or *limsy*.

A story is told of a Virginian, who had made a considerable fortune in Nova Scotia, who was met in the Railway car, hurrying southward, by a friend, who enquired if he had left the North altogether? ' Yes,' he replied, ' I am very ill; I wish to get home to die in the warm. I am frozen up. My bones are like icicles. I want to die *limber*.'

Limmer, a blackguard, a jade, still used in Scotland, but only applied to women. The word occurs in Chaucer, but means a ' hound,' possibly from the French *limier*, a blood-hound. In the Border Counties, as may be seen in the Border Minstrelsy, it is a word of reproach applied to either sex.

> What gard thee steal the Laird's Jocky horse,
> And *limmer*, what gard thee steal him, quoth he.
> > *Ballad of Dick of the Cow.*

Limmer—*continued.*

> His brother was hurt three days before,
> With *limmer* thieves, that did him prick,
> Nineteen bloody wounds lay him upon.
>> *Ballad of Rookhope Ryde.*

> Ne'er mind how Fortune waft and warp,
> Now comes the six and twentieth simmer,
> I've seen the bud upon the timmer,
> Still persecuted by the *limmer*,
>> Fra year to year.
>> *Burns : Epistle to Lapraik.*

> What's that thou sayst, thou *limmer* loon ?
>> *Minstrelsy of the Scottish Border.*

> The nurse was a false *limmer*,
> As ever hung on tree.
>> *Ballad of Lambert Linkin.*

Lin, ⎫ A mere or pool of water on the moors or among the
Linn, ⎭ mountains, of importance enough to be considered the source of a river or brook. Drayton in the Polyolbion describing the river Tivy, says :

> Tivy cometh down from her capacious *lin.*

And in the same poem ;

> And therefore to recount her rivers from her *lins.*

In Scotland, the word either signifies a fall or cataract, or the pool formed underneath it. Corra Linn on the Clyde, and the Lynn of Dee, are the two most noted for their beauty.

How fine, in the song of ' Duncan Gray,' is the description of the slighted lover, who

> Spak of lowping o'er a *linn,*

until the hard-hearted maiden relented.

Linch, to beat, or chastise, a northern English word, introduced into America as ' lynch.' Judge ' Lynch,' is a personification of the popular impulse to take summary vengeance upon a wrong doer, and not to wait for the dilatory and customary forms of law.

Ling, heath, heather, erica.

> And he saw neither rich nor poor,
> But moss and *ling*, and bare wild moor.
>> *Romance of Sir Eger, Sir Grahame, and Sir Gray Steel.*

Ling—*continued.*

> There was growing in that place where they were then encamped, very much of that kind of heath or *ling*, which the Scotch call heather.
> *Holinshed's Historie of Scotland.*

Lings, as a termination to an adverb implies going or coming in the direction of, as back*lings*, going backward ; side*lings*, going to one side ; north*lings*, going north ; east*lings*, going east ; and west*lings*, going or coming west.

Lint, flax, from the old English *linne*, whence also *linen*.

> Little he was, and wore a breast-plate made of *linne*.
> *Chapman's Homer.*

> Lassie wi' the *lint* white locks,
> *Burns.*

> Her hair it was *lint* white,
> Her skin it was milk white.
> *Hector Macneil: Saw ye my wee thing.*

Lip-wise, wise of talk or lip, as distinguished from one who is wise in brain or thought.

Lippen, to rely or depend upon, to take a liking to.

> Never *lippen* too much to a new friend or an old enemy.

> You'll beguile none but those that *lippen* to you.

> Ye may *lippen* to me, but look to yoursell.
> *Allan Ramsay's Scotch Proverbs*

Liss,
Lisse, } pleasure.

> Lord of life and of light,
> Of *lisse* and of payne.
> *Piers Ploughman.*

> *Lisse* without an ende.
> *Idem.*

Lite, few, small ; the diminutive of the word still survives as little.

Lith, moveable property. ' Nor land nor *lith*,' neither real nor personal property, was once a common phrase, long since obsolete ; see *Halliwell's Archaic Dictionary.*

Lithe, calm, quiet, soft, tender, mild.

> She tooke up her son to her,
> And happed it full *lithe.*
> *MS. Cantab, quoted by Halliwell.*

Lithe-wort, the forget-me-not.

Lithesome, } flexible.
Lissome, }

Lither, wicked, lazy, wickedly idle.

> Nay, therefore, care you not, quod Nicholas.
> A clerk hath *litherly* beset his while.
> But if he could a carpenter beguile.
> > *Chaucer: The Millere's Tale.*

> And *lither* folke to destroyen vice.
> > *Chaucer: The Cuckoo and the Nightingale.*

> Idleness most delectable to the flesh, which delighteth above measure in sloth and *lithernesse.*
> > *Northbrooke,* 1577 *(Halliwell.)*

> If he were as long as he is *lither,* he might thatch a house without a ladder.—*Cheshire Proverb.*

> The dwarf was waspish, arch, and *litherly.*
> > *Sir W. Scott.*

Lithy, pliant, supple.

Loathly, loathsome.

Lob, to drop, to fall heavily on one side; to avoid labor.

Lob, a fool, a clumsy person.

> Farewell thou *lob* of spirits.
> > *Shakspeare: Midsummer Night's Dream.*

Lob-lolly, a common colloquialism, for a lazy fool; a lolling fool; the plain Anglo-Saxon for one who indulges himself in the *dolce far niente.*

Lob's-pond, a prison, a place of confinement for one who will not work.

Lodestar, the Polar or leading star, by which ships were steered before the invention of the mariners' compass.

> Your eyes are *lodestars.*
> > *Shakspeare: Midsummer Night's Dream.*

Lodesman, a pilot.

Lodemanage, pilotage.

Loft, preterite of lift, whence a loft, something lifted upon the rest of the house; and *aloft,* lifted on high.

> The lark that sings *aloft.*

> The sweet little cherub that sits up *aloft,*
> To keep watch for the life of poor Jack.
> > *Dibden.*

Lome, frequent; 'oft and lome,' is a common phrase in old English literature, equivalent to the modern, but less elegant expression 'time and again.'

Long-home, the grave.

Longsome, tedious.

Looby, a man who lobs, or is unwilling to work.

Loof, the hollow of the hand. Apparently from the Gaelic, lamh, pronounced *laf*, the hand.

> Touch with my *lufe*.
> > *Townley Mysteries : quoted by Halliwell.*
> See, here's my *loof*.
> > *Robert Burns.*

Loon, a stupid lout, or clown.

> The devil damn thee black, thou cream faced *loon*.
> > *Macbeth.*

Loot, preterite of let, to permit.

> And aye she *loot* the tears down fa',
> For Jock of Hazeldea.
> > *Sir W. Scott.*
> Ye've *loot* the ponie o'er the dyke.
> > *Burns.*
> She'd pu'd him frae the milk white steed.
> And *loot* the bridle fa'.
> > *Motherwell's Collection.*

Looth, shelter, a sheltered place.

Lope, preterite of leap.

> Tom Rindle *lope* fra the chimley nook.
> > *Lancashire Songs, by Edwin Waugh.*

Lorefather, a man eminent for his erudition, a teacher.

> Of all men they do most evil,
> Their *lorefather* is the devil.
> > *MS. Harleian, quoted by Halliwell.*

Loresman, a teacher.

Lorel, a dissolute person.

> To love and live,
> As well *lorel* as lele.
> > *Piers Ploughman.*

Lorel—*continued.*

> Wolleward (miserable) and wetshod.
> Went I forth after,
> And yede forth like a *lorel,*
> All my life time,
> Till I wax weary of the world.
>> *Piers Ploughman.*

Lorn, lost.

> Who after that he had fain Una *lorne.*
>> *Spenser.*

This word survives in *forlorn,* utterly lost, or disconsolate, and in love-*lorn,* and lass-*lorn.*

Losengerie, flattery, lying.

> In lecherie and *losengeries,*
> Ye liven and in sleuthe.
>> *Piers Ploughman.*

> Lecherie, *losengerie,*
> And lorels tales,
> Gluttony and great othes,
> This mirth they love.
>> *Piers Ploughman.*

Lout,
Louten, } to make a curtsey, or an obeisance, to bow down.

> And then *louted* I adown,
> And he me leave granted.
>> *Creed of Piers Ploughman.*

> To which image both yonge and olde,
> Commanded he to *lout* and have in dread.
>> *Chaucer: The Monkes Tale.*

> And I am *louted* by a traitor villain.
>> *Shakspeare: Henry VI.,* part I.

From this verb comes the substantive, ' a lout,' an awkward, ungainly person, who makes an obeisance to a superior.

Loveable,
Loveworthy, } amiable.

Lovesome, amiable.

> Oh, *lovesome* ladie bright!
> How have ye fared since that ye were there?
>> *Chaucer: Troilus and Cresseide.*

Lowe, a heat, a flame, a blaze.

> Raise a great *lowe*.
>> *MS. Lincoln, quoted by Halliwell.*

> The sacred *lowe* o' weel placed love,
> Luxuriantly indulge it.
>> *Burns : Epistle to a young friend.*

Lowlyhood,
Lowlyness, } humility.

Lown, still, calm.

> ' Unbuckle your belt,' Sir Roland, she said,
>   And set you safely down.'
> ' Oh, your chamber is very dark, fair maid,
>   And the night is wondrous *lown*.'

> ' Yes, dark, dark, is my secret bower,
>   And *lown* the midnight maybe,
> But there's none waking in a' this tower,
>   But, thou, true love and me.
>> *Ballad of Sir Roland, in Motherwell's Collection ; supposed*
>> *to be quoted by Shakspeare in King Lear :*

> ' Childe Rowland to the dark tower came.'

' Keep lowne,' an old border phrase; keep it secret; keep it in the shady place, or in the modern phrase, *keep dark*.

> Violets growing in the *lown*.

Lubbard,
Lubber, } a man who might work, but will not; applied by sailors in another sense to a landsman who does not understand sea work, or does it awkwardly. Mr. Halliwell quotes from ' The Burning of Paule's Church, 1563,' a description of an abbey *lubber*, a person fed by the monks, ' one that was idle, well fed; a lazy, lewd, *lither loiterer*.

Lug, the ear; this word common in Scotland is colloquial in the east of England, but almost obsolete in literature.

> Can ye think your clumsy *lugs* so proper to decide as the delicate ears of Justice Midas.—*Midas*.

> If sorrow, the tyrant unveil thy breast,
> Draw out the foul fiend by the *lug*, the *lug*.
>> *Songs of the London Prentices and Trades, edited for the*
>> *Percy Society*

Lugsome, heavy, cumbrous, difficult, to lug or drag along.

> This *lugg*age is a little too *lugsome*.

Lum, a chimney. ' The lang *lums* of Glasgow;' i.e., the tall chimneys of the Glasgow cotton factories. This word is common in Lancashire and the Northern counties.

Lunch, in Scottish phrase, a large piece of bread, cheese, beef, &c., whence the modern English word ' lunch.' This meal in Scotland is called a *piece*, the two words being synonymous.

Lush, juicy.

> How *lush* and lusty the grass looks, how green,
> *Shakspeare : The Tempest.*

> The *lush* woodbine.—*Milton.*

The modern slang *lush*, signifying beer, wine, or other intoxicating drink, is probably derived from the adjective, so effectively employed by Shakspeare and Milton.

Lusk, a lazy lubber.

> Here is a great knave, a lither *lusk*, an idle lubber.
> *Acolastus*, 1540.

Luxome, shiny.

Lyart, ⎱ grey; a grey horse.
Liard, ⎰

This word occurs in the ' Dictionary of the Oldest Words in the English Language,' by the late Herbert Coleridge.

> I may no longer lithe, quothe he,
> And *lyard* he pricked.
> *Piers Ploughman.*

> His *lyart* haffets ; (thin grey locks).
> *Robert Burns.*

Maffle, to stammer, to stutter.

> To stammer or *maffle* in speech.
> > *Florio.*
>
> In such staggering and *maffling* wise.
> > *Holinshed.*

Maker, a poet; the Greek Πωιτης, and the Anglo-Saxon skope or scope;—a shaper or maker.

> The most curious *maker* of them all (Ben Jonson).
> > *Drayton's Elegies.*

Mal-talent, talent misapplied.

> Great grudge and *mal-talent.*
> > *Spenser : Faerie Queene.*

Malison, a curse; a malediction.

> Thus they serven Sathanas
> And soules beguileth
> Marchaunds of *malisons.*
> > *Piers Ploughman.*
>
> The curse and *malesoun* of God.
> > *Archbishop Hamilton's Catechisme.*
>
> I've won my mother's *malison,*
> Coming this night to thee.
> > *Annan Water : Border Minstrelsy.*
>
> That is a cuckold's *malison.*
> John Anderson, my Jo.
> > *John Anderson, old version in the Convivial Songster.*

Malodorous, having a bad smell.

Mammer, to hesitate, to doubt.

> I wonder in my soul,
> What you could ask me that I should deny,
> Or stand so *mammering* on.
> > *Shakspeare : Othello.*
>
> Euphues perused this letter several times, being in a *mammering* how to answer.—*Lily : Euphues to his England.*

Mammock, a shred, a fragment.

> *Mammocks* of stone.
> > *Optick Glass of Humours,* 1639.

Manfulness, virtue, or the fulness of manhood; the exact synonym of the Latin and French *virtus* and *vertu.*

Mantle, to cream or sparkle like ale, wine, or effervescent waters.

Many. The peasantry in all parts of England say, 'there was a many.' Literature says, 'a *great* many,' or 'a *good* many.'

Manymong, } of many sorts, or mixtures.
Menemong, }

> *Menemong* corn bread.
> > *Piers Ploughman.*

Mare, a demon, or imp; whence night-*mare.*—*Halliwell.*

Marrow, a mate, companion, sweet-heart; anything fellow to, or exact counterpart of another.

> Pore husbondes that have no *marrowes.*
> > *Hunting of the Hare*
>
> Thou took our sister to be thy wife,
> But ne'er thocht her thy *marrow.*
> > *The Dowie Dens o' Yarrow.*
>
> Busk ye! busk ye! my bonnie bonnie bride,
> Busk ye, busk ye, my winsome *marrow.*
> > *William Hamilton, of Bangour: The Braes o' Yarrow.*
>
> One glove or shoe is *marrow* to another.
> > *MS. Landowne, quoted by Mr. Halliwell.*
>
> None stood *unmarrow'd* save my Nan and me.
> > *Ewan Clark: Cumberland Ballads.*
>
> Let mous Meg and her *marrow* three volleys let flee,
> For love of the bonnets of Bonnie Dundee.
> > *Bonnie Dundee, Sir Walter Scott.*
>
> Meddle with your *marrow*; (i.e., hit one of your own size.)
>
> ———
>
> Your een are no *marrows;* (i.e., you squint).
>
> ———
>
> Love and lordship like nae *marrow.*
> > *Allan Ramsay's Scotch Proverbs.*

Maser, } a goblet.
Mazer, }

> A greate cuppe. brode and deepe, such as greate *mazers* were wont to be.—*Cooper's Dictionary*, 1559.

Masterful, insolent, commanding, imperious.

> A *masterful* beggar; i.e., an insolent beggar.

Math, a mowing.

Maul, a heavy hammer.

> A man that beareth false witness against his neighbours, is a *maul* and a sword, and a sharp arrow.
>
> *Proverbs*, chap. xxv. verse 18.

Maund, a basket.

Maunder, to go about with a basket, begging.

> *Maundering* for buttermilk.
>
> *Beaumont and Fletcher.*

Maup, to gape about stupidly; to 'moon.'

Maups, a silly girl; a simpleton.

Mavis, the singing thrush, as distinguished from the missal thrush, or screech thrush; a softer and more euphoneous word than that now employed; and formerly used by the best English writers, though now left wholly to the Scotch.

> Crows, popingayes, pyes, peacocks, and *mavis*.
>
> *Ashmole*, 1652.

> The swallow, martin, linnet, and the thrush,
> The *mavis* that sings sweetly in the bush.
>
> *Taylor*, 1630.

> The thrush replies; the *mavis* descant plays.
>
> *Spenser: Epithalamium.*

> When to the mirthful merle the warbling *mavis* sings.
>
> *Drayton's Polyolbion.*

> In vain to me, in glen or shaw,
> The *mavis* and the lintwhite sing.
>
> *Burns.*

Maw, the stomach. This word now signifies the stomach of birds and animals, but formerly signified that of the human species. 'Maw-bound,' says Mr. Halliwell, ' is a phrase common in Cheshire to express costiveness.'

Mawks, a slatternly, ignorant, stupid and dirty young woman.

Maw-wallop, a filthy, ill-cooked mess of victuals.

May, from the Anglo-Saxon *maeg*, a girl, a sweetheart, a maiden, and not an abbreviation for poetical and rhyming purposes as Bishop Percy supposed, of maid or maiden.

> The fairest *may* she was that ever went,
> Her like she has not left behind I weene.
>
> *Spenser.*

May—*continued.*

> Sir Caulyne loveth her best of all,
> But nothing durst he say,
> Ne descreeve his counsaile to no man,
> But dearly he loved this *may.*
> > *Ballad of Sir Caulyne, Percy's Reliques.*

> He gazed upon this bonnie *may,*
> Fairer than Bell of Oronsay,
> > *The Dance of Ballochroy.*

Mayhap, **M'happen,** **Mayhappen,** } perhaps ; a more purely English word than its modern synonym, of which the first syllable is of Latin, and the second of Saxon derivation.

> *M'happen* you thought it was me.
> > *Cumberland Ballads.*

Maze, to bewilder; whence amaze, and amazement. ' A mazed man,' is a man so confused in his mind, as to be irresponsible for his actions.

Mazy, **Meazy,** } giddy.

> Somehow it made me *meazy.*
> > *Tim Bobbin.*

Mazle, to wander about from place to place, without plan or purpose.

Meadmonth, July.

Meal, from the German mahl, a time; and applied *par excellence,* to dinner-*time,* thence known as the *meal,* or time for eating. The Germans use ein *mahl,* once; zwei *mahl,* twice; drei *mahl,* thrice ; and upwards to any number of times. In English the word, as distinguished from a repast, only survives in peace-*meal,* done by pieces at a time ; and inch-*meal,* by inches at a time.

In *Cymbeline,* the phrase occurs :

> Oh! that I had her here, to tear her limb-*meal;* i.e., to tear her to pieces, a limb at a time.

Meare, **Meere,** } a boundary.

Meden, to reward ; from whence the modern substantive, ' meed,' reward.

> And *medeth* men,
> To maintayne his laws.
> > *Piers Ploughman.*

Meere-brook, a boundary brook.

Meere-stone, a boundary stone.

Meere-tree, a boundary tree.

> The furious team that on the Cambrian side,
> Doth Shropshire as a *meare* from Hereford divide.
> *Drayton's Polyolbion.*

Meikle, } great; from the Greek: a word common to all
Mickle, } the Midland and North of England, and to Scot-
Muckle, } land.

> The name of an honest woman is *muckle* worth.

> *Meikle* water runs by, that the miller knows nothing of.

> Better be blythe with little, than sad with *muckle*.

> A proud heart wi' a poor purse, has *muckle* dolor to dree (endure).

> A wee spark may make *muckle* wark.
> *Allan Ramsay's Scotch Proverbs.*
> Oh *muckle* thinks my love o' my beauty.
> *Burns.*

Melch, mild, soft, wet, (applied to the weather).

Mell, to mix or mingle, (French, *meler*).

Mell-sylvester, the honeysuckle.

Meniality, domestic servants, menials.

Merle, the blackbird.

> To walk and take the dew by it was day,
> And hear the *merle* and mavis.
> *Chaucer: The Complaint of Cresseide.*
> The mavis made myrth for to mock the *merle*.
> *Complaint of Scotland.*
> To heir it was a poynt of paradyce,
> Sic mirth the mavis and the *merle* couth mae.
> *The Evergreen, by Allan Ramsay.*
> The *merle* upon her myrtle perch,
>   There to the mavis sings,
> Who from the top of some curl'd birch,
>   Those notes redoubled rings.
> *Drayton's Elysium.*

Mereswine, the porpoise.

Meth, courteous, mild.

> Thou wast meek and *meth*,
> A maiden mild.
> *MS. Lincoln quoted by Halliwell.*

Meth—*continued.*

> All that menye mild and *meth,*
> Went with him to Nazereth.
>
> *Cursor Mundi, Trin. Col. Cam.*

Mever, bashful.

Meverly, bashfully.

Mezzel, the leprosy.

Mezzly, blotchy.

Mevy, the gull, the sea-mew.

> About his sides a thousand sea gulls trod,
> The *mevy* and the halcyon.
>
> *Brown's Britannia's Pastorals.*

Mich or **Meech,** to skulk, act by stealth, or indulge in secret amours.

Micher, a truant or skulker; a clandestine lover.

Examples of the use of these words are frequent in Shakspeare, and in his contemporary authors. In *Euphues,* as quoted in ' Nares' Glossary,' is the passage: ' What made the gods so often to truant from heaven and *mich* here on earth?' In Henry IV., Part I., is the passage, put into the mouth of Falstaffe: ' Shall the blessed sun of heaven prove a *micher,* and eat blackberries?'

The ' Scornful Lady,' of Beaumont and Fletcher, has,

> Sure she has,
> Some *meeching* rascal in the house.

Spenser in his account of Ireland, has the passage: ' Lest any of them should struggle up and down the country, or *mich* in corners among their friends idly.' Chaucer speaks of a ' *micher* forsworn ;' and Gower of *micherie* and *miching.* In Selby's ' Mother Bombie,' 1594, quoted by Halliwell,' we find, ' How like a *micher* he stands, as if he had truanted from poverty.'

In Kent and Sussex, *meech* is still a common word to express the stealthy creeping of a cat after its prey. The word is in every way worthy of the place in literature, that Shakspeare and Spenser gave it.

Midden, a dunghill.

Midden crow, a carrion crow.

Midmorn, nine in the morning.

Midafternoon, } three in the afternoon.
Midovernoon,

Midwinter, Christmas.

Miff, a slight fit of ill-temper.

Mildhood, mildness.

Milth, to pity, or pardon, or feel compassion for.

Milthe, softness, mercifulness.

Mim, prudish, prim, and discreetly silent, applied only to women; or contemptuously to effeminate men, as in the phrase, ' He's as *mim* as a maiden.' In this sense the word is distinguished from *mum*, which means silent, or secret only, without reference to sex, as in the current slang, ' *mum's* the word.' Shakspeare says, ' the citizens are *mum* ;' and Master Slender in the Merry Wives of Windsor, complains that he went to the pretended Anne Page, and cried *mum*, and she cried budget as appointed. The word *mim* has a meaning of its own, which should preserve it in the language. It is derived by some authorities from the Greek mimeo, to imitate by action without speaking; whence mimicry, mimic, and pantomime.

> And now came the night o' feet washing,
> And Bessie looked *mim* and scarce.
> > *Jamieson's Popular Ballads.*

> Now Nancy all the while was playing prim,
> As any lamb as modest; and as *mim*.
> > *Ross's Helenore.*

> To market ride the gentlemen,
> > So do we, so do we,
> Then comes the country clown,
> > Hobbledy gee !
> First go the ladies, *mim, mim, mim ;*
> Next come the gentlemen, trim, trim, trim ;
> Then comes the country clown,
> > Gallop a trot, trot, trot.
> > *Nursery Rhymes of England.*

> Maidens should be *mim* till they're married.
> > *Allan Ramsay : Scotch Proverbs.*

> *Mim*-mou'd Meg ; (i.e., gentle or primly mouthed Meg.)
> > *Burns.*

Ming, to mix; whence the diminutive *mingle*, to mix in small quantities.

> The busy bee her honey now she *mings.*
> > *Henry Howard, Earl of Surrey.*

> *Ming* his pride and poverty.
> > *Kendall's Poems, 1577.*

Mint, to attempt, to assay; whence the *Mint*, the Assay Office.

> *Minting's* not making; i.e., attempting's not doing.
> > *Northern Proverb.*

Miredrum, the bittern.

Mirk, } dark, gloomy. This word has for upwards of a cen-
Murk, } tury been abandoned to the use of Scottish writers, although Shakspeare, Spenser, and Milton, have rendered it classic English.

> Twice in *mirk* and occidental damp,
> Moist Hesperus hath quenched her sleepy lamp.
> > *Shakspeare: All's Well that Ends Well.*

> Then to her iron waggon she betakes,
> And with her bears the foul, well-favoured witch,
> Through *mirksome* air her ready way she makes.
> > *Spencer's Fairy Queen.*

> So scented the grim feature and upturned
> His nostril wide into the *mirky* air;
> Sagacious of his quarry from afar.
> > *Milton's Paradise Lost.*

Hollinshed in his Description of Scotland, says, 'The battle lasted till *mirke* night parted them.'

Byron in the 'Corsair,' speaks of

> *Murkiness* of mind.

The Ettrick Shepherd in a fine song has,

> Twixt the gloaming and the *mirk*,
> When the kye came hame.

And Burns:

> Oh *mirk, mirk*, is this midnight hour.

Mirkshade, the evening, twilight, the gloaming.

Erroneously printed in Halliwell's 'Archaic Dictionary,' as *muck-shade*, and by Grose, as *muck shut.*

Mirthen,
Murthen, } to grow mirthful, to make merry.

> And as the wick and fire,
> Will make a warm flame,
> For to *mirthen* me now,
> That in the dark sitten.
> > *Piers Ploughman.*

Mither, to perplex, confuse, bewilder.

Mithers, perplexing. To be in the mithers, to know not what to do.

Miss, to go wrong. To do *amiss,* to do a wrong, or to act wrongfully. To miss the way, to go the wrong way. As a prefix, this syllable might be made to accommodate itself to every active verb in the language, but is not employed to the same extent among us, as it was in the youth of our literature. We have still such words as misfit, misgovern, misjudge, misinterpret, misname, miscall, misplace, misplead, mismanage, mislead, misprint, &c.; but many very convenient and expressive words, in which the prefix was formerly employed, have dropped out of books and conversation. Free-thinker for instance is a word, that would be much better rendered by misthinker, or one who thinks wrongly, for to think freely, is what every one should do : and a free thought, is not necessarily a wrong thought.

Misbelieve.

> That lewed man in *misbelief* lie and die.
> > *Piers Ploughman.*

> *Misbelief* and false suspection,
> Have truth brought to his damnation.
> > *Chaucer.*

> And coming to her son 'gan first to scold,
> And chide at him that made her *misbelieve.*
> > *Spenser.*

> And heard the hooded fathers mumbling charms,
> That made those *misbelievers* man and wife.
> > *Dryden.*

Mischoose.

> We *mischoose* the day.
> > *Stowe's Annals.*

Misdeem, to judge erroneously.

> He who misconceiveth, oft *misdeemeth*.
> *Chaucer.*

Misdo. Misdeed remains in common use, but the verb *misdo*, to do wrong, is seldom employed in any of its forms In modern phrase we say, ' I have done it wrongly, or badly,' instead of ' I have misdone it.

Misexpense, unwise expense, prodigality, reckless expenditure, money wrongly applied.

Misfall, to happen, or befall wrongly, or unfortunately.

> Thereat she gar to triumph with great boast,
> And to upbraid that chance which him *misfell*.
> *Spenser.*

Misfare, to fare or go ill, or wrong.

> Their own *misfaring* will not see.
> *Colin Clout's come Home again.*

Misgang, a failure, a going wrong.

Misgo, to go wrong, or to the wrong place.

> Alas! quo' she, I had almost *misgone*,
> I had almost gone to the clerks bedde.
> *Chaucer : The Reve's Tale.*

Mislike, to have no favourable inclination; less positive than *dislike*.

> Setting your scorn and your *mislike* aside,
> Tell me some reason why the Lady Gray,
> Should not become my wife, and England's queen.
> *Shakspeare : Henry VI.*

Mislive, to lead a wicked life.

> If he *mislive* in lewdness and lust.
> Little bootes all the wealth and the trust,
> That his father left by inheritance.
> *Spenser : Shepherd's Calendar.*

Misproud, proud for a wrong reason, or in a wrong cause.

> Impairing Henry, strengthening *misproud* York.
> *Shakspeare : Henry VI.*

Misthink, to think wrongfully.

> But I with better reason him avized,
> And show'd him how, through error and *misthought*,
> Of our like persons, each to be disguised,
> Or his exchange a freedom might be wrought.
> *Spenser · Faerie Queene.*

Misthink—*continued.*

> Thoughts ! which how fond thou harbour in thy breast,
> Adam, *misthought* of her, to thee so dear ?
> > *Paradise Lost.*

Mith, power, might.   Mr. Halliwell says the word is still in use, but gives no quotation. It would be useful as a rhyme.

Mixen, a dunghill.

Moble, to cover with a veil.

> The *mobled* queen.
> > *Hamlet.*
>
> The moon doth *moble* up herself.
> > *Shirley's Merchant of Venice.*
>
> Their heads and faces are *mobled* in fine linen.
> > *Sandys.*

Moe, ⎰ to distort the mouth in scorn, to make grimaces ;
Mow, ⎱ from the French ' faire la *moue.*'

> Unto his mother they complained,
>   Which grieved her to heare ;
> And for these pranks she threatened him,
>   He should have whipping cheer,
> If that he did not leave his tricks,
>   His jeering mocks and *mows.*
> > *The Merry Puck, quoted by Halliwell.*
>
> Sometimes like apes that *moe* and chatter at me,
> And after bite me.
> > *Shakspeare : The Tempest.*
>
> *Mows* may come to earnest.
> > *Ramsay's Scotch Proverbs.*
>
> The miller was of manly make,
> To meet him was nae *mows.*
> > *Christ's Kirk on the Green.*
>
> There was nae *mowis* them among,
> Naething was heard but heavy knocks.
> > *Battle of Harlaw, in the Evergreen.*

Moffle, to spoil work, to do anything badly, and without know-ledge.

Molt, preterite of ' melt ;' whence the past participle molten ; as ' molten gold,' molten metal.

Molt-water, drops of perspiration.

Moider } to confuse, bother, perplex, distract, bewilder. In
Moither } the 'Wit of a Woman,' 1705, occurs the passage
quoted by Nares.

> I have been strangely *moidered* e'er sin' about this same news o' the
> French king. I canna' believe 'tis true.

Moidery, confused, thick, from whence *moithery* and *mothery*,
turbid ; applied to liquors.

> It is not enough to make the clearest liquor in the world both fecu-
> lent and *mothery*.
> > *Tristram Shandy.*

> As touching the *mother* or lees of olive oil.
> > *Holland : Translation of Pliny.*

> They oint their naked limbs with *mother'd* oil.
> > *Dryden : Virgil.*

Mole, a spot on the face or skin ; formerly any kind of spot on
a garment, or piece of furniture.

> Thy best coat
> Hath many *moles* and spottes.
> > *Piers Ploughman.*

Moly, a plant known only to the poets, who ascribed to it
fabulous virtues. It is known to general readers by the al-
lusion in Milton's Comus.—*Nares.*

> The herb *moly* hath a flower as white as snow, and a root as black
> as ink.—*Lily's Euphues.*

Mome, a stupid or silly person, a blockhead.

> Parnassus is not clomb,
> By every such *mome*.
> > *Drayton.*

> I dare be bold awhile to play the *mome*.
> > *Mirror for Magistrates.*

Mong, preterite of ming, mingled : whence the preposition
among, i.e., mingled with.

Monger, a retail dealer, or mixer ; formerly applied to every
one who traded, whatever was the article he sold or mixed.
The word remains in Iron*monger*, Cheese*monger*, Coster-
monger, Tripe*monger* ; and might be advantageously combined with money, as Money*monger*, a dealer in gold and
silver ; and with slander, as a Slander*monger*, a retailer of
scandals.

Moon, to drivel, to talk in a crazy manner.

Moony, silly, affected by the moon.

Moonflaw, the wild fancy of a lunatic.

> I fear she has a *moonflaw* in her brains,
> She chides and fights that none can look on her.
> > *Nares.*

Moonling, a lunatic.

> I have a husband and a two-legged one,
> But such a *moonling !*
> > *Ben Jonson.*

Mop, ⎱ a young girl. In the West of England, a fair where
Moppet, ⎰ young girls resort, to be hired for domestic or farm service, is still called a *mop.*

Mopsey, a slovenly girl.

Mortling, an animal found on the fields, woods, or moors, still-born, or dead of disease.

> A wretched withered *mortling*, and a piece of carrion.
> > *Nares.*

Mosie, rough like the beard, hairy.

Most, an augmentation of the superlative, used with great effect by Shakspeare and the writers of his time.

> I love thee best, oh, *most* best, believe it.
> > *Hamlet.*

> To take the basest and *most* poorest shape.
> > *King Lear.*

Mote, ⎱ the original preterite of meet, to assemble, afterwards
Moot, ⎰ superseded by *met.* The word survives in Wittenage-mote, the meeting of the wise men ; and in the verb to *moot* a question ; i.e. to raise a question that only can be decided by public meeting or discussion. A Town Hall was formerly a *moot* house ; and is thus rendered in Wickliffe's Bible.

Mother-naked, stark or utterly naked, naked as a new-born babe.

> They'll shape me in your arms, Janet,
> A dove, but and a swan,
> And last they'll shape me in your arms,
> A *mother-naked* man ;
> Cast your green mantle over me,
> I'll be myself again.
> > *The Young Tamlane ; Minstrelsy of the Scottish Border.*

Mother-tongue, native language.

Mother-wit, innate ability.

Moudy, a mole catcher.

Moudy-rat, a mole; from mouldy-rat; a rat of the mould.

Moudy-warp, a mole; one that *warps* or throws up the mould.

Moudy-hill, a mole hill.

Moulter, the toll or tax taken by a miller for grinding a farmer's corn.

> The quaker's wife got up to bake,
> Her children all about her,
> She gave them every one a cake,
> And the miller wants his *moulter.*
> > *Nursery Rhymes of England.*

> It's good to be merry and wise,
> Quoth the miller, when he *moultered* twice.
> > *Allan Ramsay's Scotch Proverbs.*

Mournival, a term at cards; to have four of any of the court cards in one's hand, or to hold four aces.

> It can be no treason, to drink and sing,
> A *mournival* of healths to our new crowned king.
> > *Brome's Cavalier Song on the Restoration of Charles II.*

The word was sometimes spelled ' mornifle.'

Mow-land, grass-land; meadow-land that may be mowed, or *mown.*

Mowen,
or   } to be able; infinitive of ' may.'
Mowe,

' Thou shalt not *mowe* suffer;' i.e., thou shalt not be able, to suffer or endure.

Moy, moist.

> Mild, and *moy.*
> > *Evergreen, by Allan Ramsay.*

Mulch, straw which is half rotten, and saturated for manure.

Mung, preterite of ming, to ming or mingle; when the substantive meaning the mingled food of bread, potatoes, &c., thrown to poultry. In America, '*mung* news' is a common expression applied to false news, but probably having its de-

Mung—*continued.*

rivation from mingled (or mung) news, in which the true and the false are so mixed up together that it is impossible to distinguish one from the other.

Murch, mischief; (a Devonshire word). ' The Old Murcher,' the devil.

Murchy, mischievous.

Murge, to rejoice.

> In May it *murgeth* when idardes (dares).
> > *Advice to the Fair Sex ; Ritson's Ancient Songs and Ballads,*
> > vol. i., page 66.

Murne, mournful, sorrowful.

Murr, a cold in the head ; the influenza ; whence perhaps *murrain*, the ancient name of the rinderpest or cattle plague.

> The *murr*, the headache ; the catarrh, the bone-ache.
> > *Chapman's Mons. D'Olive.*
> Deaf ears, blind eyes, the palsy, gout, and *murr*.
> > *Rowland*, 1613.

Murrain, the cattle plague.

Mush, preterite of mash; to reduce to a consistency ; or, as the English cookery books, derived from the French, say to make a *purée*. In America, porridge either of oatmeal or of Indian corn, rice, beans, peas, or other vegetable, is called *mush*. The word is current in the North of England.

Muss, a scramble, a confusion, a difficulty. This word, though little used in England, is common in America.

> Of late, when I cried ho !
> Like boys unto a *muss*, kings would start forth,
> And cry your will ?
> > *Shakspeare : Antony and Cleopatra.*
> Striving as children play at *muss*.
> > *Florio.*

Nab, the top, or head; the same as *Knabb*—*q. v.*

From this root comes the slang phrase, to 'nab a man,' i.e., to take him by the head, or capture him.

Nake, to make naked.

> Come, be ready, *nake* your swords.
>> *Nares.*

Nantle, to fondle, to caress.

Napery, table linen; from the French *nappe*, a table cloth; whence also *Napier*, the patronymic of a very distinguished family, and synonymous with ' *draper.*' From this word also is *napkin*, a little cloth.

Nappy, comfortable, sleepy, predisposing one to 'nap;' hence applied to ale and strong beer. This word is sometimes written *noppy* and *nobby*, as derived from nob, the head; whence it is applied to liquor that mounts into the head, and which is as the French say of Burgundy wine, *capiteux.*

> With *nappy* beer I to the barn repaired.
>> *Gay.*

> Care, mad to see a man so happy,
> E'en drowned himself among the *nappy*.
>> *Burns : Tam o' Shanter.*

> While we sit bousing at the *nappy*,
> And getting fou' and unco happy.
>> *Idem.*

> Twa bottles of as *nappy* liquor,
> As ever reamed in horn or bicker.
>> *Ramsay : The Monk and the Miller's Wife.*

Nast, dirt, filth, whence the adjective, nasty.

Nash, chilly ; a Wiltshire word.

Nawl, the navel.

Nay, a negative; to be distinguished from No by many delicate shades of meaning.

No, supposes will, or prejudgment. Nay, supposes error, or something to be argued out.

Nay—*continued.*

Will you marry me? No. Are two and three six? Nay. Was Mahomet a true prophet? No, or nay. Both may be said. The one negative excludes argument, the other permits it.

Nay-word, a denial.

Ne. This form of negative was formerly prefixed to all the verbs. Chaucer uses *n'adde* for *ne hadde*, or had not; *n'is* for ne is, or is not; *n'am* for *ne am*, or am not; *n'ere* for *ne were*, or were not; and *n'ist*, for *ne wist*, or wist not. Prefixed to will, it became *nil*, noleo, ne will, to will not, to be unwilling; whence the phrase, willy·nilly, or *nolens volens.*

> *Nylling* to dwell where sin is wrought.
> > *Ashmole,* 1652.

> Their answers were nought for to hide,
> They *nolde* be of his assent.
> > *Morte Arthur.*

> And *nolde* call herself none other name.
> > *Lydgate, MS. Soc. Antiq.*

> Harme *nolde* he do none.
> > *Chron. Vilodun, quoted by Halliwell.*

> Will you, *nill* you I will marry you.
> > *Shakspeare.*

> I *nil* thine offered grace.
> > *Spenser.*

> In scorn or friendship *nill* I construe whether.
> > *Shakspeare: Poems.*

> Unto the founts Diana *nild* repair.
> > *Robert Greene: Never too late,* 1590.

Wesley attempted to revive *nill*, and wrote:

> Man wills something, because it is pleasing to him; and *nills* something, because it is painful to nature.
> > *Lectures on the English Language, by G. P. Marsh.*

Neck-weed, hemp; a common expression for a rope.

Needed, the preterite of need is still used in such phrases as, 'he needed assistance;' but is being superseded by the present tense of the verb, in such instances as, 'I told him he *need* not do it.' To avoid this incorrectness, a periphrase is often employed: 'I told him it was not necessary that he should do it.'

Neap,) a turnip. The true and original word for this vege-
Neep,) table. Mr. Halliwell quotes it as used in Cornwall.
In Scotland its use is universal. Whence the first syllable
in the ordinary English word was derived, is difficult to
discover.

Neeze, to snort; as distinguished from sneeze.

> By his (the Leviathan's) *neezing,* a light doth shine.
> *Job,* chap. xii., verse 18.

> And then the whole quire hold their hips and laugh,
> And *yexen* (hiccough) in their mirth and *neeze* and swear.
> *Shakspeare : Midsummer Night's Dream.*

Neist, the next, or nearest. Mr. Halliwell quotes this word
as current in Devonshire.

> The present moment is our own,
> The *neist* we never saw.
> *Burns.*

Nesh, fresh, tender, delicate, soft ; applied to vegetables, fruit
and foliage. Nice, which is now used in the sense of nesh,
originally meant, silly, affected, foolish, from the French
niais.

> The darker fir, light ash, and the *nesh* tops of the young hazel.
> *Crowe's Lervesden Hill.*

> Take the root of horsehelme and seethe it long in water, and then
> take the *nescheste* thereof.
> *MS. Lincoln, quoted by Halliwell.*

Never-a-dele, not a bit, never a bit—none in the least. The
word *dele,* a portion that may be divided by some other
means than the teeth, is better than 'bit,' a portion that is
bitten.

> Be it right or wrong, these men among
> Of women do complain,
> Affirming this, how that it is,
> A labor spent in vain.
> To love them well, for *never-a-dele,*
> They love a man again.
> *The Nut Brown Maid.*

Niding, a low, mean, contemptible, base wretch ; formerly the
most opprobrious word that could be applied to any body.

> When there was a dangerous rebellion against King William Rufus,
> he proclaimed that all subjects should repair to his camp, upon no
> other penalty but that, whoever refused to come, should be reputed a

Niding—*continued.*

> *niding.* * * * The people swarmed to him immediately from all
> sides.—*Camden's Remains.*

> He is a *niding*, the pulse of whose soul beats but faintly towards
> heaven.—*Howell, quoted by Nares.*

Niderling, a mean, inhospitable person.

Nieve, }
Neve, } the closed fist.

> The cudgel in my *nieve* did shake.
> > *Burns : Address to the Dei.*

Nieveful, as much as the closed hand will contain.

Neivil, }
Nevil, } a blow with the nieve or fist.

Niffer, to exchange.

> Ye shall na be *niffered* but for a better.

> It's no easy to *niffer* you for anything worse.
> > *Allan Ramsay's Scotch Proverbs.*

> You see your state with theirs compared.
> And shudder at the *niffer.*
> > *Burns : Address to the Unco guid and rigidly righteous.*

Nightertale, the night time; the whole night long.

> His men come by *nightertale,*
> With them away his body stale.
> > *Cursor Mundi ; MS. Trin. Col. Cantab., (quoted by Halliwell.)*

> By *nightertale* he was slain by king Darius.
> > *MS. Soc. Antiq.*

> The nightingale,
> Within a temple shapen hawthorn wise,
> He might not slepe in all the *nightertale.*
> > *Chaucer : Court of Love.*

> So hote he loved that by *nightertale,*
> He slept no more than doth the nightingale.
> > *Chaucer : Prologue to Canterbury Tales.*

Nim, to take.

> Fetchen I wolde of my next neighbour,
> And *nimmen* of his earth.
> > *Piers Ploughman.*

Nimster, a thief.

Shakspeare probably had the word *Nim* in his mind, when
he invented and named the famous Corporal ' **Nym.**'

Ninniver, the white water-lily.

Ninny-watch, the expectation of a fool; a vain, over-sanguine hope.

Nithe,
Nythe, } wickedness.

> In pride and treachery,
> In *nithe* and lechery.
> > *Cursor Mundi MS. (quoted by Halliwell.)*

Noggle, to walk awkwardly.

Noiles,
Noils, } coarse and inferior knots in wool; the modern
Noyls, } 'shoddy.'

> By a statute of James I., no one was permitted to put *noyles* into woollen cloth.—*Halliwell.*

Nones, the hours midway between noon and sunset.

> That eten nought but at *nones.*
> > *Piers Ploughman.*

Nori,
Nouri, } a foster child.

> For my lord's daughter she is,
> And I, his *nori*, forsooth, I was.
> > *Guy of Warwick.*

Noonscape, the escape from work at noon; when day-laborers dine and take a rest.

Noonshun, the meal taken at noonscape; whence *nuncheon,* a lunch.

> Harvest folk with curds and clotted cream,
> On sheaves of corn were at their *noonshun* dose.
> > *Browne's Britannia's Pastorals.*

Noncheon, } a lunch, or mid day refreshment; the same as
Nuncheon, } *noonshun.*

Nope, the bullfinch.

> The sparrow, the *nope,* the redbreast, and the wren.
> > *Drayton's Polyolbion.*

Noughty, having nought, poor, possessed of nothing.

Nover, high arable land, above a steep bank.

Nowl, the head of an animal, as distinguished from that of a man.

> An ass's *nowl* I fixed upon his head.
> > *Shakspeare: Midsummer Night's Dream.*

Nowte, horned cattle; Neat. *Nowte geld,* was the name formerly given in the North to a cornage, or tax upon cattle.

> Mischief begins with needles and pins, and ends with horned *nowte.*
> *Allan Ramsay's Scotch Proverbs.*

'Better sell "nowte," than nations,' retort of Lord Seafield's brother to Lord Seafield, a Scottish peer, accused of selling his country to the English government at the time of the Union between England and Scotland.

> And in your lug, most reverend James,
>   To hear you roar and rowte,
> Few men of sense will doubt your claims
>   To rank among the *nowte.*
> *Burns : Epistle to the Rev. James Stevens.*

Noy, annoyance.

> With little *noy* they can convoy,
> A matter finally.

Nub, the fist.

Nubble, to bruise with the fist.

Nubbly, or ⎰ large and rounded like the fist; a *nubbly* piece
Knubbly, ⎱ of bread.

Nug, a rude unshapen piece of timber, a block, (*Halliwell*), whence perhaps the modern word nugget, a little nug (of gold), first introduced or re-introduced into the language by the gold miners of Australia.

Nurly, ⎱ lumpy, knotty; whence, metaphorically, cross-
Gnurly, ⎰ grained, and ill-tempered.

Obdure, to become obdurate.

> Senseless of good ; as stones they soone *obdure.*
> > *Heywood,* 1609.

Oke, preterite of ache, or ake. My head aches, and my head *oke,* (ached).

Olyte, diligent. Mr. Halliwell quotes an English use of this word, from the Harleian MSS., without defining its meaning. The word is common in the Border counties of England and Scotland.

> An *olyte* mother makes a lazy daughter.
> > *Allan Ramsay : Scotch Proverbs.*

Ope-tide,) the early spring, or time when the buds begin to
Opentide,) open.

> So lavish *ope-tide,*
> Causeth fasting Lents.
> > *Nares.*

Ooth, raging mad ; from the German *wuth,* and the Scottish *wud.*

Ord, from the Celtic ord, or Ard ; a headland or promontory, as the *Ord* of Caithness : *Ard*namurchan, &c. ' In Suffolk,' says Mr. Halliwell, ' a promontory is called an *ord.*' The word has also the sense of a beginning, or a point.

> And touched him with the spear's *ord.*
> > *Romance of Sir Otuel.*

> Saul drew his sword,
> And ran even upon the *ord.*
> > *Cursor Mundi ; Trin. Coll. Cam., quoted by Halliwell.*

Orlings, the teeth of a comb.

Ouph, modernized and corrupted into *oaf,* a sprite, or goblin, less elegant, gentle, and prepossessing in appearance than a fairy.

> Urchins, *ouphes,* and fairies green and white.
> > *Shakspeare : Merry Wives of Windsor.*

Ourie, shivering in the cold.

> I thought me on the *ourie* cattle.
> > *Burns : A Winter Night.*

Outen, strange, foreign ; from without.

Outener, a foreigner.

Outrope, a sale by auction. This word survives in Scotland as ' roup,' and is derived from the German *rufen,* to call or cry ; and *ausrufen,* to cry out.

> As at common *outropes,* when household stuffe is to be solde, they cry, who gives more ?—*Dekker,* 1608.

Overcraft, deceit, too much craftiness.

Overcrafty, deceitful.

Overdreep.

> Mr. Halliwell explains this word to mean overshadow. In the Northern and Scottish Counties, ' dreep,' is to drip with moisture. The quotation given is :

> The aspiring nettles with their shady tops shall no longer *overdreep* the best herbs.—*Pierce Penniless.*

> The true meaning seems to be overdrip, and not overshadow.

Overhope, sanguineness.

Overhopeful, sanguine, enthusiastic.

Overword,
O'erword, } the chorus, burden, leading idea, or repeated
O'ercome, } phrase of a song or ballad.
Owerword,

> And aye the *o'ercome* o' his song,
> Was wae's one for Prince Charlie.
> > *Jacobite Ballad.*

> And aye the *ourword* of their song,
> Was, ' ou wee, wee, man's been lang awa'.
> > *Border Minstrelsy.*

> And aye the *o'erword* of their song,
> Was ' o'er the muir among the heather.'
> > *Jean Glover, Scottish Song.*

Overseethe, from *seethe* to boil ; to boil over.

Oversodden, boiled over.

Overworn, worn out with toil or care.

> The *o'erworn* widow.
> *Shakspeare.*

Oye, a grandchild.

Orts,
Ortings, } scraps, fragments, leavings.
Ortins,

> Let him have time a beggar's *orts* to crave.
> *Shakspeare.*

Overtimely, premature, too early.

Overthwart, opposite to, across.

> Our *overthwart* neighbours.
> *Dryden.*
> He laid a plank *overthwart* the brook.
> *Jonson.*

Overname, to call over names in a series.

> I pray thee *overname* them.
> *Shakspeare.*

Owzell, the blackbird; the word is used in Massinger, and is current through the North of England and Scotland.

> House doves are white, and *owsells* blackbirds be.
> *The Affectionate Shepherd,* 1594.
> The *owzel-cock* so black of hue.
> With orange tawny bill.
> *Shakspeare : Midsummer Night's Dream.*

Oxter, the arm-pit.

Oxy, wet, spongy, morassy, boggy; applied to land.

Paigle, a cowslip.

> Blue bells, hare bells, *paigles*, pansies.
> > *Ben Jonson.*

Paltoke, a cloak, or upper garment; the modern *paletot.*

> Proud priests came with him,
> More than a thousand,
> In *paletokes* and pyked shoon.
> > *Piers Ploughman.*

Pantler, the servant in a great household, whose business it is to attend to the bread, as it is that of a butler to attend to the wine.

> He would have made a good *pantler*, he would have chipped bread well.—*Shakspeare: Henry IV.*
>
> I will presently take orders with the cook, *pantler*, and butler.
> > *The Jovial Crew.*

Parget, to plaister or besprinkle a wall; from *spargere*, with the elision of the initial, as in parmecetty, a vulgar corruption of spermacetti, and peckled for speckled. ' Applied metaphorically,' says Nares, ' to face painting.'

> She's above fifty-two, and *pargets*.
> > *Ben Jonson.*

Passing, very, exceedingly; an abbreviation of surpassing, as in the common phrase, ' 'tis *passing* strange.'

> For Oberon is *passing* fell; (surpassingly sharp-tempered and bitter.)
> > *Shakspeare: Midsummer Night's Dream.*

Pat, preterite of put.

> The lass *pat* on her satin gown.
> > *Aberdeenshire Ballad.*

Patch, a fool; whence the common phrase, cross-*patch*, an ill-natured fool.—*Nares.*

> The *patch* is kind enough, but a huge feeder.
> > *Shakspeare: Merchant of Venice.*
>
> Call me *patch* and puppy, and beat me if you please.
> > *Beaumont and Fletcher.*

Pautch, to walk painfully in deep mud.

Pawky, witty, sly, and humourous, in speech or action, but without any evil intention. Modern English has no synonym for this Northern and Scottish word. In Suffolk, according to Mr. Halliwell, *pawky* means awkward. The modern vulgarism, ' to *poke* fun,' may possibly afford a clue to the original derivation.

> The *pawky* auld carle came over the lea,
> Wi' mony gude e'en and gude days to die,
> Says, gude wife, for your courtesie,
> Will you lodge a silly poor man.
> *The Guberlunzie Man*

In an article on ' Worcester Cathedral,' in the *Saturday Review*, June 9, 1866 ; the restorations are described as 'meagre, *pawky*, and vapid.' What could the writer mean by *pawky* in this instance?

Peason, peas. Formerly *peas* was employed in the singular, and the word *pea*, as now used, was unknown.

> Green beans and *peason*,
> Nuts, pears, plums, apples, are in season.
> *Taylor, the Water Poet*, 1630.

Pelf, rubbish ; whence ' pelf,' the philosophic term for ' money,' often applied by cynics, who by no means think money the rubbish they assert. The metaphorical use of the word, has entirely superseded the original.

> Ill-gotten gains are called *pelfry*.
> *Halliwell.*

Pelt, to rage. ' A pelting storm,' is therefore a *raging* storm. To *pelt* with stones, is, if this derivation be correct, to ' rage,' or show rage, by throwing stones.—See *Nares.*

> Poor houseless wretches, wheresoe'er ye be,
> That bide the *pelting* of this pitiless storm.
> *Shakspeare : King Lear.*

Peth, a well ; a word not very urgently required, but which, if accepted, would be useful to poets, to add to the very few rhymes to ' death,' and ' breath.'

Pin,
Pynne, } the bolt of a door.

' To tirl at the pin,' or undo the bolt, is a common expres-

Pin—*continued*.

sion in the ballad poetry of Scotland. The word *pynne* occurs in Piers Ploughman, in the sense of bolt :

> And made Peace porter,
> To *pynne* the gates.

Pinchpenny, a miser.

Pinchback, a miser, who denies himself proper raiment.

Pind, to impound a strayed animal ; to put it in the pound.

Pindar, ⎱ the officer whose duty it was to impound strayed
Pinder, ⎰ animals.

Pinfold, a pound for strayed animals.

Pingle, a small narrow enclosure.

Pingle, to eat with very little appetite, the same as ' tarrow ;' *q. v.*

> He filleth his mouth well, and is no *pingler* at his meat.
> *Topsell's Beastes*, 1607 ; *quoted by Halliwell*.

Pippin, an apple.

> A *pippin*-monger (costermonger) selling trash.
> *Hudibras Redivivus*.

Pirl, to spin like a top.

Pirle, a stream.

Pith, strength, sap, vigour. A word long obsolete, but recently re-introduced to its proper place in literature, although its claims have not been generally recognized.

> The childe was of *pith*.
> *Perceval*, 1640, *quoted by Halliwell*.

Pix, to glean in an orchard.

Pixie, a fairy ; pixy-puff, a fungus ; *pixy*-rings, fairy circles.

Plack, a piece of money. In Belgium, the *plaquette*, or little plack, is still current.

Plackless, moneyless.

> Poor *plackless* devils like myself.
> *Burns : Scotch Drink*.

Placket, a petticoat. ' Joan's *Placket* is torn,' the name of an old English melody.

> Is there no manners among maids ? Will they wear their *plackets* when they should bare their faces ?
> > *Shakspeare : Winter's Tale.*

> Keep thy hand out of *plackets,* thy pen from lender's books, and defy the foul fiend.—*Shakspeare : King Lear.*

> The bone-ache, that methinks
> Is the curse dependant on those that war for a *placket.*
> > *Shakspeare : Troilus and Cressida.*

Plainsong, a melody.

Plash, a shallow pond, pool, or running water ; whence, to ' plash ' in the water. Plash also signifies a heavy fall of rain.

> He leaves a shallow *plash* to plunge him in the deep.
> > *Shakspeare : Taming of the Shrew.*

> Obscene with filth the miscreant lies bewrayed,
> Fallen in the *plash* his wickedness had made.
> > *Pope : The Dunciad.*

> The thunder rain in large drops came *plash* after *plash* in large drops.
> > *Blackwood's Magazine,* May, 1820.

Platform, the principles agreed upon by a political party ; that on which the party stands. This word is now more common in America than in England, but was in general use in England up to the time of the Commonwealth.

> To procure himself a pardon, went and discovered the whole *plat-form* of the conspiracie.
> > *Discovery of the New World ; (quoted by Nares).*

> And lay new *platforms* to endamage them.
> > *Shakspeare : King Henry VI.*

Pleach, to intertwine.

> Walking in a thick *pleached* alley, in my orchard.
> > *Shakspeare : Much Ado about Nothing.*

> With *pleached* arms bending down.
> > *Shakspeare : Antony and Cleopatra.*

Plight, to fold, to enfold, to intertwine ; whence the phrase, ' to *plight* troth ;' to intertwine or fold the faith, word and promise of lovers.

The modern ' plait ' seems to be a corruption of this word.

Plight—*continued*.

> Creatures of the element,
> That in the colours of the rainbow live,
> And play in the *plighted* clouds.
>> *Milton : Comus*.

Plim, plump.

> He boiled a great number of groats with a design, as he said to make them *plim*, i.e., thicker.
>> *Loche on Lowering Interest*.

Plout,
Plouter, } to wade or flounder through water or mire ; to stir dirty water, or figuratively ; to be engaged in a dirty or miry business.

> *Plouting* though thick and thin.
>> *Grose*.
> Many a weary *plouter* she'd cost him,
> Through gutters and glaur.
>> *Jameson's Popular Ballads*.

Posie, a nosegay, a bouquet, a motto. It was formerly the custom for the gallant, who sent a nosegay to a lady to affix a paper, with a ' poesy,' or poetical quotation to the stalk, whence the ' posy ' or 'poesy' afterwards came to signify the flowers themselves.

> And if some infrequent passenger crossed our streets, it was not without his medicated *posie* at his nose.
>> *Bishop Hall*, 1625.
> An' its a' to be a *posie* to my ain dear May.
>> *Burns*.

Potsure, sure with the confidence of drunkenness.

> When they beheld her thus secure,
> And armed against them like a man *potsure*.
>> *Legend of Captain Jones*, 1650 (*quoted by Nares*).

Poult, a chicken ; from the French *poulet*.

> 'Tis believed, coz,
> You do not feed on pleasant (pheasant ?) *poults*.
>> *Chapman's Revenge of Homer*, 1654.

Poulter, a dealer in chickens and fowls ; corrupted to poulterer, a word that is as irregular as *grocerer* would be if used instead of *grocer*.

> Over against the parish church of St. Mildred, have ye divers faire houses inhabited by *poulters*.
>> *Stowe's London*.

Pow, the head, the pate. An abbreviation of poll. To *poll* at election, is to count by heads; a poll-tax, is a personal tax, or tax on heads.

> God bless thy snowy *pow.*
>> *Waugh's Lancashire Songs.*

> But blessings on thy frosty *pow,*
> John Anderson, my Jo.
>> *Burns.*

Prank, to dress in the fashion, to adorn.

> Some *prank* their ruffs, and other trimly dight,
> Their gay attire.
>> *Spenser.*

> *Prankings* and adornings.
>> *Sir Thomas More.*

> False tales, *prankt* in reason's garb.
>> *Milton: Comus.*

Pranker, a dandy, a ' swell.'

Pranksome, full of tricks and pranks, lively, frolicsome.

Prink, to behave in a pert, saucy, manner; to adorn one's self jauntily. Dr. Johnson defines the word to be a diminutive or modification of prank.

> *Prink* their hair with daisies.
>> *Cowper.*

Prinkle, the flesh is said to *prinkle,* when there is a tingling sensation, consequent upon a temporary suspension of the circulation.—(*Jameson.*)

> My blood ran *prinkling* through my veins,
> When I beheld my dear, O.
>> *Hogg's Mountain Bard.*

> I found the very hairs of my head begin to creep, and a *prinkling* through all my veins and skin, like needles and pins.
>> *The Brownie o' Bodsbeck.*

Proclive, leaning to, addicted to, having a ' proclivity ' for.

> Frail and *proclive* unto all evil.
>> *Latimer's Sermons.*

Prog, to poke, push, and peer about; to maraud, for the purpose of plunder; whence the modern slang ' *prog,*' originally meaning food taken from the people by an invading army; but now food in general, as in the phrase, ' my *prog* and my grog,' i.e., my food and my drink.

Prog—*continued.*

> We travel sea and sail, we pry, we prowl,
> We progress and we *prog*, from pole to pole.
> > *Quarles' Emblems.*

> What less than fool is man to *prog* and plot.
> > *Idem.*

> And that man in the gown, in my opinion,
> Looks like a *progging* knave.
> > *Beaumont and Fletcher.*

Prow, brave, courageous : whence *prowess*, bravery, strength.

> For they be two, the *prowest* knights on ground.
> > *Spenser : Faerie Queene.*

Proyne, to clean or prune the feathers as birds do.   The flori-
cultural word *prune* in the sense of lopping off redundan-
cies from trees or plants, does such multifarious duty, that
the ancient word *proyne* of which it is a corruption, might
advantageously be restored to that restricted meaning which
it had in the poetry of Chaucer's age :

> And after this the birds everich one,
> Toke up one other songe full loude and clere,
> And with a voice said, ' Well is us begone,
> That with our makis are together here,
> We *proyne* and play without doubt and dangere.
> > *The King's Quair.*

> Up stode and *proined* him the bird.
> > *Chaucer's Dreame.*

> The royal bird
> *Prunes* the immortal wing and cloys his beak.
> > *Shakspeare : Cymbeline.*

Quack, to be noisy; whence quack doctor, one who makes a noise of his pretensions by advertisement, or otherwise.

Quaddy, squat; short and thick.

Quaisy, tough and indigestible.

Quar, a stone quarry.

> The very agate
> Of slate and polity, cut from the *quar*
> Of Machiavel; a true cornelian
> As Tacitus himself.
>> *Ben Jonson.*

Quarr, to block up.

> But as a miller having ground his grist,
> Lets down the flood-gates with a speedy fall,
> And *quarring* up the passage therewithal;
> The waters swell in spleene and never stay
> Till by some cleft they find another way.
>> *Browne's Britannia's Pastorals.*

Quash, to break; to smash, to subdue; whence bequash, to break into little pieces.

> Lest we should too happy be,
> Even in our infancy,
> Our joys are *quashed*, our hopes are blasted.
>> *Cotton. On Death.*

> Thus Britain's hardy sons of rustic mould,
> Patient of arms, still *quash* th' aspiring Gaul.
>> *Philip, Cerealia.*

> The earth for heaviness,
> That he would suffer,
> Quoke as a quick thing,
> And all *bequashed* the rocke.
>> *Piers Ploughman.*

Quave, to shake, to quiver.

> The day for dread withdrew,
> And dark became the sun,
> And all the world *quaved*.
>> *Piers Ploughman.*

Quave-mire, a quag-mire, or a shaky bog.

> A greate deepe marsh or *quave-mire*.
>> *North (Nares).*

Queach, a bog, a morass.

> All sylvan copses and the fortresses of thorniest *queaches*.
>> *Chapman's Homer.*

Queachy, shaking, quavering.

> Goodwin's *queachy* sands.—*Drayton's Polyolbion.*
> Rent the holly woods, and shook the *queachy* ground.
> > *Idem.*

Quean, a woman, a wench, a strong girl.

> Grey, great-headed *queans.*—*Piers Ploughman.*
> I wat she was a cantie *quean.*
> > *Burns: Roy's Wife of Aldivalloch.*

In Shakspeare's time *quean* ceased to be a word of respect, as it used to be in the days of Piers Ploughman and Chaucer; and as it still is in Scotland, and became a term of contempt and reproach.

> A witch, a *quean,* an old cozening *quean.*
> > *Shakspeare: Merry Wives of Windsor.*
> That Troy prevailed, that Greeks were conquered cleane,
> And that Penelope was but a *queane.*
> > *Harington's Ariosto.*

Queme, to please; pleasant, convenient, fitting, appropriate; the modern German *bequemlich* has the same meaning.

> To be accepted thee to *queme* and please.
> > *Lydgate MS., Ashmole; quoted by Halliwell.*

Queming, pleasure. These two words occur in the Dictionary of the Oldest Words in the English Language, by Herbert Coleridge.

Querl, to spin round, to coil, to twirl.

Quern, a hand mill, a churn.

> Are ye not he,
> That frights the maidens of the villages,
> Skims milk, and labors in the *quern?*
> > *Midsummer Night's Dream.*

Quert, joyful, in good spirits.

> He was now in *quert,*
> And all hale of wille and herte.
> > *Iwayne and Gawin, (Jameson.)*
> All but the Earl they were full fain,
> In *querte* that he was comyn hame.—*Sir Eglamour.*

Quethe, to say, speak, declare. The preterite of this verb still remains in the language, in the well-known and well-worn phrase, 'quoth he.' From the same root comes, *bequeath,* to give to your survivors in your last will and testament; to *say* that they shall have such and such portions of your property.

Quick, alive.

'The *quick* and the dead,' is a scriptural phrase, familiar to every body. The word in this sense is fast becoming obsolete; and 'quick' in its modern signification is simply active, the reverse of slow. The common expression, 'Look alive,' is synonymous with 'be *quick*.'

> If ever the dead come to the *quick*,
> Be sure, Marg'ret, I'll come to thee.
> > *Clerk Saunders : Minstrelsy of the Scottish Border.*

Quillet, a play upon words ; a facetious subtlety of argument, without logical force.

> Let not human *quillets* keep back divine authority.
> > *Milton : Of Reformation in England.*
>
> Ply her with love-letters and billets,
> And bait them well with *quirks* and *quillets.*
> > *Butler : Hudibras.*

Quip. This word enshrined in Shakspeare and Milton, dropped out of use for a century, but is again becoming a favorite. It means a quick, sharp, jest, or stroke of raillery.

> And notwithstanding all her sudden *quips*,
> The least whereof would quell a lover's hope.
> > *Shakspeare : Two Gentlemen of Verona.*
>
> *Quips* and cranks and wreathed smiles.
> > *Milton.*

Quirk, an unfair turn in an argument ; an evasion or twisting of the truth.

> For my part, I have studied the law ; * * * these be but *quirkes* intended to delay matters.
> > *Fox : Book of Martyrs.*

Quirky, tricky ; unfair, pettifogging.

Quoke, preterite of quake, to tremble.

> An ugly pit, deep as any hell,
> That to behold thereon, I *quoke* for fear.
> > *The King's Quaire.*
>
> The whole land of Italy trembled and *quoke.*
> > *Douglas : Translation of the Eneid.*

Quoy, a northern word, signifying a piece of enclosed land on a common. "In Orkney, a circular enclosure of the kind is called 'a ringit *quoy.*'—(*Jameson*)."

Rack,
Wrack, } cloud ;—a bank of clouds, vapour.

> Can permit the basest clouds to ride,
> With ugly *rack* on his celestial face.
> > *Shakspeare : The Tempest.*
>
> Swifter than the sailing *rack* that gallops
> Upon the wings of angry winds.
> > *Beaumont aud Fletcher.*
>
> Now we may calculate by the welkin's *wrack*,
> Eolus hath chast the clouds that were so black.
> > *Heywood's Marriage Triumph.*

Raddles, pieces of supple underwood, twisted between upright stakes to form a fence.

> Our fathers did dwell, either in houses of staves, or in houses of *raddles*.
> > *Holinshed.*

Raid, a predatory incursion on horseback.

> The *raid* of Ruthven.
>
> The *raid* of Reidswire.
>
> Riding a *raid*, browsing.

This Scottish word has gradually been establishing itself in the favor of the best writers and speakers, both in England and in America.

Rakel,
Raucle, } rough, coarse, rugged, rash.

Rakelness, roughness, coarseness, rashness.

This word, derived from the German and Anglo-Saxon rauh, rough, or from the Latin raucus, hoarse, survives in Scotland. Burns in the 'Jolly Beggars,' describes the wench, who sings the song of 'A Highland lad my love was born,' as a 'raucle carline.' In his 'Earnest cry

Rakelness—*continued.*

and prayer to the Scottish representatives in Parliament,'
he speaks of Scotland as having ' a *raucle* tongue, when she
is offended.' In Chaucer the word appears as *rakle*, as in
' Manciple's Tale :'

> O *rakle* hand ! to do so foule amis
> O troubled wit ! O ire reccheless !
>
> * * * * *
>
> O every man beware of *rakelness.*

Mr. Halliwell quotes from a MS. in the Bodleian:

> The soudan sayd it is not so
> For your prestes that suld vertus trace,
> They syn *raky*ᴵl out of gud grace,
> Give ille example and lie in synne.

In the West of England, ' rackle ' signifies rough, noisy
talk ; and in Cumberland, ' rackle-deed,' is loose, unruly
conduct. These examples serve to show that the word is
not derived from reck, and *reckless*, as Worcester and other
lexicographers suppose : as in addition to the sense of
heedlessness and suddenness, it always implies coarseness
and roughness. From the same source is derived the corrupted form of *rake-hell.*

> With a handful of *rake-helles*, which he had scummed together in
> this our shire, whilst the king was on his return from Tewbury.
> *Lambarde's Perambulation*, 1596.

The Americans of the present day, call *rake-hells*, roughs,
thus going back unconsciously to the original source of the
word.

Rance, a prop, a stake ; support, or scaffold.

Ranch, a deep scratch or wound with the sword upon the body,
with a plough upon the earth, or with the claws of a wild
animal.

> A *ranche* or clinche with a beast's paw.
> *Cotgrave.*
>
> *Ranched* his hips with one continued wound.
> *Dryden.*

Dr. Johnson was at a loss to explain the etymology or
meaning of this word ; and Worcester defines it to be a
corruption of *wrench.* ' A Northamptonshire rustic,' says

Ranch—*continued.*

Mr. Sternberg in his Glossary, 'would have had no difficulty in understanding that line of "*Glorious John*," which so puzzled the learned Johnson. Dryden was a Northamptonshire man, and might have heard the word during one of his many sojourns in that county.'

Rand, the rushes and long grass on the banks of a stream, or on the margin of a lake or pool.

Rant, a public meeting, or fair; whence, perhaps, the word *ranter,* a priest or layman who preached to the crowd on such occasions.

> Thou art the life o' public haunts,
> But then what were our fairs and *rants.*
> > *Burns: Scotch Drink.*

Rape, haste.

Rapely, readily.

Rapen, to prepare, make ready.

> Two risen up in *rape.*
> > *Piers Ploughman.*

> *Rape* thee to ride.
> > *Idem.*

> *Rape* thee to shrifte.
> > *Idem.*

> With that saw I another.
> *Rapelich* (rapely) run forth.
> > *Idem.*

> Ran ramping, swearing, rude and *rape.*
> > *The Cherry and the Sloe.*

Rath, ⎫ early, soon. The comparative of this adjective is in
Rathe, ⎭ common use; but the positive and superlative have both been allowed to drop out of the language. Milton in Lycidas speaks of the '*rathe* primrose;' Drayton in his Polyolbion, has '*rathe* as he could rise.'

> To serve that lady both late and *rathe.*
> > *Piers Ploughman.*

> Oh dear, cousin mine, dear John, she said,
> What aileth you so *rathe* for to arise?
> > *Chaucer.*

> Too *rathe* cut off by practice criminal
> Of secret foes.
> > *Spenser.*

Rath—*continued.*

> A *rathe* December, blights my lagging May.
> *Bartley Coleridge.*

Bishop Hall mentions ' *rathe* ripe wits, that prevent their own perfection ;' and in the cider districts there is a well known species of apple called the *rathe-ripe.* Nares quotes but one example of the use of the superlative *rathest :* ' Barley almost ripe to be cut in June, whereas in England they seldom cut the *rathest* before the beginning of August.'

In the Glossary of the Provincialisms of Sussex, by W. Durrant Cooper, it is stated that the word *rath* is in frequent use and well understood in that county.

Rax, to reach ; to stretch.

Raught, reached, stretched.

This is doubtless the ancient form of the modern word to reach, or stretch, the x being softened to ch, as has happened in such words as church from kirk ; churn, from kern. The advantage of retaining it is shewn in the proverb : ' Never *rax* aboon your reach :' which, if translated into modern phraseology, would be, ' never *stretch* above your *reach,*' a phrase as full of meaning, but scarcely so forcible.

The word still exists in the South of England. A street at Bridport is called the *Rax,* or stretch of ground.

> And ye may *rax* corruption's neck,
> And give her for dissection.
>> *A Dream, by Burns.*

> Their three mile and half-mile graces,
> A *raxing* conscience.
>> *Epistle to Rev. John McMath by Burns.*

> He stert up and would have him *raught.*
>> *Merlin, Early English Metrical Romances.*

> Upon my life, by some device or other,
> The villain is o'er *raught* of all my money.
>> *Shakspeare : Comedy of Errors.*

> The auld gudeman *raught* down the pock.
>> *Burns : Halloween.*

Raven, to devour greedily, or to be eager to devour ; apparently derived from the Saxon *reave* or *rieve,* to steal or take away violently ; from whence the word ' *Ravener,* a plunderer ; used by Gower, Chaucer, and other

Raven—*continued.*

writers of that time; and the still current adjective, ' raven-
ous,' hungry for food, enjoyment or revenge.

> Benjamin shall *raven* as a wolf.
>> *Genesis,* chapter xlix.

> Better 'twere
> I met the *raven* lion when he roared
> With sharp constraint of hunger.
>> *Shakspeare: All's Well that Ends Well.*

> Our natures do pursue ;
> Like rats that *raven* down their proper bane.
>> *Shakspeare : Measure for Measure.*

> Maw
> Of the *ravened* salt sea shark.
>> *Shakspeare : Macbeth.*

Reave, to take away, only used at present in its augmentative
form of be-reave.

> If he *reveth* me my right,
> He robbeth me by maistrie.
>> *Piers Ploughman.*

> Next we *reave* this sword,
> And give the armless to their enemies,
> For being foe to goodness and to heaven.
>> *Beaumont & Fletcher : Knight of Malta.*

> To *reave* the orphan of his patrimony,
> And have no other reason for his wrong,
> But that he was bound by a solemn oath.
>> *Shakspeare : Henry VI.*

> Butcher sire that *reaves* his son of life.
>> *Shakspeare: Venus and Adonis.*

> That which God will give,
> The Deil canna *reave.*
>> *Allan Ramsay : Scotch Proverb.*

Reavery, robbery.

> Wallace was near, when he such *reaverie* saw,
> He spake to them with manly countenance.
>> *Wallace.*

Reft, preterite of reave.

> These poor, world wandering men,
> (Of all hope to return their country *reft,*)
> Sought shores whereon to set the little there was left.
>> *Drayton's Polyolbion.*

From this word comes the northern *reiver,* a thief, a
taker-away. At Newcastle, the evening before the fair the

Reft—*continued.*

Great Bell of St. Nicholas called the *Thief and Reaver Bell* is rung, to notify to the fair-frequenting public the approaching commencement of business, and consequently of the advent of the thieves.

Ream. This word expresses the effervescency of liquor, like the French word *mousser*, to sparkle, and is a better word than creaming, of which it is the original. ' Creaming champagne, and creaming ale,' should be, ' reaming champagne, or ale,' for there is no cream in wine or beer, unless they be made into possets. Ream was formerly used in the sense of cream, as may be seen in the passage quoted from the Legendæ Catholicæ in Halliwell's Archaic Dictionary :

> Methinks this pain is sweeter,
> Than any milk's *ream.*

In Scottish poetry the word is of frequent occurrence, and by Robert Burns more especially is used with excellent effect. Tam o' Shanter sits by the Ingle side, on a market night ;

> With *reaming* swats that drink divinely.

Afterwards the swats (ale)

> So *reamed* in Tammie's noddle,

when he looked in at the window of the haunted kirk and saw Maggie leaping in her ' cuttie sark,' that he was emboldened to utter the famous cry that brought the whole of the grotesque crew after him.

In his celebration of Scotch Drink, he speaks of ale or porter, that

> *Reams* o'er the brink,
> In glorious foam.

And in the same poem, he says of whiskey ;

> That merry night we get the corn in,
> Oh sweetly then thou *reams* the horn in.

Reck, to take heed ; or care ; whence *reckless* and *recklessness.*

> I *reck* as little what betideth me,
> As much I wish all good befortune you.
> *Shakspeare.*

Reck—-*continued.*

> With that care lost,
> Went all his fear of God or hell, or worse,
> He *recked* not.
>
> > *Milton.*

> And may ye better *reck* the rede,
> Than ever did the adviser.
>
> > *Burns : Epistle to a Young Friend.*

Rede, to advise, to counsel.

Redel, a thing or subject to be taken into counsel ; or consideration, whence ' riddle,' a little rede.

> Are ye ————————
> Yernen to *rede redels,*
> I shall bring you a Bible,
> A book of the old lawe.
>
> > *Piers Ploughman.*

> When King Orfed heard this case,
> Then he said alas ! alas !
> He asked *rede* of many a manne.
>
> > *MS. Ashmole, quoted by Mr. Halliwell.*

> Why yes, fore God, quoth Henry Nicholas,
> If thou wilt werken after love and *rede.*
>
> > *Chaucer : The Miller's Tale.*

> And therefore I *rede,*
> My son that thou flee and drede
> This vice.
>
> > *Gower : Confessio Amantis.*

> Himself the primrose path of dalliance treads,
> And recks not his own *rede.*
>
> > *Shakspeare : Hamlet.*

> Therefore I *rede* you three go hence.
>
> > *Gammer Gurton's Needle.*

> Short *rede* is good *rede.*
>
> > *Allan Ramsay.*

> And may you better reck the *rede.*
> Than ever did th' adviser.
>
> > *Burns : Epistle to a Young Friend.*

> Ye gallants bright, I *rede* ye right,
> Beware o' bonnie Anne.
>
> > *Burns : Songs.*

Two hundred and nine marched out ; one escaped at the end of the bridge ; yet behold when you count the corpses, they are two hundred and ten. *Rede* us this riddle.

> *Carlyle's History of the French Revolution,* vol. 3, page 272.

Redel—*continued.*

> The man is blest that hath not lent
> To wicked *rede* his ears.
>> *Sternhold : Version of the Psalms.*

The etymology of the name of the village of Leather-head, in Surrey, has puzzled whole generations of local antiquaries, but as it was originally written Leoderede, the name seems to offer no difficulty, and to bespeak for itself a very respectable antiquity, as well as a very honorable derivation. *Leod* is the Anglo-Saxon for people, from the same root as the German *leute*, and conjoined with 'rede,' means the ' Council of the people.' Probably it was the place of meeting of some great popular assemblage ; not a *wittenagemote*, or meeting of the wise men ; but of the multitude.

Reek, smoke, vapor, or exhalation ; from *rauch*, smoke. '*Auld Reekie*,' 'old smoky ;' i.e., Edinburgh.

> You common cry of curs, whose breath I hate,
> As *reek* o' the rotten fens.
>> *Shakspeare.*

> Few chimneys *reeking* you shall spy.
>> *Spenser.*

> Which with his beams, the sun
> Soon dried, and on the *reeking* moisture fed.
>> *Milton.*

> The *reek* of my ain house is better,
> Than the ingle of my neighbour's.
>> *Allan Ramsay's Scotch Proverbs.*

> The thick abomination,
> Spreads *reeking* to the sky.
>> *The Souls of the Children.*

> Come hitherward my maidens fair,
> Come hither unto me,
> Through this *reek*, and through this smeek.
>> *Motherwell's Ancient Minstrelsy.*

Rept, preterite of reap.

> After the corn is *rept.*
>> *Nomenclator, quoted by Nares.*

Revel-coyle, noisy merriment.

> To dance, sing, sport, and to keep *revel-coyle.*
>> *Taylor's Workes,* 1630.

Revel-rout, confused and noisy sport; the same as *revel-coyle.*

> There is a strange thing like a gentlewoman,
> Crept into the nunnery, we know not which way,
> Plays *revel-rout* among us.
> > *Monsieur Thomas.*

Rewth, } pity, compassion; from whence *ruthless,* pitiless, and
Ruth, } *ruthful,* compassionate.

> Then said he by Saint John,
> It is great *rewth* for to slon (slay),
> That God has bought so dear.
> > *Romance of Amys and Amylion.*

> Tho' she can weep to stir up gentle *ruth,*
> But for her noble blood and for her tender truth.
> > *Spenser: Faerie Queene.*

> If *ruthful* gods have any power.
> > *Surrey: Virgil's Eneis.*

Ribb, } a wrinkle, a furrow. Sternberg, in his Northamp-
Ribble, } tonshire Glossary, quotes the popular phrase: 'His
forehead was *ribbled.*'

Coleridge, in a note to the Ancient Mariner, says he was
indebted to Wordsworth for the lines :

> And he was, lank and lean, and bare,
> As in the *ribb'd* sea-sand.

Rindle, to sparkle like running water; a mountain stream.

> The dainty *rindles* dancing down,
> Fro' the mountains to the plain.
> > *Waugh's Lancashire Songs.*

> By primrose banks,
> Where *rindling* weet was shining.
> > *Idem.*

Rift, to belch, to blow.

> Three times the carline groaned and *rifted.*
> > *Allan Ramsay.*

Rift, a fissure, a break, that which is riven or rift.

Rift, to cleave or break asunder.

> Then I'd shriek, that even your ears
> Should *rift* to hear me.
> > *Shakspeare: Winter's Tale.*

> Flauchts (lightnings) did *rift*
> Frae the black vizard o' the lift.
> > *Allan Ramsay : The Vision.*

Rink.—A course or arena for public sports. The word is principally used in connection with skating, and applied either to an open pond, frozen over, where a ring is made, or to a covered inclosure for the same purpose. The word is common in America and Scotland, though but little used in England. It formerly signified a distinct charge, or encounter in a tournament.

> Trumpets and shalms with a shout
>   Played ere the *rink* began,
> And equal judges sat about
>   To see who tint or wan.
> *The Evergreen.*

Roaky, } hazy, misty, nebulous, dull, coarse, not clear; from
Roky, } the French *rauque ;* une voix rauque, a hoarse, thick voice.

In Shakspeare, act iii., scene 2, of Macbeth, the passage occurs :

> Light thickens ; and the crow
> Makes wing to the *rooky* wood.

It is probable that ' rooky' was formerly a recognized English word, or is a misprint for roaky. If there were much doubt on the true meaning of the passage, it might be removed by a reference to Jameson's Dictionary of the Scottish Language,' where 'roaky' is spelt 'rooky' and defined as ' misty.'

> A *rooky* mist fell down at break of day,
> Then thought he fit to make the best o's way.
> *Hamilton's Wallace.*

Richardson defines the word in Shakspeare to mean ' covering.' Johnson in like manner failed to perceive the real meaning, as did also Webster and Worcester, both of whom define ' rooky' to mean inhabited by rooks.

Rooky is a not more legitimate word than ' crowy' would be ; and why the crows should fly to the rooks at daylight, is not easy to discover. But 'roaky or rooky ' in the sense of misty, makes the passage intelligible.

Rode, a healthy complexion ; the redness of one red with the blood of life ; whence *ruddy.*

Rode—*continued.*

> His *rode* is like scarlet in grayn.
> > *Chaucer.*

Rogue-house, a prison, a penitentiary.

Rone, to comfort; (Herbert Coleridge's Dictionary of the Oldest Words in the English Language.)

Roop, a sore throat, the croop.

Rooped, } hoarse, as with bronchitis or a cold in the throat.
Roopit, }

> What's the matter now with him ?   What a *roope* ails he ?
> > *Terence in England,* 1614.

> Alas, my *roopit* Muse is hoarse.
> > *Burns: The Author's Earnest Cry and Prayer.*

Roose, } to praise ; to drink a health.
Rouse, }

This word is still current in the North of England and Scotland, in its original sense of to praise or extol.   In England, in the Elizabethan age, it meant to drink a bumper to any one's health; on which occasions, as now when people drink a toast, it was customary and necessary to praise the person, in whose honor the bumper was drank.

> *Rouse,* a mode of drinking, in which the full cup or other drinking vessel was to be emptied at a draught; a bumper toast.
> > *Rev. A. Dyce: Glossary to Ben Jonson's Works.*

> No jocund health that Denmark drinks to-day,
> But the great cannon to the clouds shall tell,
> And the kings *rouse* the heavens shall bruit again,
> Respeaking earthly thunder.
> > *Shakspeare : Hamlet.*

> *Roose* the ford as ye find it.

> *Roose* the fair day at e'en.
> > *Allan Ramsay's Scotch Proverbs.*

> When Redisdale and Wise William,
>   Were drinking at the wine,
> They fell a *roosing* them among,
>   On one unruly time.

> Some of them hae *roosed* their hawkes,
>   And other some their hounds,
> And other some their ladies fair.
> > *Motherwell's Ancient Minstrelsy.*

Roose—*continued.*

> And we'll have a *rouse* in each of them, anon ; for bold Britons
> i' faith.—*Ben Johnson.*

> I have took since supper
> A *rouse* or two too much.
> > *Beaumont and Fletcher.*

> Shall bauld Lapraik, the king o' hearts,
> *Roose* ye sae well for you deserts,
> In terms sae friendly,
> Yet ye'll neglect to show your parts,
> And thank him kindly.
> > *Burns : Epistle to Lapraik.*

Roove, to rivet, to clinch.

> If this nail be once *rooved*, we with our teeth will never get it drawn
> > *Baillie's Letters, (quoted by Jameson.)*

Rooven, riveted.

> Ships composed of meane stuffe, having their keeles and ribs made
> of slight timber, and the rest of the hull *rooven* up with osiers, covered
> with leather.
> > *The Soveraigntie of the British Seas ; by Sir John Borough,* 1633.

Rote, a wheel. To learn a thing by rote, is to learn it mechanically, ' as the wheel turns.'

> His rewel and respondes,
> But be pure *rote.*
> > *Piers Ploughman.*

> And if by chance a tune you *rote.*
> > *Drayton.*

Rother, a rudder : whence Rotherhithe, the haven of rudders i.e., ships.

Rove, preterite of rive, to split, to rend asunder.

Route,
Rout, } to assemble ; a company.

> In all that land no Christian durste *route.*
> > *Chaucer : The Man of Lawe's Tale.*

> Even he rode the hinderest of the *route.*
> > *Chaucer : Prologue to the Canterbury Tales.*

> Of women many a *route.*
> > *Chaucer : The Marchante's Tale.*

Routh, abundance.

> For *routh* shall cherish love, and love shall bring,
> Mae men t' improve the soil and serve the king,
> > *Allan Ramsay : The North Sea.*

> God grant your lordship joy and health,
> Long days, and *rowth* of real wealth.
> > *Idem, Epistle to Lord Dalhousie.*

> They that have *rowth* o' butter, may lay it thick upon the scone.
> (cake).—*Allan Ramsay's Scotch Proverbs.*

> Rich folk have *routh* o' friends.
> > *Idem.*

> A *rowth* of bonnie bairns and brave.
> > *Idem, Masque on the Marriage of the Duke of Hamilton.*

> Fortune ! if thou wilt gie me still.
> Hail breeks, a scone, a whiskey gill,
> And *rowth* o' rhyme to rave at will.
> > Take a' the rest.
> > *Burns : Scotch Drink.*

Rowan-tree, the mountain ash.

Rown, to talk privately ; to whisper in the ear; from the Anglo-Saxon, rune ; a letter, a secret; a whisper.

> And ryt righte to reason,
> And *rowneth* in his ear.
> > *Piers Ploughman.*

> Two risen up in rape,
> And *rowned* together ;
> And praised this pennyworth.
> > *Idem.*

> The archbishop then called to him a clerk, and *rowned* with him.
> > *Wordsworth's Ecclesiastical Biography.*

> The steward on his knees set him down,
> With the emperor for to *rown.*
> > *Romance of Cœur de Lion.*

> But if it like you that I might *rowne* in your eare.
> > *Skelton.*

This word in Shakspeare's time had become corrupted into *round*, just as the word drown in our time is by vulgar people pronounced drownd. The phrase to ' round in the ear,' appears in much of the literature of that day ; and has not been corrected, as it ought to be, in the modern reprints of Shakspeare. Polonius says to the King in Hamlet :

Rown—*continued.*

> Let his queen mother all alone entreat him
> To show his griefs ; let her be *round* with him.

Mr. Stanton in a note on this passage, explains this to mean, ' let her be blunt and plain spoken with him.' Possibly the true meaning is to be sought in the word *rown,* and not in *round.*

> As God's own soldier, *rounded* (rowned ?) in the ear,
> With that same purpose-changer.
> > *Shakspeare : King John.*

> Disease, age, death, still in our ears thus *round* (rown).
> > *Puttenham.*

> But being come to the supper place, one of Kalender's servants
> *rounded* (rowned) in his ear.—*Pembroke's Arcadia.*

> They're here with me already, whispering, *rounding.*
> > *Shakspeare : Winter's Tale.*

Rowte, to roar or bellow like cattle.

The word rout in the phrase, ' rabble rout,' or the roar of the multitude, may possibly be derivable from this source rather than from ' rout,' confusion.

In Sternberg's Northamptonshire Glossary, *rout* is said to be a noise made by sheep.

Chaucer in the House of Fame, uses the word to express the roaring of the sea.

> Like the beating of the sea,
> Against the rockys hollow,
> And that a man stande
> A mile off thence and hear it *rowte.*

In the Miller's Tale, the Carpenter ' dede asleep,' is said to *grone* and *rowte.* 'The Miller snorted in his sleep, and his wife provided a burden or bass to the music, so loud that 'men might hear her *rowtings* at a furlong's distance.'

Allan Ramsay in his Pastoral on the death of Addison, has :

> Maggie has baked the supper scones,
> And muckle kye stand *rowting* in the loans (lanes).

Rowte—*continued.*

Burns imitated or adopted the expression in the 'Twa Dogs:'

> The bum-clock (beetle) hummed in lazy drone,
> The kye stood *rowting* in the *loan.*

Royle, } *v.* to trouble, or create a commotion in the waters
Roil, } until they become turbid; also to ruffle a person's temper; to reproach. The word, often pronounced *rile,* is common in all the Midland Counties. 'He's been *royling* at me all day;' is a phrase quoted in Sternberg's Northamptonshire Glossary. 'He loves to fish in *roiled* waters,' is a common proverb in many parts of England. The Americans have adopted the word, with its corrupt spelling rile, in which form it has come back again to the land of its birth, where it might do good service if the proper pronunciation could be restored. *Sam Slick* has done much to make it familiar. In the 'Clockmaker in England,' he says: 'I won't say your country or my country, and then it won't *rile* nobody.' And in 'Human Nature:' 'It *riled* me so, that I first steps up to him, as savage as a meat-axe, intending to throw him down stairs.'

Lowell in the 'Bigelow Papers,' has the stanza:

> We begin to think it's nature,
>   To take sarse and not be *riled,*
> Who 'd expect to see a tater.
>   All on end at being biled.

The word in America is also used as an adjective: 'The boys and girls were laughing at my scrape, and the pickle I was in, that I gan to get *riley,*' *Robb., Squatter Life.*

Royne, the mange: from the French *rogne.*

Royny, } mangy.
Roynish, }

> The *roynish* clown, at whom so oft,
> Your Grace was wont to laugh.
>   *Shakspeare: As You Like it.*

Roxle, to grunt.

'Herbert Coleridge's Dictionary of the Oldest Words in the English Language.'

Ruck, to roost like a bird ; to haunt.

> The furies made the bridegroom's bed,
>   And on the house did *rucke*
> A cursed owl, the messenger
>   Of ill success and lucke.
>
> *Golding's Ovid,* 1603.

> The raven *ruck'd* her in the chimney's top,
> And chattering pyes in dismal discords sung.
>
> *Shakspeare : Henry VI.*

Ruddock, the robin redbreast.

> The *ruddock* would with charitable bill,
> Bring them all this.
>
> *Shakspeare : Cymbeline.*

> The mavis descant plays,
> The ouzell trills, the *ruddock* warbles soft.
>
> *Spenser : Epithalamium.*

Ruff, a triumph ; the ancient name for a trump card.

> And in the *ruffe* of his felicitie,
> Pricked with ambition.
>
> *Mirror for Magistrates.*

Rug, } the back of a man or animal; also a protuberance ;
Rugge, } hence applied to a rock or mountain ; the root of the
adjective ' rugged.'

> Should no curious clothe
> Comen on his *rugge.*
>
> *Piers Ploughman.*

> The knight to the boar is gone,
> And cleveth him to the *rugge-bone.*
>
> *MS. Cantab., quoted by Halliwell.*

> At his *rugge* bones end.
>
> *Piers Ploughman.*

Ruly, obedient ; as good and necessary a word as *unruly,* which
remains in the language.

Rumorous, murmurous.

> Clashing of armour, and the *rumorous* sound,
> Of the stern billows.
>
> *Drayton,* 1604.

Rune, a letter ; a discourse, a conversation, a whisper.

Mr. Herbert Coleridge includes this word among the
oldest in the English Language.

Rung, the step of a ladder.

> And layeth a ladder thereto,
> Of lesyngs are the *rungs.*
>> *Piers Ploughman.*

Rung, a cudgel, a shillelah. Something that hits a ringing blow.

> Auld Scotland —————————
> She's just a devil wi' a *rung.*
>> *Robert Burns.*

Runt, an ox; German rint. Metaphorically applied in the North to a strong, rough, ignorant, bull-headed fellow.

Rure, a noise ; Anglo Saxon, (whence the modern word, *up-roar.*)

Ryn, Anglo Saxon, to whisper, to tell secrets ; the same as the Anglo-Saxon, *rune* and *rown,* q. v.

Sag, to bend or give way under great pressure; like marshy land under the foot; to fail in health, to droop, to wither.

> The mind I sway by, and the heart I bear,
> Shall never *sag* with doubt or shake with fear.
> > *Shakspeare.*

> That it may not *sag* from the intention of the founder.
> > *Fuller's Worthies.*

Sog, preterite of sag.

Samely, monotonous, unvaried; always the same.

> Oh *samely*, naked leas, so bleak and strange.
> > *Clare's Village.*

Samite, silk velvet.

> In silke *samite* she was light arrayed,
> And her fair locks were woven up in gold.
> > *Spenser's Faerie Queene.*

> Clad in white *samite*, mystic, wonderful.
> > *Tennyson.*

Sark, a common word all over Scotland and the North and East of England, for a shirt; and either derived from the Greek σαρξ, the body next to which the shirt is worn, or as Richardson supposes, from Σηρικος, silk; of which material *sarks* were first made. Dr. Arbuthnot, in John Bull, says, 'Flaunting beaux with their breasts open, and their *sarks* over their waistcoats.'

> She shoulde unsowen her *serk*.
> > *Piers Ploughman.*

> My *sark's* dear to me, but my skin's dearer.
> > *Allan Ramsay's Scotch Proverbs.*

Saw, a saying.

> Full of wise *saws* and modern instances.
> > *Shakspeare.*

From the same source comes after*saw*, a rejoinder.

Scafe, to lead a roving, vagabond life ; to beg, to swindle.

> They scaffed (*scafed*) through all Scotland, oppressing the leal man
> as well as the thief, for their particular commoditie.
>> *Pitscottie's Chronicle.*

> A *scafing* varlet, wanting shame.
>> *Legend of the Bishop of St. Andrews.*

Scale, to disperse ; like a crowd or congregation.

> They would no longer abide,
> But *scaled* and departed away.
>> *Holinshead.*

> Whereupon the troopers *scaled.*
>> *Ibid.*

This word, lost in England, is common in Scotland : ' The kirk is *scaling* ;' i.e., the congregation is leaving the church. ' When the school *scales* ;' i.e., when the school hours are over, and the children are let loose.

Scart, to scratch.

> Yea, weighty reason me inclines,
> To thank some eminent divines ;
> Make their assenting here to thwart,
> And one another's cheeks to *scart.*
>> *Cleveland.*

> They that bourd (jest) with cats may count upon *scarts.*
>> *Allan Ramsay.*

> Biting and *scarting* is Scotch folks wooing.
>> *Ferguson's Proverbs.*

To *scart* the buttons, or draw one's hand down the breast of another, so as to touch the buttons with one's nails, is a mode of challenging to battle among boys ; perhaps a relic of some ancient mode of hostile defiance.—*Jameson.*

Scart-free, without a scratch, or the slightest injury.

> All whom the lawyers do advise,
> Get not off *scart-free.*
>> *Cleland.*

One is said to have come off *scart-free*, who has returned safe from a broil, or battle, or any dangerous situation.

Scartle, to scratch or scrape together by small strokes ; diminutive of *scart*. In the South of Scotland, an instrument resembling a hoe, used for clearing out a cow-house, is called a *scartle*.

Scathe, or *skaith ;* to injure, blast, destroy ; and *scathe,* injury, harm, destruction, together with the adjectives *scatheful,* injurious ; and *scatheless,* harmless. These words have been used by the best writers since the days of Chaucer ; though they have not succeeded in retaining their place in ordinary conversation, the pulpit, or the stage.

> It doeth him double *scathe.*
> > *Piers Ploughman.*

> My foes ——————————
> Are buckled to do me *scathe.*
> > *Earl of Surrey.*

> Was some deal deaf, and that was *scathe.*
> > *Chaucer : Wife of Bath.*

> This trick may chance to *scathe* you.
> > *Shakspeare : Romeo and Juliet.*

> Had I twenty times as many foes,
> And each of them had twenty times their power,
> All these could not procure me any *scathe,*
> So long as I am loyal, true, and harmless.
> > *Shakspeare : Henry VI.*

> *Scathed* the forest oaks and mountain pines.
> > *Milton.*

> Gude faith,
> Ye're may be come to stop my breath ;
> I rede ye weel, take care of *skaith,*
> > See ! here's a gully !
> > > *Burns : Death and Doctor Hornbook.*

> One man does the *scathe,* and another gets the scorn.

> ————————

> Better learn from your neighbour's *skaith* than your own.

> ————————

> Better *skaith* saved than amends made.

> ————————

> Scorn commonly comes wi' *skaith.*
> > *Allan Ramsay's Scotch Proverbs.*

> Nor with neglecting prudent care,
> Do *skaith* to your succeeding heir.
> > *Allan Ramsay's Epistle to Robert Yarde, of Devonshire.*

Scathy, } mischievous; applied to a wild, excited, or frantic
Skathy, } person.

> Let him alone, he's *scathy*.

Scaur, } a bare rock without vegetation. *Nab-Scar*, in West-
or **Scar,** } moreland, opposite Rydal Mount; 'the head of the
bare rock.' From the same root, the Gaelic, *skerries*, the
rocks; and Skerrievore, the 'great, bare rock,' on the West
Coast of Scotland.

Scarborough, in Yorkshire, derives its name from this word.
In Cumberland and Westmoreland it is commonly used.

> Round a rocky *scaur* it strays.
> > *Burns : Halloween.*

Scaw, the elder tree.

Scoad, } to scatter earth, manure, or broken rubbish.
Scode, }

Scoil, loose stones, rubbish; the head of a quarry.

Scope, Anglo-Saxon for poet; from sceopen, to make.

Scorce, to exchange.

> But Paridell sore bruised with the blow,
> Could not arise the counterchange to *scorce*.
> > *Spenser : Faerie Queene.*

> Will you *scorce* with him? You are in Smithfield, you may fit
> yourself with a fine, easy-going street nag.
> > *Ben Johnson.*

Scouth, room; elbow-room, space.

> And he'll get *scouth* to wield his tree,
> I fear you'll both be paid.
> > *Ballad of Robin Hood.*

> By break of day he seeks the dowie glen,
> That he may *scouth* to a' his morning len'.
> > *Allan Ramsay : Pastoral on the Death of Matthew Prior.*

Screeve, } to glide swiftly along.
Scrieve, }

> The wheels of life go down hill *scrieving*,
> Wi' rattling glee.
> > *Burns : Scotch Drink.*

Screak,
Screik, } a cry, or sound ; harsher and sharper than a skriek.
Scrike, } ' The *scriek* of the railway whistle.

> Which lie in torments, yet die not,
> With many woeful *scrikes*.
> > > *Halliwell.*

Scritch, to screech.

> Perhaps it is the owlet's *scritch,*
> Or what can ail the mastiff bitch ?
> > > *Coleridge : Christabel.*

Scrog, a stunted bush ; furze.

Scroggy, abounding in underwood; covered with stunted bushes or furze, like the Scottish mountains.

> The way toward the city was stony, thorny, and *scroggy.*
> > > *Gesta Romanorum.*

Sir Walter Scott, when in his last illness in Italy, was taken to a wild scene on the mountains that border the Lago di Garda. He had long been apathetic, and almost insensible to surrounding objects ; but his fading eyes flashed with unwonted fire at the sight of the furze bushes and scrogs that reminded him of home and Scotland ; and he suddenly exclaimed in the words of the Jacobite Ballad :

> Up the *scroggy* mountain,
> And down the *scroggy* glen,
> We dare na gang a hunting,
> For Charlie and his men.

Scroil,
Scroyle, } default ; rubbish ; a mean fellow.

Queen Elizabeth thanked Sir Harry Wallop, ' for some other services than common commissions for which in *skroile* of other memorials, I fail not to lock in my best memorye.' *Chalmer's Apology*, 1797.

In King John, Falconbridge uses the word, and says :

> By heaven, these *scroyles* of Angiers, flout you, kings.

Mr. Stanton derives the word from the French, ecrouelle, a ' scabby rogue.'

Scroil—*continued.*

Mr. Halliwell defines it to mean ' a mangy fellow,' and quotes from Taylor the water poet :

> Then upon Sabbath days the *scroyle* begines,
> With most unhallowed hands to weed up sinnes.

Sculsh, any trashy sweetmeats or green fruit : such as children are fond of eating.

Scutch, to bruise slightly ; whence, by corruption, to ' scotch.' In the sense of to bruize flax, the word is still pronounced *scutch*, in the English manufacturing districts.

> We've *scotched* [scutched] the snake, not killed it.
> *Shakspeare : Macbeth.*

Second-grand-father, a word used by the peasantry to express what in common but less correct, and elegant English is called a ' great grandfather.' A *third* great grandfather, means in like manner, a ' great, great, great grandfather.' As the phrase is capable of indefinite extension into antiquity, it seems a loss to literature that its use should be left wholly to the unwritten speech of the people. A tenth remove of great grandfatherhood would be difficult to designate by ten repetitions of the word ' great,' but easy, as well as graceful by the popular method.

Seethe, to boil; a word in common use before French cookery introduced the French *bouillir.*

> Thou shalt not *seethe* a kid in its mother's milk.
> *Deuteronomy.*
> The priest's servant came while the flesh was a *seething.*
> *1 Samuel*, ii. 13.
> And he said unto his servant, set on the great pot, and *seethe* pottage for the sons of the prophets.
> *2 Kings*, iv. 38.
> The boiling baths at Cairbadon,
> Which *seethe* with secret fire eternally.
> *Spenser.*
>
> Go suck the subtle blood o' th' grape,
> Till the high fever *seethe* your blood to froth,
> And so 'scape hanging.
> *Shakspeare : Timon of Athens.*

Seethe—*continued.*

He that lends his pot may *seethe* his kail-broo' [cabbage] in his loof (hand).

> *Seethe* stanes in butter, the two will be good.
>> *Allar Ramsay : Scotch Proverbs.*
>
> My eyes are *seething* in my head,
> My flesh roasting also.
>> *The Fire of Frendraught.*

The absence of the name of General Rosecrans from the lists of recent promotions has caused much comment. The reason need be no secret. Between Grant and Rosecrans there is waging an irrepressible conflict. Courteous in words, they fairly *seethe* with concealed hatred.
>> *New York Daily News,* May 7, 1866.

Seld,
Selde, } seldom.
Selden,

Selkouth, } from kouth, couth, or kythe, to show, appear, or
Selkethe, } be known ; meaning seldom seen ; strange, or unusual.

Seremonth, August. The month when the leaves begin to dry or be *sere.*

Shack, to rove about idly, to loiter, to go on the tramp ; or in American phrase to ' loaf.'

Shackaback, } an idle vagabond.
Shackler, }

> They call me *shackaback,*
> And knave and lazy loon,
> Because, though hale and strong,
> I'm idle all day long ;
> And carol to the glimmer of the moon.
>> *Under Green Leaves,* 1860.

This word is derived from the Anglo-Saxon, sceacere (or shacker), a thief. In Jamieson's Scottish Dictionary, to *shack,* is described as meaning to shape or form anything in an oblique way. Thus, an idle vagabond, who goes on the tramp rather than do any work, *shacks,* or goes off obliquely from the true path of honesty.

Shackle, the wrist; whence the verb, to shackle, to fetter. The modern shackle was formerly schackle-lock or schacklock, i.e., wrist lock.

Shaftmond, the measure of the palm of the hand with the thumb extended.

> A *shaftemonde* large.
>
> *Morte Arthur.*

The word is still current in Scotland and the North of England.

Shad, preterite of shed.

> Then for us He *shad* His blood,
> And also dyed on the rode.
>
> *Old Christmas Carols, edited by T. Wright, for the Percy Society.*

Shale, a husk; whence the modern word shell; to shell peas, &c., a word not required in this sense, as it has another meaning, as in, shells of the sea. Worcester in his Dictionary says shale is corrupted from shell. The reverse is the fact.

Shalm, a trumpet.

> In cornemuse and *shalmie,*
> And many another pipe.
>
> *Chaucer.*

> He caused all the players of *shalmes* to come out of the city.
>
> *North's Plutarch.*

This word was also written *shawm,* as in the following quotations;

> What stately music have you?
> You have *shawms ?*
>
> *Beaumont and Fletcher.*

> In prayers and hymns to Heaven's eternal King,
> The cornet, flute, and *shawm,* assisting as they sing.
>
> *Otway: Windsor Castle.*

Shapester,
Shepster, } a milliner; one who shapes the dress to the form.

> Mabyll the *shapster* maketh surplys, shirts, breeches, keverchifs and all that may be wrought of linen cloth.
>
> *Caxton's Booke for travellers, (Nares).*

Shard,
Sherd, } fragments of brittle substances, such as stone, marble, slate, glass, pottery, &c.; from the Anglo-Saxon, *scear,* to shear, or cut off. Hence the scales of serpents, or the shining wing cases of beetles, and other insects, hard, and as if made of a different substance from the rest of their bodies, were metaphorically called *shards* or *sherds.*

Shard—*continued.*

Thou shalt break the *sherds* thereof.
Ezekiel xxiii. 34.

For charitable prayers,
Shards, flints, and pebbles, should be thrown on her.
Shakspeare : Hamlet.

Where the pig's (earthenware vessel) broken, let the *sherds* lie.
Allan Ramsay's Scotch Proverbs.

For longe tyme it so befelle,
That with his sworde, and with his spere,
He might mete the serpent dere ;
He was so *sherded* all aboute,
It helde all edge toole withoute.
Gower : Confessio Amantis.

Guid observation they will give them,
And when the auld moon's gain to leave them,
The hardmost *shaird* they'll fetch it with them.
Burns : Epistle to W. Simpson.

Sherd, **Shard,** **Sharn,** the dung of cattle, when dried by exposure in the fields. Considerable controversy has arisen as to the sense in which Shakspeare used the phrase ' *shard*-born beetle,' in Macbeth ; whether he meant shard-born, i.e., born amid cow dung ; or *shard*-borne, borne in the air on shards or wings. In Cymbeline, he says :

And often to our comfort we shall find,
The *sharded* beetle in a safer hold,
Than is the full-winged eagle.

This passage seems to refer to ' shard,' a wing, rather than to ' shard,' dung. The Anglo-Saxon for cow-sherd or shard, was *scearn* or *sharn ;* which pronunciation still survives in the North of England, and Scotland.

Sharm, **Swarm,** to make a buzzing, confused, chattering noise ; as of a crowd of people, children, or birds.

And though they *sharme* and crie, I care not a might.
Digby Mysteries (Halliwell.)

Shaw, a small wood, thicket, or plantation of trees ; from the Anglo-Saxon scuwa, a shady place. This word was once common in English literature, and still subsists in the patronymics of many families ; as, Shawe, Aldershawe, Hinshaw, Abershaw, Hawkshaw (or Oakshaw), and others ; and is still used by the peasantry in most parts of England, and Scotland.

Shaw—*continued.*

> Whither ridest thou under this green *shawe?*
> Said this yeman.
>> *Chaucer: The Frere's Tale.*

> Gaillard he was a gold-finch in the *shaw,*
> Brown as a bery, a proper short felaw.
>> *Chaucer: The Coke's Tale.*

> Close hid beneath the greenwood *shaw.*
>> *Fairfax: Translation of Tasso.*

> In summer when the *shawes* be shene,
>> And leaves be fair and long,
> It is full merry in fair forest,
>> To hear the fowles sing.
>>> *Ballad of Robin Hood.*

> The braes ascend like lofty wa's,
> The foaming stream deep roaring fa's,
> O'erhung wi' fragrant spreading *shaws,*
>> The birks of Aberfelds.
>>> *Burns.*

> Gloomy winter's now awa,
> Saft the westlin' breezes baw,
> Mang the birks o' Stanley *shaw,*
>> The mavis sings fu' cheery, oh.
>>> *Tannahill.*

Shawp, an empty husk; a pea-pod.

Sheal,) to put under cover. To *sheal* the sheap, i. e., to put
Shiel,) them under cover.

Sheen. Nares defines this word to mean, shining as an adjective, or brightness as a noun; but the true derivation is
from the German *schön,* beautiful. It is used by Shakspeare
and Milton in the sense which Nares attributes to it.

> By fountain clear or spangled starlight *sheen.*
>> *Shakspeare: Midsummer Night's Dream.*

> And thirty dozen moons with borrowed *sheen.*
>> *Shakspeare: Hamlet.*

Chaucer, King James I. of Scotland, Spenser, and the
early metrical romancers, use it in its true sense of *schön,*
or beautiful.

> Your blissful sister Lucina, the *sheen,*
> That of the sea is chief goddess and queen.
>> *The Franklin's Tale.*

Sheen—*continued.*

> Her garment was so bright and wondrous *sheene*,
> That my fraile wit cannot devise to what
> It to compare.
>> *The Fairy Queen.*

> After sharpe showers,
> Most *sheen* is the sun.
>> *Piers Ploughman.*

In the King's Quair, the author describes 'the Sphere of Love,' and its presiding divinity Cupid, and his three arrows of gold, silver, and steel; and adds that:

> On his long yellow lockis *sheen*,
> A chaplet had he, all of levis green.

In the romance of Guy of Warwick, the word is used in the same sense:

> The wedding ring was forth brought,
> Guy then and fair Felice thought,
> He had her nigh forgotten clean,
> Alas! he said, Felice the *sheen!*
>> Penance I crave,
> None other maid my love shall have.

And in Sir Bevis of Hampton:

> Her skin that was both bright and *sheen.*

Richmond in Surrey received the name of *Sheen*, from its beauty, not from its brightness.

Byron, though following Shakspeare, seems to be wrong in using the word *sheen* in the sense of *shine* in the following passage:

> The Assyrian came down like a wolf on the fold,
> And his cohorts were gleaming in purple and gold.
> And the *sheen* of their spears was like stars on the sea.
>> *Hebrew Melodies.*

Tennyson in his poem of Love and Death, is also wrong in the use of the word *sheeny*, which is in reality a mere mis-spelling of shiny:

> You must begone! said Death, 'these walks are mine,'
> Love wept and spread his *sheeny* vans for flight.

Coleridge uses it correctly in the 'Ancient Mariner:'

> The upper air burst into life,
> And an hundred fine flags *sheen*,
> To and fro they were hurried about.

Shend, *v.* to rebuke ; to blame ; to shame.

Shent, rebuked.

Dryden, according, to Dr. Johnson, was the last author of note who used this word.

> Vengeance, vengeance,
> Forgiven be it never,
> That *shente* us, and shedde our bloode.
> *Piers Ploughman.*

> What say you, sir ?
> I am *shent* for speaking to you.
> *Shakspeare : Twelfth Night.*

> Sorely *shent* with this rebuke.

> Sorely *shent* was the heir o' Linne.
> *The Heir of Linne.*

> Ye for no bidding, or for being *shent*,
> Would he restrained be from his attendement.
> *Spenser : Faerie Queene.*

> Though bending from the blast of eastern storms ;
> Though *shent* their leaves, and shattered are their arms.

> He that shames let him be *shent*.
> *Allan Ramsay's Scotch Proverbs.*

Shevel, to distort; to walk in an oblique and unsteady manner.

Shieling,
Shealing, } a shepherd's hut ; a covering.

> Ten miles from any town this *shieling* lies.
> *Ross's Helenore.*

Shinicle, a bonfire. A distant fire or light ;—a little shine.— (*Jameson.*)

Shive,
Sheeve, } a large slice.

Shiver, a small slice.

> A man shall not find a *sheve* of it to fetch fire in.
> *Bevis' works : Halliwell.*

> Have I not of a capon but the liver ?
> And of your white bread nought but a *shiver*.
> *Chaucer : The Sompnour's Tale.*

> Easy it is
> Of a cut loaf, to steal a *shive* we know.
> *Shakspeare : Titus Andronicus.*

Shiver—*continued.*

> Bannocks and a *sheeve* of cheese,
> Will make a breakfast that a laird might please.
>
> *Allan Ramsay : The Gentle Shepherd.*

Shoon, ancient plural of shoe.

> And how should I your true love know,
> From many another one ?
> O, by his cockle hat and staff,
> And by his sandal *shoon.*
>
> *Shakspeare : Hamlet.*

The disuse of the Anglo-Saxon plural in n and en, is one of the greatest losses which the English language has suffered ; and combined with the simultaneous disuse of *eth*, in the third person singular in the present tense of verbs, aggravates the tendency to sibillation or hissing, which makes English the most unvocal of all modern tongues. In the version of God save the Queen as commonly sung there are no less than twenty-nine distinct and cacophonous sibillations. In the first verse there are eight,—as follow .

> God *S*ave our graciou*S* Queen,
> Long live our noble Queen,
> God *S*ave the Queen !
> *S*end her victoriou*S*,
> Happy and gloriou*S*,
> Long to reign over u*S*,
> God *S*ave the Queen !

Shope, preterite of shape or create.

> God *shope* the world.
>
> *Wickliffe's Bible.*
>
> Lord that *shope* both heat and cold.
>
> *Guy of Warwick.*
>
> Wymmen were the best thing,
> That *shope* our high Heaven King.
>
> *Advice to the Fair Sex. Ritson's Ancient Songs and Ballads.*
>
> The king and the commune,
>   *   *   *   *   *
> *Shopen* laws.
>
> *Piers Ploughman.*

Shote, a young hog.

In America a very common expression of contempt applied to a man, is that, ' he is a poor *shote.*'

Shram, to shrivel with cold.

> Shrammed; benumbed with cold.
>
> *Halliwell.*

> It was a cold, damp evening, and I found four miles an hour on 'Shanks' pony' only enough to keep me warm; but I am glad to say that his Majesty was the only one of the party in two open carriages who did not, to use a Wiltshirism, look '*shrammed* with cold.'
>
> *Daily Telegraph,* Nov. 1, 1866.

Shreed, to clothe, to cover.

Shred, clothed, covered.

Shrowd, a garment, a covering.

> Bevis of his palfrey alight,
> And *shredde* the palmer as a knight.
>
> *Bevis of Hampton.*
>
> In a kirtel of silk he gan him *shreede.*
>
> *Guy of Warwick.*
>
> Worthy to be *shredde* and shrined in gold.
>
> *Morte Arthur.*
>
> I shope me in a *shrowde* as I a shepherd were.
>
> *Piers Ploughman.*

> The princes were even compelled by the hail, to seek some *shrowding* place.—*Sidney: Arcadia.*

> There was a place called the *shrowds* at Paul's Cross; a covered space on the side of the church to protect the congregation in inclement seasons.—*Pennant's London.*

The word *shroud* applied to the clothing of the dead body is still used. *Shred,* a rag or remnant of attire, is derived from the same root.

Shrew, this word, as a substantive, seems to have been originally applied to both sexes, and to have meant, an ill-conditioned, ill-natured, malicious, bad person, a blackguard, a knave, a rascal. As a verb, with the prefix, *be,* it was used as an imprecative, signifying to curse, as, ' beshrew me, if I do;' i.e., ' curse me if I do.' Some lexicographers have erroneously derived the word from the *shrew*-mouse; but shrew-mouse really means an ill-natured and ferocious kind of mouse. In ' Blount's Glossographia, or Dictionary of Hard Words,' 1680, occurs the following passage, in support of this absurd derivation:

> "*Shrew,* a kind of field mouse, which, if he go over a beast's back, will make him lame in the chine; and if he bite, the beast swells to the heart and dies. From hence came our English phrase, ' *I beshrew thee,*" when we wish ill to any one. And we call a curst woman a *shrew.*"

Shrew—*continued.*

Chaucer in the ' Wife of Bath's Tale,' says :

> I *beshrewe* me,
> But if I telle tales two or three of Freres.

In the Early Metrical Romance of ' Sir Otuel,' the angel answers the prayer of the Christen Knight Roland, in his combat with Mahound, and says :

> Arise, Roland, and fight,
> And shed the *shrew's* blood,
> For he was never good,
> By land nor by sea.

In the Romance of Merlin, the young Merlin's play-fellows, taunting him with the mystery of his birth, exclaim :

> Thou black *shrew,*
> Thou art a foul thing, gotten amiss,
> No man wot who thy father is.

In the ' Evergreen, or Poems written by the Ingenious before 1600,' the author of the ' Pedder Coffes,' calls cheating pedlars,

> Shameless *shrews.*

Shakspeare uses the word for both sexes :

> By this reckoning he's more *shrew* than she.

And in ' Love's Labour Lost,' the Princess says :

> I *beshrew* all *shrews.*

The current meaning of the word, and of its adjective *shrewish*, as applied to a scolding wife, seems to be due entirely to its use by Shakspeare.

Cotton in the ' Joys of Marriage,' has :

> If too wary then she'll *shrew* thee
> If too lavish she'll undo thee.

The Americans use the word *curse*, or as they pronounce it ' cuss,' in a similar sense, both as verb and noun. ' A Yankee,' said an indignant slave owner at New Orleans, ' is a mean *cuss.*' A *shrewish* woman is also called a *cuss.*

Shrew, in Piers Ploughman, seems to mean, ' bad ' as distinguished from ' good,' as in the following passage :

> Whereby wist men which were white,
> If all things black were ;
> And who were a good man,
> But if there were some *shrewe.*

Shrive, to confess.

Shrove ⎫
Shriven ⎬ confessed.

The infinitive and past participle of this verb are not quite obsolete. Shrove, the preterite, survives in Shrove Tuesday.

Shore, ⎫ preterite of shear; the past participle *shorn*, remains
Shure, ⎭ in the language.

> Robin *shure* in harvest.
> *Burns.*

> Boston was the Delilah that allured him (Daniel Webster). Oft he broke the withes of gold, till at last, with a pension she *shore* off the seven locks of his head, and his strength went from him.
> *Theodore Parker's Discourse on the Death of Daniel Webster.*

Shunt, to turn off, or aside; a word lately re-introduced into the language by Railway engineers and workmen.

Shruck, preterite of shriek; to cry out.

Sib, related to by blood or marriage. ' An ancient Saxon word,' says Ray, ' signifying kindred, alliance, or affinity.' The Cheshire proverb, quoted by Halliwell, has : ' we are no more *sib* than sieve and riddle, that both grow in the woods together.' A Scotch proverb in Allan Ramsay's collection, says : ' A' Stuarts are no *sib* to the king ;' ' a vaunter and a liar are right *sib* ;' and ' it's good to be *sib* to siller ;' i.e. money.

> Which is *sib* to Christ himself.
> *Piers Ploughman.*

> An ye be but *sib* to some of these sisters seven.
> *Piers Ploughman.*

> He was *sib* to Arthur of Bretayne.
> *Chaucer.*

> He is no fairy born or *sib* to elves.
> *Spenser.*

> Let the blood of mine that's *sib* to him, be sucked from me with leeches ; let him break and fall off me with that corruption.
> *Beaumont and Fletcher.*

Sile,
Syle, } to run over, to slide down, or subside ; as sand in water.

Silth, that which has subsided ; as the *silth* of a river or lake.

Siss,
Sissie, } a term of endearment; applied to a female child in America: from the first syllable of ' sister.' This word is supposed by some to be purely American, and to be derived from *siss* and *asiss*, signifying *little*, in several Indian dialects. Mr. Halliwell, partially aware of the English, and unaware of the American use of the word, appears to lean to the opinion that *siss* is an abbreviation of *Cicely*, ' a common name for a girl.' He quotes:

> The showman that in times past was contented to russet, must now-a-days have his doublet of the fashion, with wide cuts, his garters of fine silk of Granada, to meet his *siss* on Sunday.
>
> *Lodge's Wit's Miserie,* 1598.

Sistren,
Sustren, } the ancient plural of sister. Chaucer speaks of the fates, or weird sisters, as ' the fatal sustren.' Bartlett's Dictionary of Americanisms, says that the word is a ' vulgarism, sometimes heard from uneducated preachers at the West;' and quotes from ' Carlton's New Purchase,' the following example :

> Brethren and *sistren*, it is a powerful great work, this here preaching of the gospel.

It appears, however, that the word was not vulgar in Chaucer's time. It is, as such, as well entitled to a place in pulpit eloquence, as its equally antique partner—brethren.

> All *sustren* and bretheren,
> That beth (be) of our ordre.
>
> *Creed of Piers Ploughman.*

Sithence,
Sith, } since.

> I came to my lady kith,
> I was yet sobre never *sith*.
>
> *Gower : Confessio Amantes.*

> *Sith* 'twill no better be,
> I trust I have within my realm
> Five hundred good as he.
>
> *Ballad of Chevy Chase.*

> *Sith* 'twas my fault to give the people scope.
>
> *Shakspeare : Measure for Measure.*

Sith—*continued*.

> *Sith* thou hast not hated blood, even blood shall pursue thee.
> > *Ezekiel*, chap. xxxv.

Sith,
Sithe, } time or times.

> And humbly thanked him a thousand *sith*.
> > *Spenser : Faerie Queene*.

> Of his coming the king was blith,
> And rejoiced a hundred *sith*.
> > *Bevis of Hampton*.

Sithcundman, the oldest inhabitant ; one who knows what has happened a long time since ; one known for a long time. The chief man in a town, district, or parish.

Skam, preterite of skim ; to take off the froth or upboiling of a liquid ; whence also *scum*.

Skart, the cormorant.

> Like *skarts* upon the wing, by the hope of plunder led.
> > *The Invasion of the Norsemen*.

Skelly, to squint.

> The very man, said Bothwell, he *skellies* fearfully with one eye.
> > *Sir Walter Scott*.

Skene, a knife, a sword, (Gaelic) ; early used as an English word.

> The Saxons * * the very noblest were,
> And of those crooked *skains* (skenes) they used in war to bear.
> > *Drayton's Polyolbion*.

> His arme is long,
> In which he shakes a *skene*, bright, broad, and long.
> > *Heywood*.

Skew, to turn aside ; whence to look *askew*.

> *Skew* your eye toward the magnet.
> > *Halliwell*.

> The water *skeweth*.
> > *MS. Cotton : quoted by Halliwell*.

Skime, to look at a person furtively ; or with half shut eyes, pretending not to see.

Skenk, } to draw or pour out liquor ; from the German *schen-*
Skink, } *ken*, to pour out.

Skinker, a waiter.

> Such wine as Ganymede doth *skink* to Jove.
> > *Shirley*.

Skinker—*continued.*

> *Skink* out the first glass.
>
> *Ben Jonson.*

> Sweet Ned, * * * I give thee this pennyworth of sugar, clapt
> even now into my hand by an under-*skinker.*
>
> *Shakspeare : Henry IV.*, part 1.

> Until he falls asleep he *skinks* and drinks.
>
> *Taylor, The Water Poet,* 1630.

> But no fear affrights deep drinking,
> There I toss'd it with my *skinkers.*
>
> *Drunken Barnaby's Journal.*

> The bowl went round the board,
> Which empty'd the rude-*skinker* still restored.
>
> *Dryden's Homer.*

> The gods laughed out, unweary'd as they spy'd,
> The busy *skinker* hop from side to side.
>
> *Tickell.*

> The wine! there was hardly half a mutchkin, and puir fusionless
> *skink* it was.
>
> *Sir Walter Scott.*

In the glossary to Ramsay's poems, (1723), *skink* is described as strong broth, made of the shins of beef. ' Skink,'
says Blount's Glossographia (1684) " is, in Scotland, a kind
of pottage of strong nourishment made of knuckles and
sinews of beef long boiled."

Skirl, to shriek, to cry out; or to make a loud noise on a wind
instrument. This word is never used to express the shriek
or scream of pain, but is suggestive either of anger or boister-
ous glee. In Tam o' Shanter, the ' deil' on the window-ledge
of Alloway Kirk, screwed up the bagpipes, and made them
' skirl,' so loudly that the vibration shook the rafters.

> Ye have given the sound thump, and he the loud *skirl ;* (i.e., you
> have punished the man, and he shows it by his roaring.)
>
> *Allan Ramsay's Scotch Proverbs.*

> When *skirling* weanies see the light,
> Thou makes the gossips clatter bright.
>
> *Burns : Scotch Drink.*

Skirm, to fence ; from the French *escrime*, whence also *skir-
mish.*

Skug, to hide, to skulk; to keep under shade or cover; from
the Danish, Swedish, and Icelandic, ' skyg,' ' skog,' and
' skugga ;' a forest, or shady place.

Skyme, a glance or gleam of light.

> The *skyme* o' her e'en was like dewy sheen.
> > *Lady Mary of Craignethan.*

Skyte, to drive and pelt like rain or hail before the wind.

> When hailstones drive wi' bitter skyte.
> > *Burns : The Jolly Beggars.*

Slade, a narrow valley on a mountain side.

> Down through the deeper *slade.*
> > *Drayton.*

Slake,
Sloke, } to cool with water; to quench, to extinguish.
Sloken,

> From henceforth my rest is my travaile,
> My dry thirst with teris must I *sloken.*
> > *The King's Quair.*

> Some hidden place wherein to *slake* the gnawing of my mind.
> > *Earl of Surrey.*

In Richardson's Dictionary, *slake* and *slack*, to slacken, retard or make slow, are held to be of the same signification.

Todd's Johnson gives the following examples of its use by early writers in a different sense.

> And *slake* the heavenly fire that raged evermore.
> > *Spenser.*

> If I digged up thy forefathers' graves,
> And hung their rotten coffins up in chains,
> It could not *slake* mine ire.
> > *Shakspeare.*

> And with the crystal stream their thirst at pleasure *slake.*
> > *Blackmore.*

Sleeple, to slumber; to have a little sleep.

> Mirthe of their mouthes,
> Made me there to *sleeple.*
> > *Piers Ploughman.*

Sleech, the mud or soft sand at the bottom of lakes or rivers, when taken away and used as manure.

Sleech, to ladle or dip out water or broth.

Sleepaway, to die without disease, peaceably, and by gradual decrease of the powers of nature.

Sleeve, a favor ; a badge, a love token ; something given for *lief* or *lieve,* love or gallantry.

> And I'll grow friend with danger.   Wear this *sleeve.*
> *Troilus and Cressida.*
> Shining in armour bright before the tilt,
> And with thy mistress' *sleeve* tied on thy helme.
> *Nares.*

Sleeveless, without love-token, badge, favor, or sign of favor ; whence the common phrase, not yet obsolete, ' a *sleeveless* errand,' one from which no reward, encouragement, or favor is to be got.

Sleight, skill, a trick ; whence the modern phrase, 'sleight of hand.'

> By muckel *sleight,*
> As it becometh a conqueror,
> To konne manye *sleights,*
> And many wiles and wit.
> *Piers Ploughman.*

Sleith, slyness, contrivance, cunning.

Sleithly, slily, cunningly.

> What whenest thou Him who knowest all,
> To deceive with thy *sleithly* wile ?
> *Lydgate, quoted by Halliwell.*

Slent, }
Slant, } to jest slily or untruthfully ; to lie.

'He *slants* a good deal,' a proverbial expression in the North, quoted by Brockett ; i.e., he lies, or *slants* from the right line of truth.

> And when Cleopatra found Antonius' jests and *slents* to be but gross and soldier like, * * * "she without fear taunted him thoroughly.
> *North's Plutarch.*

> One Proteus, a pleasant conceited fellow that could *slent* finely.
> *Idem.*

Sleuth, to track an animal, or a person to a shelter or hiding place ; whence the word ' sleuth-hound,' formerly used in Scotland.   In the South of England, *leuth,* signifies a shelter ; and sleuth is probably a contraction of *disleuth,* to *dis*lodge from a place of shelter.   In the Border ballad of ' Hobbie Noble,' the word is spelt *slough*-hounds.   In the spirited ballad of the 'Fray of Suport,' one of the characters is represented as sitting

Sleuth—*continued.*

> Wi' his *sleuth-dog* in his watch-right sure ;
> Should the dog gie a bark,
> He'll be out in his sark,
> And die or win !

In Thomson's English Etymons, *slouth* is said to mean a company of wild beasts, a troop of bears or wolves, which suggests another derivation ; *slot*, in the same volume is defined, the track or beat of a deer ; and in Yorkshire, to *slate* a beast is to set a dog at him.

> *Sleuthe* with his slyng,
> A hard assault he made.
> > *Piers Ploughman.*

Slick, smooth, glossy. This word is not a vulgarism or an Americanism, as generally supposed, but a more ancient and genuine English word than its synonyme *sleek*, by which it has been partially superseded. The ancient pronunciation appears in Chaucer, who makes it rhyme to *chick*.

> Her flesh tender as is a chicke,
> With bent browes, smoothe and *slike*.
> > *Chaucer : Romance of the Rose.*

> The mole's a creature very smooth and *slick*.
> > *Book for Boys and Girls*, 1636.

The word has recently acquired an extension of meaning both in America and England, and signifies : rapidly, effectually, thoroughly, clean.

> The railroad company, out of sheer parsimony, have neglected to fence in their line, which goes *slick* through the centre of your garden.
> > *Blackwood's Magazine*, July, 1847.

> I've heard tell that courtin's the hardest thing in the world to begin ; though it goes on *slick* enough afterwards.
> > *Traits of American Humour.*

Slid, slippery.

Sliddery, slippery.

Slidness, slipperiness.

> Ye hae sae saft a voice and *slid* a tongue.
> > *The Gentle Shepherd.*

> There's a *sliddery* stane before the ha' door ; (i.e., they who visit above their station, may slip.)
> > *Allan Ramsay's Scotch Proverbs.*

Slide, to disappear from sight; to go out of one's thought or concern.

'Let it *slide*,' is a common phrase in America, and supposed to be an Americanism; but the word occurs in the same sense in Chaucer and Shakspeare.

Lord Walter in the Clerke's Tale, was so addicted to the sport of hawking, that

> Well nigh all other cures let he *slyde*.
>> *Chaucer.*

Dorigene, in the Frankelin's Tale, says:

> Let her sorrow *slide*.
>> *Chaucer.*

And Shakspeare, in the Taming of the Shrew, has:

> Let the world *slide*.

Slive, to do anything furtively or slily; to sneak, to skulk.

Slive, to slip down.

Slove, } slipped down; loosened like an untidy garment;
Sloven, } whence the word *slovenly*.

Sliver, to cut in long shreds or slices.

> The harme of which I would fain deliver,
> Alas! that he all whole, or of him *sliver*,
> Should have his repute.
>> *Chaucer: Troilus and Cressida*, book iii.

> She that herself will *sliver* and disbranch,
> From her material sap, perforce must wither,
> And come to deadly use.
>> *Shakspeare : King Lear.*

> There on the pendant boughs her coronet weeds,
> Clambering to hang, an envious *sliver* broke.
>> *Shakspeare : Hamlet.*

This word is always pronounced in America, as Chaucer seems to have pronounced it, with the i short. In modern English the i is usually long.

Sloach, to drink heavily.

Slock, to entice away; to inveigle.

Slockster, one that slocks or entices away another man's servants.—*Blount's Glossographia*, 1684.

Slodder, slippery, tenacious; adhesive mud or slush.

Slogan, the war-cry of a Scottish clan; a word not to be confounded with *pibroch*, a musical composition for the bagpipes, as has been done by some English writers.

Sloke, preterite of slake, to appease; ' to slake one's thirst.'
> He *sloke* his thirst at the running stream.

In some parts of the Midland Counties and the North, it is common to say that a ' fire is sloken,' i.e., extinguished.

Sloom, to sleep heavily and soundly; distinguished from *slumber*, to sleep lightly.

Sloomy, dull, lazy.

Slop, preterite of slip.

Sloppe, a garment; something slipped on. *Slop* clothes and *slop* tailors, are current phrases in the present day; but it appears from Chaucer, that in his day, any loose garment was called a *sloppe*.

> His overest *sloppe* it is not worth a mite ;
> *   *   *   *   *
> Why is thy lord so sluttish I thee pray ?
> > *Chaucer : The Chanones Tale.*

Slorp, to eat greedily and with a guttural noise.
> There's gentle John and Jock the *slorp*,
> And curly Jock, and burly Jock,
> And lying Jock himsel.
> > *Jacobite Relics.*

Slote, the pit of the stomach.
> Through the brain and the breast, with his bright weapon,
> Slant down to the *slote* he slittes at once.
> > *Morte Arthur.*

Slotter, to make a noise with the palate in eating. To feed like an animal.

Slotterhodge, a coarse-feeding clown.
> > *Jamieson.*

Sloy, a slatternly woman.
> How tedious were a shrew, a *sloy*, a wanton, or a fool.
> > *Nares.*

Slub,
Slab, } thick mire.

Shakspeare, in the Witch Scene in Macbeth, makes the witch say :
> Make the gruel thick and *slab*.

Slug, to be lazy and sleepy; whence 'sluggard;' and 'slug' applied to the earth worm from its slow motions.

> He used to *slug* and sleep in slothful shade.
> *Spencer's Faerie Queen.*

Slut, preterite of slit.

Smatter, a heap of small objects in motion; also, to be busily engaged about small affairs; whence a *smattering* of knowledge.

Smatters, small matters, trifles: small sums of money.

Smeddum, meal, grit; a northern word; applied in Scotland to signify sense, wit, or capacity, in the same way as 'grit,' is used in America.

Smeke, to flatter a man to his face, and overdo it.

Smell-feast, a parasite; an habitual diner out, a spunge, a sorner.

Smerl, a smock, a shift, a chemise.

Smerly, demure looking.

Smeth, the preterite of smooth; a word still used in many parts of England for a depilatory, that *smoothes* the skin of its hair. The unguent is sometimes called a *smoothery*.

Smither, a small fragment; whence the vulgar colloquialism, '*smithereens.*'

Smirl, a mischievous or roguish trick.

> I'll play him a *smirl* for that yet.
> *Jamieson.*

> And in some distant place,
> Plays the same *smirl*.
> *T. Scott.*

Smock, a woman's under-garment; from the German schmücken to adorn; a much better word than the modern *chemise;* and the odious vulgarism, *shimmy*. The word survives in '*smock*-frock,' a farm laborer's overgarment. 'Lady's *smock*,' is the common name, preserved in Shakspeare, of the white convolvulus. This word also signifies an over- as well as under-garment; a dress; a robe; as in the following:

Smock—*continued.*

> Believe me if my wedding *smock* were on,
> Were the gloves bought and given,
>   The licence come,
>   *   *   *   *
> I would not wed that year.
>   *Beaumont and Fletcher : The Scornful Lady.*

Smolt, smooth, shiny, glossy; from *smolten* metal.

Smore, to smother.

Smure, smothered.

Smore, a swarm or gathering of a people; not so many as to be called a crowd.

Smuly, }
Smooly } sly and demure.

Smoothen, to smoother.

> Mrs. Transome worked to *smoothen* the current of his dialogue.
>   *Felix Holt the Radical*, 1866.

Snack, quick, active; whence a ' snack,' a hasty meal.

Snag, a tooth standing in the mouth by itself, or a projection on a tree where a branch has been lopped off at some distance from the trunk.   To this word the Americans owe their name for the peculiar danger of the Mississippi.

> How thy *snag* teeth stand orderly,
> Like stakes by the water side.
>   *Wit's Interpreter*, 1671.

> His weapon was a tall and *snaggy* oak.
>   *Heywood*, 1609.

Snape, to blight.   ' Snaped by the East wind.'

> A poor unfortunate wean *snaped* by its step-mother.

Snarl, a difficulty, an entanglement; a knot.   This word, almost obsolete in England, is common in America.

> Let Hymen's easy *snarls* be quite forgot.
>   *Quarles' Emblems.*

> And from her head oft reft her *snarled* hair.
>   *Spenser's Faerie Queene.*

> You *snarle* yourself into so many and such heinous absurdities as you shall never be able to winde yourself out.
>   *Cranmer's Answer to Bishop Gardiner.*

Snathe, to prune trees.

Snaught preterite of snatch; on the same principle as *caught*, from catch.

Sneap,
Sneb,
Snib,
Snub,
} to check, chide, or rebuke angrily ; nip with unkindness; whence *snub*, the preterite of this verb, now used as the present tense and infinitive.

The first of these four words has almost disappeared from literature and conversation, to make room for the last ; though ' snub ' is scarcely worthy of the honor, considering how much Shakspeare and other poets have done to make *sneap* familiar to us.

> No *sneaping* wind at home to make us say,
> This is put forth too early.
> > *Shakspeare: Winter's Tale.*

> Biron is like an envious *sneaping* frost,
> That bites the first born infants of the spring.
> > *Shakspeare: Love's Labour Lost.*

> I will not undergo this *sneap* without reply.
> > *Shakspeare: Henry IV.*

> Do you *sneap* me too, my Lord ?
> > *Brome's Antipodes.*

> And on a time he cast him for to scold,
> And *snebbe* the good oak.
> > *Spenser : Shepherd's Calendar.*

Sneath, the handle of a scythe.

Snell, sharp, active, lively, piercing ; from the German *schnell*, quick. Johnson affirms the word to be obsolete, and Richardson ignores it altogether.

> A handy man and *snell*
> In tournament, and eke in fight.
> > *Morte Arthur.*

> Fought stout and *snell*,
> And stood about him in the stour.
> > *The Reid's Quair.*

> One rough night the blattering winds blew *snell*.
> > *Allan Ramsay.*

> Shivering for cold, the season was so *snell*.
> > *Gawin Douglas, Translation of Virgil.*

> He answered *snell*,
> Berynus I am named.
> > *Chaucer.*

Snell—*continued.*

> More *snell* than all the pelts of Knox.
> > *Allan Ramsay.*

> This *snell* lass that came with me.
> > *Ross's Helenore.*

> And when the day was done,
> They rode out *snell*.
> > *Ritson.*

> Not Boreas that so *snelly* blows.
> > *Ferguson.*

Snew, preterite of snow.

'It blew and it snew' is an Americanism. Chaucer uses the word '*snewe*,' which is as consonant to the genius of the language as *blew* from blow, and *crew* from crow.

Snid, to prune, lop, shear, mow.

Snod, preterite of snid; mown, shorn, pruned. Snodgrass, a well known name, means mown, or shorn grass.

> Your *snod* remarks and pointed style.
> > *Galloway's Poems.*

Snidge, to hang and spunge upon a person; to sorn.

Snipe, a cutting remark; a sarcasm.

Snipsy, sarcastic.

Snirl, to shrivel up.

Snirp, to wither.

Snirt, a short, suppressed laugh.

Snirtle, to attempt to suppress one's laughter.

Snite, a snout or nose.

Snite, to blow the nose; of which the preterite was 'snot,' a word that has become vulgar, to signify not the blowing of the nose, but what is blown from it.—See *Nares*.

Snithe, cold, sharp, and cutting; said of the East wind.

> Let's spang (close) our gates,
> It's varra *snithe*,
> It will be frost believe.
> > *Yorkshire Dialogue, 1667.*

Snood, a band or fillet for the hair, worn by unmarried girls. This word is still common in Scotland, and the North of England.

> You gentlewoman with the saffron *snude*.
> > *Two Lancashire Lovers, 1640.*

Snool, to dispirit by constant chiding ; or to depress the energies of life by excess of bodily toil. Mr. Halliwell explains a '*sneul*' and a '*snool*,' to mean a poor pitiful fellow.

> It's ass and fuil and silly *snuil,*
> Its naething but a noodle.
> > *Miss Blamire : The Cumberland Scold.*

Snoke, to pry meanly into holes and corners, to poke one's nose where it has no business.

Snoove, to pry, to sneak.

Snurl, to ruffle the surface of the waters with a wind ; metaphorically applied to the temper of man or woman.

> Northern blasts the ocean *snurl.*
> > *Allan Ramsay.*

Snurle, an influenza: catarrh or cold in the head.

Snurles, from *nose-thurles,* the nostrils.

Sny, snug.

Sodden, past participle of seethe, to boil. ' Gin-sodden,' a phrase applied to a low drunkard, sodden, seethed, boiled in gin.

Soggy, very wet, soft, swampy ground. The word occurs in Ben Jonson, and is in common use in America.

Solaine, } a solitary person ; one all by himself.
Soleyne, }

> He sat neither with Saint Johan,
> > *   *   *   *   *
> Ne with maidens, not with martyrs,
> > *   *   *   *   *
> But by himself as a *soleyne.*
> > *Piers Ploughman.*

Somedeal, a little ; in some part.

> A poor widow, *somedele* stooped in age.
> > *Chaucer.*

Sonce, prosperity.

Soncy, } fortunate ; also used in the sense of comely, well-
Sonsie, } favoured, healthful, and agreeable.

> Three are aye *sonsy.*
> > *Allan Ramsay.*

Soncy—*continued.*

> The *unsonsy* fish gets the unlucky bait.
>> *Scotch Proverbs.*
>
> A *sonsie* and a bonnie lassie.
>> *Burns.*

Sool, anything eaten with bread or potatoes for a relish. Nares derives the word from the French *soule,* satiated, full, or drunk; 'se souler' to get drunk. The English and Scottish *sool* is not applied to liquids.

Soom, to drink a long draught, with a sucking noise of the mouth ; as if in great thirst, or with great relish.

Sooth, truth.

> He looks like *sooth,*
> He says he loves my daughter.
>> *Shakspeare : Winter's Tale.*
>
> If thy speech be *sooth,*
> I care not if thee dost for me as much.
>> *Shakspeare : Macbeth.*

Soothfast, strong and steady in the truth.

Sorn, a word common in Scotland to express the art of fastening one's self upon another, to feast and lodge, unasked and unwelcome; almost equivalent to the word, to *sponge* in England.   In Scotland, 'to go and *sorn* upon a man for a dinner;' would be in England, 'to go and take pot-luck with him;' he not expecting you.   No exact synonyme exists, south of the Tweed.

In Thompson's 'Etymons of English Words,' it is said to be a corruption of *sojourn* and *soiorn,* to tarry from day to day, and to have been derived from the ancient practice in unsettled times, of bands of armed men, living at free quarters upon the people when passing through a country.

Sot, preterite of set.   I *sot* him a task ; obsolete in England, but current in America.

Sothery, soothing; but defined by Nares to mean sweet.

> And as I wene,
> With *sothery* butter their bodies anoynted.
>> *Four P's, Old Play, (Nares.)*

Sough or **sugh.** In Nares's Glossary, this beautiful and useful word is defined to mean, 'perhaps a *sound.*' He quotes from Ben Jonson's Epigrams:

> The well greased wherry now had got between,
> And bade her farewell *sough* unto her burden.

Mr. Halliwell comes nearer to the mark, and describes a *sough* or *sugh*, as a buzzing, a hollow murmuring, a roaring. Johnson, in his Dictionary, though quite unaware of the derivation of the word, defines it to mean the whistling of the wind ; and quotes from the History of the Royal Society, Vol. IV., p. 225 : the phrase, 'A noise like that of a great *soughing* wind.' In the Scottish dialect the word is spelt and pronounced *sugh*, (with the guttural pronunciation,) and means the sound of the wind upon the seashore or among the trees, or amid the long grass, or the sedges on a river's brink ; in all of which senses, it is used both in the highest order of poetry, and in the most ordinary conversation. It is evidently from the same root as *sigh*, or the Greek, *psyche*, the breath, or soul. According to Richardson the word was anciently written 'sike,' thus betraying its etymology.

> November chill blaws loud wi' angry *sough.*
> *Burns : Cotters' Saturday Night.*

> Like a rash-bush stood in sight,
> Wi' waving *sough.*
> *Burns : Address to the Deil.*

> The wavy swell of the *soughing* reeds.
> *Tennyson : The Dying Swan.*

Sounder, a herd or company of wild swine.—*Blount's Glossagraphia,* 1681.

> If by any chance there is a *sounder* of them (boars or swine) together ;
> then if any break sounder, the rest will run.
> *Gentle Recreation, (quoted by Nares.)*

Souse, pickled pork or other meat ; also brine for pickling.

> Thus they went all along unto the miller's house.
> Where they were seething of puddings and *souse.*
> *Percy's Reliques, the King and the Miller of Mansfield.*

> Nor is a breast of pork to be,
> Despised by either thee or me ;
> The head and feet will make good *souse.*
> *Poor Robin,* 1738.

Souter, a shoemaker.

> Ploughmen and pastorers,
> And other common laborers,
> *Souters* and shepherds.
>
> *Piers Ploughman.*
>
> *Soutar* Johnny.
>
> *Robert Burns.*

Spade-graft, the depth to which a spade will dig.

Spae, to tell fortunes ; to predict.

Spae-wife, a fortune-teller.

Spaed, } that which is gelded or castrated.—*Blount's Glossa-*
Spade, } *graphia,* 1681. 'To call a spade, a spade, was a
popular phrase for to be plain spoken,' says Nares. He
adds, 'why the spade was especially chosen to enter into
this figurative expression is not so clear.' Perhaps Blount's
explanation may throw light upon the obscurity. To call a
spaed man, a *spaed* ; i.e., to call a eunuch, a eunuch, is the
probable, and certainly a possible derivation.

> Small eloquence men must expect from me,
> My scholarship will name things as they be ;
> I think it good plain English without fraud,
> To call a *spade* a *spade*, a bawd, a bawd.
>
> *Taylor, the Water Poet's Works,* 1630.

Spalt, brittle ; whence spelter.

Sparthe, an axe, a halberd.

Spate, } a flood or freshet from the overflow of a river or lake.
Spait, } *Spat* or *spate*, from the same root as spatter, to disperse, or shed abroad a fluid, means, according to Mr. Barnes,
in his English Roots, a 'heavy down-casting of rain.' Flood,
the quasi synonyme of *spate*, may, and does mean, a torrent
of water in its usual channel ; whereas, a *spate*, is water
that has overspread its channel.

> The water was great and mickle of *spate*.
>
> *Ballad of Kinmont Willie.*

> Even like a mighty river, that runs down in *spate* to the sea.
>
> *W. E. Aytoun, Blackwood's Magazine.*

Speedful, prosperous, fortunate. 'I wish you good *speed ;*' is
still a common expression.

Sperage, the herb asparagus, or as it is vulgarly called by the street criers, 'sparrow-grass, and ' grass.'

> This herb is so called by Gerard and all the old botanists, as its English name. It is an indigenous plant.—*Nares.*

Spert,
Spirt, } a sudden fit of energy or spirit.
Spurt,

> And some of them led`here and there by *spirts*,
> Shifting their lodgings oftener than their shirts.
> > *Taylor's Works,* 1630.

Speer, } to ask, to enquire. This word is now seldom heard
Spier, } out of Scotland, but was formerly universal in England.

> She *speer'd* his name; ' I come from far,
> My name is called Dissowar.'
> > *Romance of Roswal and Lilyan.*

> I am *Spes,* quoth he,
> And *spier* after a knighte,
> That took me a mandement,
> Upon the mount of Sinai,
> To rule all reams (realms) with.
> > *Piers Ploughman.*

> Many a one *speers* the way he knows full well.
> > *Scotch Proverb.*

Spike, } lavender.
Spikenard, }

> The gilliflower, the mint, the hyacynthe, the *spike*.
> > *Affectionate Shepherd,* 1594.

Spilth, that which is spilt or overflown. ' The *spilth* of the river covered the meadow lands.'

> Our vaults have wept,
> With drunken *spilth* of wine.
> > *Shakspeare : Timon of Athens.*

Spink, a finch, a small bird; the gold*spink,* the goldfinch.

Splairge, } to splash, or splatter in the water. Mr. Halliwell
Splurge, } quotes *splairge,* as a Northumbrian word. In America the word is written *splurge* ; and means to make a dash, or splash, or sensation, by great expenditure of energy or money ; equivalent to the English phrase, ' cut a dash.'

Splat, a row of pins, as they are sold in the paper.

Splay, from display, to spread or extend unnaturally; as a 'splay foot,' a 'splay mouth.' Splay in some parts of England means to 'castrate.'

Splent, steel armour for the shoulder and arms.

> With spur on heel, and *splent* armour on the shoulder.
> *Ballad of Kimont Willie ; Minstrelsy of the Scottish Border.*

Splint, to support, whence the word used in surgery, a 'splint,' to support a weak or broken limb.

Splore, a riotously merry meeting; to make a *splore*, to create a sensation.

> In Poosie Nancy's held the *splore*,
> Wi' quaffing and laughing,
> They ranted and they sang.
> *Burns : The Jolly Beggars.*

> We've had some bits of *splores* together.
> *Sir Walter Scott.*

Spoffle, to make one's self very busy over a matter of very little consequence. An Eastern Counties word.—(*Halliwell.*)

Spole, from the French *epaule ;* the shoulder.

Spolt, a heavy blow; struck from the *spole* or shoulder; to strike a blow from the shoulder.

> Speedes them to *spolt* with speeres y-new.
> *Morte Arthur ;* quoted by Mr. Halliwell, who gives the word as *spolett*, without explanation.

Spook, a common word in America for a ghost, or goblin; derived from Puck and Pook.

Spoom, a nautical word, signifying to go right before the wind.

> When virtue *spooms* before a prosperous gale,
> My hearing wishes help to fill the sail.
> *Dryden : Hind and Panther.*

Spore, a trace, a mark; a foot *spore*, a foot mark.

Spousal-breach, adultery.

Sprack, } sprightly, quick, alert.
Sprag, }

Sprad, preterite of spread.

Spreath, active, nimble ; from the same root comes sprightly, and the American word ' spry.'

Sprene, to sprinkle ; whence sprinkle as a diminutive. The word in its original form has long been obsolete ; but besprent, the past participle of be-*sprene* is common both in ancient and modern poetry.

Sprentle, to flutter.

> *Sprentled* with her wings tway.
> > *Gower MS., Soc. Antiq. (Halliwell.)*

Springald, ⎱ a youth, a young man ; one newly sprung to ma-
Springall, ⎰ turity.

> A lusty *springald*, or younkere.
> > *Douglas's Virgil.*

> Then came two *springalds*, full of tender years.
> > *Spenser : Faerie Queene.*

> Good, observe me,
> I do not rail against the hopeful *springall.*
> > *Beaumont and Fletcher.*

Sprink, to dash water ; whence the diminutive *sprinkle*, to cast water in small drops.

Sprith, rushes, coarse grass.

Sprithy, rushy, grassy.

> His dead master was lying in a little *sprithy* hollow, not above a musket shot from the peat stack.
> > *Blackwood's Magazine*, March, 1823.

Sprote, a fragment.

Sprote-wood, small twigs and sticks, and windfalls of trees gathered for fire-wood.

Sprunt, neat, well-grown, well-formed, and lively.

Spruntly, gaily, becomingly.

> How do I look to-day ?
> Am I not dressed *spruntly ?*
> > *Ben Jonson.*

Spry, nimble, active, sprightly. A Somersetshire and Southern English word, very common in America.

Spry—*continued.*

> You're not so small as I,
> And not half so *spry.*
>> *R. W. Emerson.*

> As *spry* as a cricket.
>> *Judd's Margaret.*

Spuddle, to go about a trifling business as if it were a matter of grave importance. To assume airs of importance without occasion.

Spunk, a spark of life, or fire.

Spunky, mettlesome, brisk, brave, fiery of spirit.

> In that snug room, where any man of *spunk,*
> Would find it a hard matter to get drunk.
>> *Peter Pindar.*

> The *spunk* of life is in him yet.
>> *Jameson.*

Spunkie, the ignis fatuus, or Will o' the Wisp.

Spurge, froth ; to emit froth.

> The bodys something noisome,
> Good troth, it *spurgeth* monstrously.
>> *Nares,* 1651.

Spurtle, a round stick, or piece of wood ; used in the Northern counties and in Scotland to stir the porridge in the pot when boiling. To have the scraping or licking of the *spurtle,* is the reward of a good child in the districts where oatmeal porridge is still the food of the young.

Spur-way, right of way for a man on horseback, as distinguished from *foot*-way or *carriage*-way.

Squab, an unfledged bird. In America the word signifies more particularly a young pigeon, fit for the market.

Squash, an unripe pod, before the peas are formed.

> Not yet old enough for a man, nor young enough for a boy ; as a *squash* is before 'tis a peascod.
>> *Shakspeare : Twelfth Night*

In America the word is applied to a coarse kind of pumpkin.

Squawk. This word bears the same relation to squeek, as squeel does to squall; to squeek but with a deeper note.

> Good gracious! said Mrs. Bedalt, if you'd heard Miss C. sing you'd a gin up. The way she *squawked* it out, was a caution to old gates on a windy day.—*Bartlett's Dictionary of Americanisms.*

Squelch, this word is so common in America, and so little used in England, as to be supposed an Americanism. It occurs in English literature in the sense of to ' crush by a fall,' or by a severe blow.

> He was the cream of Brecknock,
> And flower of all the Welsh,
> But St. George he did the dragon fell,
> And gave him a plaguy *squelch.*
> > *St. George and the Dragon.*

Quelch is another form of the same word, but less commonly used.

Squintard, a person who squints.

Squirm, to wriggle like a worm; a common word in the South of England, and in general use in the United States.

> Some gentleman is suddenly seized with the retrenchment gripes, and *squirms* around, like a long red worm on a pin-hook.
> > *Speech of Mr. Pitt in the Missouri Legislature,* June, 1859.

Staddle, the stain left on metal after the rust is removed.

Stadle, young trees left growing in an underwood: *v.,* to cut a wood in such a way as to leave *stadles.*

Stanch, to suppress, put an end to, abolish.

> An act of the first year of the reign of King James I. was passed for the *stanching* of all masterful and idle beggars.'—*Chambers.*

This word, obsolete in the above sense, survives in ' stanch the blood of a wound,' i.e., to stop the bleeding.

Stang, a large wooden bar or post; called in America, a rail. To ride the *stang* in England, and to ride the *rail* in America, is a rural punishment often inflicted by Lynch law, upon some offender against the proprieties whom other law cannot reach.

Stall,
Staule, } to decoy.
Stale,

Stall—*continued.*

A *stall* pigeon in the English sense of a decoy duck, is a common phrase in America.

> *Stales* to catch kites.
>> *Beaumont and Fletcher.*

> The trumpery in my house, go fetch it hither,
> For *stall* to catch the thieves.
>> *Shakspeare : The Tempest.*

Stalwart,
Stalworth, } strong, lusty.

Stark, strong, lusty.

> *Stark* beer, boy, stout and strong beer.
>> *Beaumont and Fletcher.*

> How found you him? *stark* as you see.
>> *Shakspeare : The Tempest.*

> Going a fishing on a *stark* calm morning.
>> *Robinson Crusoe.*

This word has seemingly lost its original meaning, and instead of strong, is employed to express the adverb *strongly,* utterly, or *very.*

The phrases *stark* naked, utterly naked, and *stark* dead, stiff, or utterly dead, still survive : but *stark* is scarcely ever used in its original sense at the present day, except in America, where such expressions as *stark* treason and *stark* murder, are occasionally heard.

Stathe,
Staithe, } a wharf, or pier.

Stede, a place ; whence *stead,* in such words as farm-*stead,* road-*stead,* bed-*stead,* home-*stead,* in*stead* of, i.e., in place of ; *stead*-fast, fast to the place ; steady ; and in the termination of names of places, as Hamp*stead.*

Spencer has the lines :

> His gorgeous rider from his lofty *stede,*
> Would have cast down, and trode in dirty mire.

In the days of chivalry, a knight's *place* was on horseback ; whence a knight and his *stede,* i.e., place.

> He was then so courteous and free,
> That doun off his *stede* he light.
>> *Morte Arthur.*

Stede—*continued.*

> Lady he said ——————————
> For me, (ne give thee nothing ill,)
> In another *stede* my heart is set.
> > *Morte Arthur.*

From these examples it appears that the modern word, *steed*, as applied to a horse, has grown out of a misconception or perversion of *stede*, which no more means a horse than it does a house.

Steeve, strong, firm, stiff, well-made, and active.

> Thou ance was i' the foremost rank,
> A filly, buirdly, *steeve*, and swank.
> > *Burns: The Auld Farmer to his Auld Mare Maggie.*

Steik, to shut up.

Stoke, shut up.

> As I have spoke,
> Then hadst thou the gates *stoke*.
> From such folly.
> > *Chaucer.*

> Taverns should be *steiked* at nine hours.
> > *Skenne's Acts.*

> When one door *steiks*, another opens.
> > *Allan Ramsay.*

> *Steik* the awning and the kist,
> Or else your gear will soon be mist.
> > *Sir Walter Scott.*

Stoker, a shutter up of the doors of a furnace ; a modern word of ancient derivation, applied in railway language to the man who feeds the furnace with coal, and *steiks* or shuts up the door.

Stell, to place; from the German *stellen*, whence stall, a place for horses.

Stent, *v.a.* cease, desist, leave off.

> And of this cry, ne would they never *stent*.
> > *Chaucer : The Knights' Tale.*

> By process and by length of certain years,
> All *stenten* in the mourning and the tears.
> > *Idem.*

> When they this song had sung a little *thraw* (while),
> They *stent* awhile.
> > *The King's Quair.*

Stent—*continued.*

> Then *stented* she as if her song were done.
> > *Gascoigne.*

From this root comes the modern word to *stint* one's self or any one else; i.e., to cease giving.

> How much wine do you drink in a day? My *stint* in company is a pint at noon.—*Swift.*

Stent, an allotted portion of work. A daily task, a portion.

> *Stente* or certeine of value, ordered and other lythe taxation.
> > *Harleian MS., quoted by Halliwell.*

This word, like many others, lost to English literature, survives in America :

> Little boys in the country, working against time with *stents* to do, long for the passing by of some tall brother, who in a few minutes shall achieve what the smaller boys took hours to do.
> > *Discourse on the Death of Daniel Webster, by Theodore Parker,* 1853.

Sterve, to die; the German *sterben*, corrupted into *starve*; and restricted in the latter form, to die of hunger, though in the Northern counties the people still speak of ' starving with cold.' The modern word, *starvation*, half corrupt English, and half Latin, ought to be expelled from the language if a proper synonyme could be found or made for it, from an English root. ' Clem' or 'clam,' *q.v.*, is the original word for dying of hunger, but the attempt to reintroduce so thorough a localism would probably be all but hopeless.

> Choose out some noble dame, her honour thou and serve,
> Who will give ear to thy complaint, and pity ere thou *sterve.*
> > *Romeus and Juliette, (quoted by Nares.)*

> To her came message of this wunderment,
> Wherein her guiltless friends should hopeless *sterve.*
> > *Fairfax : Tasso.*

> He stood until such time he *sterved,*
> And so God send all murderers may be served.
> > *Percy's Reliques, Titus Andronicus.*

Steven, a voice. The rhymes to ' heaven ' in the English language are few, and this word would be useful.

> With dreary heart and sorrowful *steven.*
> > *Morte Arthur.*

> She shall be queen of my land,
> And all bow unto her hand,
> And none withstand her *steven.*
> > *Sir Isumbras.*

Steven—*continued.*

> So blithe he was to hear that *steven,*
> That his heart became all light.
>> *Florice and Blanchflour.*

> Then thanked her God in heaven,
> And Mary with mild *steven,*
> That had so y-wrought.
>> *Sir Otuel.*

> Say to him with mild *stevyn,*
> He will not say you nay.
>> *MS. Harl. quoted by Halliwell.*

Stichel. 'This word,' says Nares,' is a term of reproach, implying want of manhood.' The word Twitchel, or twychild, twice a child, a very old man, q. v.; might have helped him to the derivation. He quotes:

> Barren *stichel!* That shall not serve thy turn;

but misses the root of the word, 'stay-child,' one who cannot procreate.

Stickle, to arbitrate; whence *stickler,* an arbitrator; and figuratively, one who makes a point of trifling matters, and will take nothing for granted.

Stightle, to confirm, to strengthen.

> To *stightle* the people,
> Preaching and praying.
>> *Piers Ploughman.*

Stith, robust, strong, firmly-fixed, and not to be easily shaken.

> The stremys are so stiffe and *stythe,*
> That many men there lose their lyfe.
>> *MS. Lincoln, (Halliwell.)*

> On stedes that were *stithe* and strong,
> They ridden together.
>> *Amis and Amiloun.*

> A turnament,
> With knightes *stithe* on stede.
>> *Sir Tristram.*

Stithe,
Stithy, } an anvil.

Stithy—*continued.*

> A head where Wisdom mysteries did frame,
> Whose hammers beat still in that lively brain,
> As on a *stithe*, whereon some work of fame,
> Was daily wrought to turn to Briton's gain.
> > *The Earl of Surrey on the Death of Sir Thomas Wyatt.*

> By the forge that *stithy'd* Mars' helm,
> I'll kill thee everywhere; yea, o'er and o'er.
> > *Chaucer: Troilus and Cressida.*

> And my imaginations are as foul,
> As Vulcan's *stithy*.
> > *Shakspeare: Hamlet.*

A pig's sty, was formerly called a *stythe* in the North, as may be seen in the ballad of Fause Foodrage, in the Border Minstrelsy.

> She wandered up, she wandered down,
> > She wandered out and in,
> And at last into the swine's *stythe*,
> > The queen brought forth a son.

Stodge, to stuff too full.

Stodge-full, so full as to be unable to contain any more; like the ground after heavy and continuous rains; or like a glutton at a feast.

Stoly, dirty, confused, disordered.

> A *stoly* house.—*Grose's Provincial Glossary.*

Stot, a young bullock.

> Grace gave Piers,
> Of his goodness, four *stotts*.
> > *Piers Ploughman.*

> A *stot* unto your plough.
> > *Sir Isumbras.*

> But if the lover's raptured hour,
> Shall ever be your lot,
> Forbid it every heavenly power,
> You e'er should be a *stot*.
> > *Robert Burns.*

Stoup,
Stoop, } a pitcher.

> Set me the *stoop* of wine upon the table.
> > *Shakspeare: Hamlet.*

> And surely ye'll be your pint-*stoup*,
> And surely I'll be mine.
> > *Burns: Auld Lang Syne.*

Stound, a hurt, a severe pain.

> And aye the *stound* and deadly wound,
> Came from her een sae bonnie blue.
> > *Robert Burns.*

> It does boom off, nevertheless sending a *stound* through all hearts.
> > *Carlyle's French Revolution.*

Stound, an hour; a little while ; from the German *stunde.*

> What booth wilt thou have ? our king reply'd ;
> Now tell me in this *stound.*
> > *Percy's Reliques, The King and the Tanner of Tamworth.*

> Listen to me a little *stound.*
> > *Percy's Reliques : The Carle of Carlisle.*

Stoure, dust stirred by the wind, or by the trample of feet ;
and from whence, metaphorically, strife, contention. The
word is common all over Britain, from Devonshire where
it is pronounced *sture,* to Caithness, where, as in Scotland
generally, it is *stoure.*

> The lord that great was of honour
> > Himself, Sir Lancelot do take
> Above the gates upon the tower ;
> > Comely to the king he spake :
> My Lord ! God save your honour,
> > Me is woe now, for your sake,
> Against thy kin to stand in *stour ;*
> > But needs must I this battle take.
> > > *Morte Arthur.*

> He is stalwarth in *stoures,*
> By Saint Martin of Towers.
> > *MS. Lincoln, (Halliwell.)*

> The *stoure* was strong, enduring, long,
> The Romans had there the field,
> The Sarrazings they slew among,
> Ten thousand and more with speare and shielde.
> > *Ferumbras.*

> Alas ! Fortune she that whilom was,
> Dreadful to kings and to emperours ;
> > *   *   *   *   *
> And she that helméd was in stark *stoures,*
> And won by force towns, strong, and towers.
> > *Chaucer : The Monke's Tale.*

Stoure—*continued*.

> Wee, modest, crimson tipped flow'r,
> Thou'st met me in an evil hour,
> For I maun crush among the *stoure*,
>   Thy slender stem,
> To spare thee now is past my power,
>   Thou bonnie gem.
>
> *   *   *   *   *
>
> Such is the fate of artless maid,
> Sweet flow'ret of the rural shade,
> By Love's simplicity betrayed,
>   And guileless trust,
> Till she, like thee, all soiled is laid,
>   Low i' the dust.
>   *Robert Burns.*

Stow, a place; whence *Stowe*, the seat of the Duke of Buckingham, *the* place. Whence, also, Waltham*stow*, Bishop*stowe*, and several other names of towns, villages, and places.

Stow-away, a person who *stows*, or places himself in hiding on board of an emigrant ship, to escape the roll-call of the passengers ; and who, by showing himself when the vessel is far out at sea, forces the Captain to take him to his destination for humanity's sake. The Captain on such occasions endeavours to get some value out of a stowaway by compelling him to do the menial offices of the ship.

Straight-fingered ; one whose fingers will not crook to seize or hold dishonest gains ; thoroughly honest.

Straught, preterite of to stretch.

Strake, to wander about.

> With stern staves and strong,
> They over land *straketh*.
>   *Piers Ploughman.*

Strene, to generate.

Strend, a generation.

> For he said in his hearte nought sae I wende,
> Withouten evil fra *strende* to *strende*.
>   *Cotton MSS. (Halliwell).*

Strene, } lineage. Chaucer uses *strene* in the sense of *strend,*
Strain, } to signify a race or generation. In the late Herbert Coleridge's Dictionary of the First or Oldest Words
in the English Language, '*stren*' is defined as progeny;
and *streon,* the knot in the yolk of an egg, the point where
generation commences.

> Benedick is of a noble *strain,*
> Of approved valor, and confirmed honesty.
> > *Shakspeare : Much Ado about Nothing.*

> He is bred out of that bloody *strain,*
> That haunted us in our familiar paths.
> > *Shakspeare : King Henry V.*

Strome, to walk backwards and forwards with long strides, as
some do in anger and perplexity.

Stromp, } to tread heavily, or pace about; whence, probably,
Strump, } *strumpet,* a street walker.

> I heard 'un *strompin'* down stairn ; i.e., I heard him walking heavily
> down stairs.—*Sternberg's Northamptonshire Glossary.*

In Ford's Play of 'The Fancies Chaste and Noble,' when
the ladies are entreated to bear with Secco, who is 'a foul
mouth'd man,' Secco calls one of them by the most opprobrious epithet that can be applied to a woman, and adds :
' a fox-bitch, a *treddle.*' The last word thus appears to have
the same meaning as *strumpet,* and suggests treading, walking or *strumping* the streets.

Stunt, past participle of *stent,* to allowance, or apportion :
corrupted into the modern word *stunted,* applied to persons,
animals, and vegetables of imperfect, and prematurely ended
growth.

Stub, a thick short stump of a tree left in the ground, when
the trunk is cut down. Stubble, the diminutive of this
word means the small stalks of corn, when cut.

> All about old stocks and *stubs* of trees.
> > *Spenser.*

> Upon cutting down of an old timber tree, the *stub* hath sometimes
> put out a tree of another kind.—*Bacon.*

Stub—*continued.*

> We
> Live on tough roots and *stubs ;* to thirst inured ;
> Now to much misery and hardship born.
> *Milton.*

> Striking his foot against some *stubbe* or stone.
> *Topsell's Four-footed Beasts,* 1611, (*Halliwell*).

The late President Lincoln, was met by a friend in Pennsylvania Avenue, at Washington, who seeing that he limped a little, asked what was the matter ? ' Oh, not much,' replied the President, ' I have only *stubbed* my toe,' i.e., 'knocked my toe against a *stub.*'

Stubby, short and thick, like the stump of a tree.

Sturt, } to trouble, annoy.
} strife, annoyance ; from the same root as *stoure,* battle or contention.

> The merriest man that lives in life,
>   He sails upon the sea,
> For he knows neither *sturt* nor strife,
>   But blythe and glad is he.
> *The Evergreen, edited by Allan Ramsay.*

> *Sturt* follows all extremes.
> *Allan Ramsay.*

> *Sturt* pays no debt.—*Ibid.*

> I've lived a life of *sturt* and strife,
>   I die by treachery.
> *Burns : Macpherson's Farewell.*

> And aye the less they hae to *sturt* them,
> In like proportion less will hurt them.
> *Burns : The Twa Dogs.*

Suckerel, an unweaned infant.

Suckets, confectionery, sweetmeats, called in England sweet-stuff ; in America, 'candies,' and in Scotland, ' sweeties.'

> And in some six days' journey does consume,
> Ten pounds in *suckets.*
> *Drayton.*

> Bring hither *suckets,* candies, delicates.
> *Antona and Mellida, quoted by Nares.*

Suckets—*continued.*

> Well filled with *suckets* and sweetmeats.
> > *Taylor, the Water Poet.*

> In the fifth course were confects and *suckets.*
> > *History of Francion,* 1655, *quoted by Nares.*

Sud, the drift sand or slush left in the meadows by an overflow of rivers; meadows are said to be *sudded* after a flood, or '*spate.*'

Sugh, preterite of sigh; whence the *sugh* of the wind, or of the willows, or reeds, when the wind passes over or through them.—See *Sough.*

Sumph, a fool, a blockhead; a common Scottish and Northern word. Mr. Halliwell says, that in Suffolk, a very heavy weight is called a *sump;* and that hence, a heavy stupid fellow is so designated. In Scotland, a heavy fall of rain is called a '*sump,*' as in the following:

> Of thunder July speaks, and *sumps* of rain,
> And August winds uproot the growing grain.
> > *Blackwood's Magazine,* January, 1821.

> Better thole a grumph, than a *sumph ;* (i.e., better endure a surly, or grumpy man, than a fool.)
> > *Allan Ramsay's Scotch Proverbs.*

> The *sumpish* mob of penetration *schawl ;* (i.e., the foolish mob of shallow penetration.)—*Allan Ramsay.*

Sundriness, diversity.

Sunstead, the solstice; the place, or *stede*, of the sun.

Swad, a lout, a raw recruit, a lubber; a person who has to be brought into order and discipline, and to be *swaddled*, strapped, and laced.

> No better could the silly *swad* than this.
> > *Robert Greene : Perimedes the Blacksmith,* 1590.

> Let country swains and silly *swads* be still.
> > *Idem.*

Swaff, to come one over the other, like waves upon the shore.

> Drenched with their *swaffing* waves.
> > *Taylor's Works,* 1630.

Swale, to distend and wave in the wind, as a plume, a flag, or a sail; a more appropriate word for the purpose than its quasi synonyme, swell, which means to increase in real, whereas, to *swale* is to increase only in apparent, bulk.

Swale, a shady valley.

Swank, vigorous, hale, and hearty.

> Steeve and *swank*.
> > *Burns : The Auld Farmer to his mare Maggie.*

Swarf, the grit worn away from the stone in grinding.

Swarth, ⎱ the corn cut by one stroke of the scythe; the reach
Swath, ⎰ of the scythe.

> The Greeks, ripe for his edge,
> Fall down before him like the mower's *swath.*
> > *Shakspeare.*

The devil a puritan that he is, or anything constantly but a time pleaser; an affectioned (affected) ass, that cons state without book; and utters it by great *swaths.—Shakspeare : Twelfth Night.*

> Here stretched in lengths, the levelled *swarths* are found.
> > *Pope.*

> So Time the mower, cuts his fatal *swath,*
> And mortals see him not across their path
> > *W. R. Alger: The poetry of the East.*

Swash, to swell, to protrude, to swagger, to bully, to affect bravery; also used as a substantive and an equivalent to the modern word ' a swell.'

> Or score out husbands in the charcoal ashes,
> With county knight, not roaring city *swashes.*
> > *Translation of Ovid's Art of Love,* 1677.

This word was formerly applied in the sense of swell, or swelling, to a water-fall, ' a great *swash* of water.' To *swash* water, is a phrase still employed in the sense of ' *splash*,' but with the latent meaning of greater force.

Swasher, a rowdy, a bully, a braggart.

> I have observed these three *swashers.*
> > *Shakspeare : Henry V.*

> A *swashing* blow.
> > *Ben Jonson.*

Swash-buckler, a bully, a fellow whose sword makes a noise against his buckler.

Swash-bucket, a clumsy servant girl, who *swashes* or spills the milk or the water over the pail.

Swarble, to climb a straight tree, on which there are no branches to help the ascent. The word ' swarm ' has in some parts of England the same meaning.

Sware, to pass backwards and forwards, to wave to and fro ; whence to *swerve.*

Swat, preterite of sweat, to perspire.

Swatch, a specimen, a sample.

> That's just a *swatch* o' Hornbook's way.
> > *Burns : Death and Dr. Hornbook.*

Swatter, to scatter abroad extravagantly ; to waste.

> He *swattered* away all his money.—*Grose.*

Swattle, to drink voraciously, and with a noise, as a duck does, applied metaphorically to a drunkard.

Sweer, ⎫ hard, heavy, difficult to move, loth to move, unwill-
Swere, ⎬ ing ; from the Anglo-Saxon and German *schwer.*

> Thou art as young a man as I,
> And seem to be as *sweer.*
> > *Ballad of Robin Hood.*
>
> Work for nought makes folk dead *sweer.*

> *Sweer* in the bed, and *sweer* up in the morning's, no a good house-wife.

> An olite (over diligent) mother makes a *sweer* daughter.

> Pride and *sweerness* take muckle uphadding (upholding).
> > *Allan Ramsay's Scotch Proverbs.*

Sweeting, sweet-heart, lover.

> Ah, my sweet *sweeting,*
> My little pretty *sweeting,*
> My *sweeting* will I love wherever I go.
> She is so proper and pure,
> Full steadfast, stable, and demure,
> There is none such, you may be sure,
> As my sweet *sweeting.*
> > *MS. Temp. Henry VIII.*
>
> All's well *sweeting,*
> Come away to bed.
> > *Shakspeare : Othello.*

Sweeting—*continued.*

> Oh, mistress mine,
> Trip no further, pretty *sweeting*,
> Journeys end in lovers' meeting,
> Every wise man's son doth know.
> > > *Shakspeare.*

> One I could hear appointing with his *sweeting*,
> A place convenient for their secret meeting.
> > > *Drayton: The Owl.*

> Let not any maiden here,
> Dare to turn away her ear,
> Unto the whisper of her love,
> But give bracelet, ring, or glove.
> As a token to her *sweeting*,
> Of an after secret meeting.
> > > *Beaumont and Fletcher : Cupid's Revenge.*

Sweg, to sway to and fro by its own weight; whence the modern slang-word, 'swag,' as applied to plunder, when it is plenteous and heavy.

Swelt, to perish.

> Death came drying after,
> And all to duste perished ;
> Kynges and knyghtes,
> Kaysers and popes,
> Lered and lewed,
> He loot no man stand.
> Many a lovely ladye,
> And leman of knyghtes,
> Swound and *swelted*,
> For sorrow of his dintes.
> > > *Piers Ploughman.*

Sweltersome, very hot, close, sultry, and damp, applied to the weather. 'Sweltering heat,' is a common expression. The modern word sultry is apparently derived from ' swelter.'

Swelter, to suffer from the heat.

Swelth, the swollen flood of mud, slush, and foul water.

> Rude Acheron, a loathsome lake to tell,
> That boils and bubs with *swelth* as black as hell.
> > > *Sackville: Mirror for Magistrates.*

> A deadly gulf where nought but rubbish grows,
> With foul blacke *swelthe* in thickened lump that lies.
> > > *Idem.*

Swent, smooth, regular, even, quiet, placid.

> Of a *swent* nature, amiable.
> > *Nares.*

Sweven, to dream; a dream or vision.

> At night when Arthur was brought in bed,
> He should have battle upon the morrow,
> In strong *swevens* he was be-stead,
> That many a man that day should have sorrow.
> > *Morte Arthur.*

> Now, by my fay, said Jolly Robin,
> A *sweven* I had this night.
> > *Robin Hood and Grey of Gisborne.*

> My heart with grief will brast,
> I had thought *swevens* had never been true,
> I have proved them true at last.
> > *Percy's Reliques.*

Swike, to deceive, betray, play false.

Swikedom, treachery.

Swikeful, deceitful, treacherous.

Swile, to wash.

Swill, to drink gluttonously.

Swill-bowl, }
Swill-tub, } a drunkard.

Swill, a wash, or that which is washed.

Swill-pail, a pail in which the washings of the pantry are preserved. In the United States, almost every house in town or country has the swill-pail into which the Irish servants, very commonly throw as much food daily as would feed an English laborer's family. The '*swill*-woman' comes round regularly, and purchases the plunder.

Swime, from swim; a swimming or dizziness in the head; a swoon.

> Intill his logge he hyed that tyme,
> And to the earth he fell in *swyme*.
> > *MS. Lincoln (Halliwell).*

Swink, to labor over-hard.

> Upon a book in cloister alway to pore,
> Or *swinken* with his hand.

*   *   *   *   *

Swink—*continued.*

> A true *swinker* and a good was he,
> Living in peace and charitie.
> > *Chaucer: Prologue to the Canterbury Tales.*

> For all the night he shope him for to *swinke*,
> In carrying of the gold out of that place.
> > *Chaucer: The Pardnere's Tale.*

> In setting and sowing,
> *Swinken* full harde,
> > *Piers Ploughman.*

> But now I *swinke* and sweate in vain,
> My labor hath no end,
> And moping in my study still,
> My youthful years I spend.
> > *Marriage of Wit and Wisdom,* 1579.

> Riches, renown, and principality,
> Honor, estate, and all this world's good,
> For which men *swink* and sweat incessantly.
> > *Spenser: Faerie Queene.*

> We'll labor and *swinke*,
> We'll kiss and we'll drink,
> And tithes shall come thicker and thicker.
> > *Beaumont and Fletcher: The Spanish Curate.*

> Is there no patron to protect the muse,
> And fence for her Parnassus' barren soil?
> To every labor its reward accrues,
> As they are sure of bread who *swink* and moil.
> > *Thomson; Castle of Indolence.*

> The laboured ox,
> In his loose traces from the furrow came,
> And the *swink'd* hedge at his supper sat.
> > *Milton: Comus.*

Swither, *n.* uncertainty, perplexity; to be in a 'swither,' to be uncertain whither to go.

> Considering the *swiddering*
> Ye forced me first into.
> > *Montgomery: The Cherry and the Sloe.*

> The errant knight
> Bestrides his steed,
> And stands some time in jumbled *swither*,
> To ride in this road or that ither.
> > *Allan Ramsay.*

> I there wi' something did forgather,
> That put me in an eeriee *swither*.
> > *Burns: Death and Dr. Hornbook.*

Swirl, an eddy in a stream; the rapid and noisy revolution of a wheel; and in the East of England, according to Halliwell, any whirling, wavy, motion.   In the North, *swerl,* signifies to twist or twirl about.

> Out shot his hand, alas! alas!
> Fast in the *swirl* he screeched.
>> *The Mermaid, Finlay's Collection of Scottish Songs,* 1808.

Swith,
Swithe, } quickly, rapidly, very.
Swythe,

> When she herde the chylde crye her beforne,
> It comforted her full *swythe.*
>> *MS. Cantab. (Halliwell).*

> This messenger,
> Unto the king's mother rideth *swithe.*
>> *Chaucer : The Man of Lawe's Tale.*

> And he that hath the cut, with herte blithe,
> Shall remove to the town, and that full *swithe.*
>> *Chaucer : The Pardneres Tale.*

> All so *swythe,*
> As grasse falleth fro' the scythe.
>> *Romance of Richard Cœur de Lion.*

> *Swith* away;
> Or learn, like us, to be thought more gay.
>> *Allan Ramsay.*

> I am wounded *swithe* sore.
>> *Sir Bevis of Hampton.*

Swoll, preterite of swell; a word for a long time disused in favor of swelled, but gradually re-assuming its lost place.

Syle, to overflow, to boil over; to pour down in large quantities.

> He *syled* a gallon of ale down his throat.
>> *Grose's Provincial Glossary.*

Tang, a sharp sound; from *tang*, the preterite of ting, to sound.

> A tongue with a *tang*.
> > *Nares.*

> Let thy tongue *tang* arguments of state.
> > *Shakspeare.*

Tanglesome, quarrelsome, querulous, or unreasonable in argument.

Tanker, a cross humour.

Tankerous
Tankersome, } ill-natured, peevish, unreasonably quarrelsome.

These words, in common use in the Eastern Counties of England, are probably the origin of the English and American expression, *cantankerous*.

Tantle, to walk feebly, like an invalid or old person.

Tantrell, an idle unsettled person, who will not fix to any employment.—*Grose*.

Tapsalteerie, topsiturvy.

> Gie me a canny hour at e'en,
> My arms about my dearie O ;
> And worldly cares and worldly men,
> May a' gang *tapsalteerie* O.
> > *Robert Burns.*

Targe, a shield.

> When I was thus armed, I put the *targe* to my side.
> > *Romance of the Monk, Sion College, MS.*

> By his side,
> There hang his *targe*, with gashes deepe and wide.
> > *Sackville: Mirror for Magistrates.*

In Herbert Coleridge's Dictionary of the Oldest Words in the English Language, ' *targe* ' is defined to be ' a combination of shields, like the Roman testudo.'

Tarn, a lake high up in the mountains.

Tarriance, the act of tarrying; a word formed on the same principle as dalliance from dally.

> While lazy time his turn by *tarriance* serves,
> Love still grows sickly and hope daily starves.
> *Drayton*, 1637.

> After somewhat more than a fortnight's *tarriance*.
> *Southey.*

Tarrow, to be over-dainty for want of appetite.

> A *tarrowing* hen was never fat.
> A *tarrowing* bairn has had oure muckle.
> *Allan Ramsay.*

> I have seen their coggies fu',
> That yet have *tarrowed* at it.
> *Burns.*

Tarrysome, lingering, tarrying long.

> Of her long sorrow and *tarrysome* dede.
> *Douglas's Æneid.*

Tartle, to hesitate, to view a person or thing dubiously, as if not recognizing him, or it, with certainty.—*Jamieson.*

> A toom (empty) purse makes a *tartling* merchant.
> *Allan Ramsay's Scottish Proverbs.*

Tasse, a cup.

Tassie, a little cup.

> Go fetch to me a pint of wine,
> And fill it in a silver *tassie* ;
> And I will drink before I go,
> A service to my bonnie lassie.
> *Burns.*

Tath, the luxuriant grass which rises in tufts where the dung of cattle has been deposited.—*Jamieson.*

Tathy-grass, rough grass.—*Halliwell.*

Taverner, the keeper of a tavern.

Taut, neat, clean, tight, tidy; the word survives in English nautical phrase.

> Sae *taut*, sae taper, tight, and clean.
> *Burns : The Vision.*

Tauted, } made taut, or tight; or matted together like hair or
Tautie, } wool.

> She was na get o' moorland tips,
> Wi' *tauted* kep and hairy hips.
> *Burns : Poor Maitie's Elegy.*

Tead, a light, a lamp.

> Phœbus doth his beams display,
> And the fair bride forth to lead,
> Makes his torch their nuptial *tead*.
> *Spenser.*

Taw,
Tawe, } To beat and dress leather with alum to harden it.

> I'll *taw* the hide of thick-skinned Hugenes.
> *Marston's What You Will.*

In Scotland and the northern counties of England, the *taws* signifies a piece of hard leather, with which children at school are punished for ignorance, inattention, or bad behaviour. Formerly, if not now, every schoolmaster's desk was provided with the implement.

Teat, a small quantity; whence to teat or 'ted' the hay, to spread it out in small quantities to dry; to spill.

> I wish our folks meet na some dool,
> Meg *tedd* the salt upon thee.
> *Picken's Poems.*

Teathe, the dung of cattle dropped on the field by the animals when feeding; also to manure with dung.

Ted, to spread hay for its better drying.

> The smell of *tedded* grass.
> *Milton.*

> *Tedding,* turning, cocking, raking,
> And such business in haymaking;
> The lads and lasses sweat and fry,
> As they the grass do toss and dry.
> *Poor Robin,* 1746.

Tee-hee, to giggle.

> You *tee-heeing* pixie; (i.e., you giggling witch or gipsy.)
> *Exmoor Dialect.*

Teem, to pour out.

Toom, poured out, emptied.

As a verb neuter, in the sense of pouring out or bringing forth the natural increase; this word finds a place in every English Dictionary. 'The earth *teems* with plenty;' 'the landscape *teems* with beauty;' 'the sea *teems* with fish;' &c.

> If she must *teem,*
> Create her child of spleen, that it may live
> And be a thwart, disnatured. to torment her.
>> *Shakspeare: King Lear.*

> *Teem* out the remainder of the ale into the tankard.
>> *Swift.*

Toom, the original preterite of teem, has become the infinitive in Scottish and Northumbrian phrase. It is also used as an adjective.

> They *toom'd* their pocks and pawned their duds.
>> *Burns: The Jolly Beggars.*

> Better a *toom* house than a bad tenant.
>> *Scotch and Northumbrian Proverb.*

Teld, to build, to erect; a building. — (*Wright's Provincial Glossary.*)

Telt, erected, set up, built.

Tent, to heed; to take care of.

> Our Matty helps my mother, and sews, and *tents* our Joe.
>> *Waugh's Lancashire Songs.*

> But warily *tent* when ye come to court me.
>> *Burns.*

> When the tod (fox) preaches, take *tent* of the lambs.
>> *Northern Proverb.*

> Think ye we are less blest than they,
> Who scarcely *tent* us in their way ;
> As hardly worth their while.
>> *Burns: Epistle to Davie ; a brother poet.*

> I'll *tent* thee, quoth Wood,
> If I cannot rule my daughter,
> I'll rule my good.
>> *Cheshire Proverb, (Grose.)*

Tent, caution, care ; take *tent,* i.e., take care, *prenez garde.*

Tenty, careful, cautious, anxious.

Tentless, inattentive.

> I'll wander on wi' *tentless* heed.
>> *Burns: Epistle to James Smith.*

Temse, a sieve. In French, a sieve is a *tamise,* the same word that designates the river Thames.

Teth, temper, disposition.—(*Jamieson.*)

Tethy, ill-tempered; whence by corruption the modern word *techy.*

Thairms,⎫ fiddle-strings.　Nares and Richardson define the
Thermes,⎬ word to mean the intestines of bullocks or other
Tharmes,⎭ animals, and quote from *Archaius Toxophilus*, p.
140 : ' In olde time they made their bow-strings of bullock's
thermes.'　Skinner calls it a word in common use in Lincolnshire.

> He who has a wide *thairm*, never has a long arm ; (i.e., the man who
> has much to do, never has the means of doing it.)
> *Allan Ramsay's Scotch Proverbs.*

> MacLauchlan, *thairm* inspiring sage !
> *Burns : The Brigs of Ayr.*

> Come screw the pegs,
> And o'er the *thairms* be trying.
> *Burns : The Ordination.*

Thane, an earl or baron.

> All hail, Macbeth ! thou shalt be *Thane* of Cawdor.
> *Shakspeare : Macbeth.*

> Thane was a dignity among our ancient Saxon ancestors of two
> sorts : meset *thanes* (mass *thanes*), were priests qualified to say mass ;
> worold (worldly or temporal) *thanes*, were a kind of secular or temporal
> lords.—*Blount's Glossographia*, 1681.

Thar, to need.

> Have then ynough, thee *thar* not plainen then.
> *Chaucer: Wife of Bath's Prologue.*

Theak, to thatch.

> Bessie Bell and Mary Gray,
> They were twa bonnie lasses,
> They bigget (built) a bower in yon burn brae,
> And *theekit* it owre wi' rashes.
> *Ballad of Bessie Bell and Mary Gray.*

Theat, firm, close, sound.　' A *theat* barrel,' is a barrel that
does not leak.

> ' Out of *theats*,' i.e., out of order, or use, is a phrase, as
to any one who is rusted, as to any art or science, for want
of practice.—*Jamieson.*

Thepes, gooseberries.

Therle, gaunt, ill-fed.—(*Wright's Provincial Dictionary.*)

Thester, dark.

Thesterness, darkness.

> On a Thursday in *thesternesse,*
> Then was he taken;
> Through Judas and Jews,
> Jesus was his name.
> > *Piers Ploughman.*

Thews. Shakspeare speaks of ' *thews* and sinews;' and the two words, after his example are generally found combined in modern literature; and are taken to be synonymous. But *thew* in more ancient writings appears to signify culture, manners.

> His virtues and good *thews,*
> And good example that he shewes.
> > *MS. Cotton, quoted by Halliwell.*

> To be brought up in gentle *thewes* and martial might.
> > *Spenser.*

> In virtuous *thewes* and friendly constancie.
> > *Mirror for Magistrates.*

> For Nature, crescent does not grow alone,
> In *thews* and bulk.
> > *Shakspeare: Hamlet.*

Thibble, a stick for stirring porridge or gruel, *Scottice* a spurtle.

> To borrow their *thibble* to stir the furmety with.
> > *Tim Bobbin.*

Thig, to beg, to spunge, to sorn, to take advantage of friends and acquaintances for food and lodging as long as decency admits on the one side, or patience on the other.

> Better *thig* their meat,
> Than ony good in that wise get.
> > *Harleian MSS.*

> You've come to the goat's house to *thig* wool.
> > *Allan Ramsay's Scotch Proverbs.*

> The father buys, the son biggs (builds),
> The oye sells, and his son *thiggs.*
> > *Idem.*

Thigster, a beggar.

Thight, the same as *theat,* q.v.; closely planted; as trees in a hedge, or turnips in a field; firmly fixed like staves in a barrel.

Thill, the shaft.

Thill-horse, the shaft-horse.

> Thou hast got more hair on thy chin, than my *thill-horse* Dobbin has on his tail.—*Shakspeare : Merchant of Venice.*

Thirdendeal, a third part of anything.

Thirle, ⎱ *n.* a small hole ; to *drill* a hole, to pierce through.
Thurle, ⎰

> Sore yhurt,
> And with a spear was *thirled* his breast bone.
> *Chaucer : The Knight's Tale.*

Mr. Halliwell quotes from a Lincolnshire MS. :

> If thou were in a mirke house * * * and all the *thirles,* doores and wyndows were stokyne, that no one might enter.

St. Thomas in the MS. of *Cursor Mundi* at Trinity College, Cambridge, says of the Saviour's wounds :

> Till I see and feele his fleshe,
> The *thurles* both of hands and feete.

The narrow passages in coal-pits are in the North called *thurlings;* and in Kent the rabbit hole, is the rabbit *thirle.* In Dorsetshire, the martin and swift are said to have their nests in *thirles.* From ' nose *thirle,*' is derived nostril.

Thirlable, penetrable ; that through which *thirles* or holes can be made.—*Wright's Provincial Glossary.*

Thitherto, for the future. ' I have acted honestly *hitherto ;* and shall act honestly *thitherto.*'

Thole. This word, is common in Old English and Scottish poetry, and lingers not only in Scottish, but in the Cumbrian and Northumbrian dialect. It signifies to endure or suffer, and has been wrongfully thrust out of English to make room for modern substitutes derived from the French. A still current Saxon synonyme is bear : ' I cannot bear it,' which has the double disadvantage of being a weaker form of expression, and of using a word already pre-occupied in another sense. The Scotch and Northumbrians say of a thing they cannot endure : ' I canna *thole* it.'

> So muckle wo as I with you have *tholed.*
> *Chaucer.*

> What mischief and mal ease Christe for man *tholed.*
> *Ibid.*

Thole—*continued.*

> She shall the death *thole.*
>> *Gower: Confessio Amantis.*

> These three without doute,
> *Tholen* all povertie.
>> *Piers Ploughman.*

> All that Christe *tholed.*
>> *Piers Ploughman.*

> The montayne cedar *tholes* the blusterous winds.
>> *The Evergreen.*

> But in vain,
> I still maun doat and *thole* her proud disdain.
>> *Allan Ramsay.*

> Better *dree* out the inch when you have *tholed* the span.

> He that has a good crop ought to *thole* a few thistles.

> Better *thole* a grumph (a surly man) than a sumph (a fool).

> A good heart maun *thole* mickle.

> He who *tholes*, conquers.
>> *Allan Ramsay's Scotch Proverbs.*

Tholance, endurance, sufferance, toleration.

Tholeable, endurable.

Thone, ⎱ moist, damp, limp, soft, pliable ; probably derived
Thoney, ⎰ from the Gaelic *thon*, a wave.

Thorp, a village. This word still survives as the terminal syllable of the names of many places in England.

> There stood a *thorpe* of sight delitable.
>> *Chaucer : The Clerke's Tale.*

> As we were entering at the *thorpe's* ende.
>> *Chaucer : The Persone's Prologue.*

> By twenty *thorps*, a little town,
> And half-a-dozen bridges.
>> *Tennyson.*

Thorpsman, a villager.

> To call in from the fields and waters, shops and work-housen, from the inbred stock of more homely women, and less filching *thorpsmen.*
>> *Fairfax*, 1674.

Thoughty, meditative, pensive.

> Fanny is two years younger than I am ; and not so *thoughty*, as Philip says.—*Petticoat Tales, Jamieson.*

Thrall, a slave ; whence *enthrall*, to enslave ; and thraldom, slavery ; words still current in literature.

> When they have turned them to the faith they make his *thralles* free out of *thraldom.*—*Chaucer : The Persone's Tale.*

> > This kyng as thou herdest ere this,
> > Hed a *thrall* that dede amiss.
> > > *Religious Poems, Fifteenth Century ; quoted by Mr. Halliwell.*

> > Look gracious on thy prostrate *thrall*.
> > > *Shakspeare.*

> > No *thralls* like them that inward bondage have.
> > > *Sidney.*

> > Till he redeemed had that lady *thrall*.
> > > *Spencer's Faerie Queen.*

> > He drinketh the wine, but at the last,
> > The wine drinketh him and bindeth him fast,
> > And laith him drunke by the walle ;
> > As him which is his bond *thralle*,
> > And all in his subjection.
> > > *Gower : Confessio Amantis.*

Thrail, } a flail.
Thrale, }

Thrang, busy, thronged with many customers.

> > Two dogs that were na' *thrang* at hame,
> > Forgathered once upon a time.
> > > *Burns : The Twa Dogs.*

Thratch, to gasp convulsively.

> > If I but grip you by the collar,
> > I'll gar you gape,
> > And *thratch* for want of breath.
> > > *Beattie : John o' Arnha'.*

Thrave, } a bunch, a bundle, a lot, a company.   Twenty-four
Threve, } sheaves of wheat.

> > And after cometh a knave,
> > The worst of a *thrave*.
> > > *MS. Lansdown, quoted by Mr. Halliwell.*

> > And I have thoughts a *thrave*.
> > > *Piers Ploughman.*

Thrave—*continued.*

> He sends forth *thraves* of ballads to the sale.
> > *Bishop Hall : Ritson's Ancient Songs.*
>
> A daimen icker in a *thrave*; (a random ear of corn from the sheaf.)
> > *Burns : To a Mouse.*
>
> A *thrave* of corn is two shocks of six, or rather twelve sheaves a piece. The word comes from the British *threva*, twenty-four. In most counties of England, twenty-four sheaves do now go to a *thrave*. Twelve sheaves make a stook, and two stooks make a *thrave*.
> > *Blount's Glossographia,* 1681.

Thraw, *s.*, a turn, a little whirl, a turn of time. To twist, to thwart, to be perverse, or contrary.

> When I a little *thrawe*, had made my moan.
> Bewailing mine infortune and mischance.
> > *The King's Quair.*
>
> And when she walked had a little *thrawe*,
> Under the sweete, greene bowis bent,
> Her fair fresh face, as white as any snawe,
> She turned.
> > *Ibid.*
>
> St. Stephen's boys wi' jarring noise,
> They did his measures *thraw*, man.
> > *Burns : The American War.*
>
> There are twa hens into the crib,
> Have fed this month and mair ;
> Make haste and *thraw* their necks about,
> That Colin weel may fare.
> > *Wm. Julius Mickle : There's nae luck about the house.*

Thrawn, cross, perverse ; ill-tempered, twisted out of humour.

> I'll be as *thrawn* as you ; though you were as *thrawn* as the woodie ;
> i.e., I'll be as cross as you, though you should be as cross as the gallows.
> > *Scotch Proverb.*

Thrawardness, perversity

> But, instead of thankful hearts and good obedience, her Highness's clemency is commonly abused with *thrawardness* and ingratitude.
> > *Proclamation of Mary Queen of Scots.*

Threesome, triple.

> There's *twasome* reels, and *threesome* reels,
> There's hornpipes and strathspeys man.
> > *Burns.*

Threne, a lamentation.

> Whereupon it made this *threne*,
> To the phœnix and the dove.
> > *Shakspeare : The Passionate Pilgrim.*

Threpe, to argue or dispute. In the ancient ballad, 'Take thine auld cloak about thee;' quoted by Shakspeare in Othello; claimed both by Scotland and by England, and common to both, the husband says:

> Bell my wife, she loves not strife,
> Yet she will lead me if she can,
> And oft to lead a quiet life,
> I'm forced to yield though I'm good man;
> It's not for a man with a woman to *threpe*.

Chaucer seems to use the word in a different sense, when he says:

> The bodies seven   *   *   *
> Sol gold is, and Luna silver we *threpe*,
> Mars iron, Mercurie quicksilver, we clepe.

But Chaucer would not employ two synonymous words to rhyme his couplet, and if 'clepe' means to call, *threpe* may mean, argue, insist, or assert. 'Sol gold is, and we argue (or *threpe*) that Luna is silver.'

The word is often used in Scottish poetry and romance, and deserves a place in the English vocabulary, to which it strictly belongs. Burns in his Epistle to W. S(impson), Ochiltree, says:

> Some herds well learn'd upo' the book,
> Wad *threap* auld folks the thing mistook.

Bishop Fisher in a sermon cited in Todd's Johnson, says:

> Some cry upon God, some other *threpe* that he hath forgotten them.

In Lord Surrey's paraphrase of the 55th Psalm, we find:

> My foes they bray so loud,
> And eke *threpe* on so fast.

In Grose's Provincial Glossary; a shopkeeper's phrase is quoted: 'This is not *threaping* ware;' meaning, that the ware, or goods, is so obviously of first quality that it needs no arguing about.

Thrimmel, to pay a debt reluctantly; to part with money in a niggardly and mean manner.

Threaden, } made of thread.
Thridden, }

> Which did reveal him then to be indeed,
> A *thridden* fellow in a silken weede.
> *Stephens's Essays and Characters,* 1615; *quoted by Halliwell.*

Thrid, preterite of the verb to thread.

> Some *thrid* the mazy ringlets of her hair.
> *Pope.*

Thrid, to divide into three parts.—*Jamieson.*

Thrin, three together, a triplet, a trio. This ancient English word, if of no use to prose writers, might be valuable to rhymers.

Thring, to press, to crush ; whence the preterite *thrang*, pressed, and the substantive *throng*, a crowd.

Thripple, to labour hard.

Thrist, difficulty, hard pressure ; stress of circumstance.

> Withdraw thee from no perils or hard *thrist*,
> But even enforce more strongly to resist.
> *Douglas's Eneid.*

Throaty, guttural.

> Certain hard *throaty* words which I was taught lately.
> *Howell's Familiar Letters,* 1650.

Throdden, to grow, to thrive, to increase.

Throme, a gang, company, or drove.

Throughgang, a thoroughfare.

Throughgoing, active, lively ; going through with a thing.

> She seems to be a plump and jocose little woman ; gleg, blythe, and *throughgaun'* for her years.—*Blackwood's Magazine.*

> Betty Lanshaw was an active, *throughgoing* woman.
> *Galt's Annals of the Parish.*

Throughly, thoroughly.

Throve, preterite of thrive, to prosper.

Thrum, green and vigorous ; applied to herbage.

Thrum, the tufted part beyond the tie, at the end of the warp in weaving ; any collection of tuft or short thread.—*Nares.*

> O fates, come, come,
> Cut thread and *thrum.*
> *Shakspeare : Midsummer Night's Dream.*

Thrum—*continued.*

> A child and dead? alas, how could it come!
> Surely thy thread of life was but a *thrum.*
> > *Wit's Recreation.*

> Thou who wilt not love, doe this,
> Learne of me what woman is,
> Something made of thred and *thrumme,*
> A meere botch of all and some.
> > *Herrick.*

Thrummed, made of coarse refuse thread or wool.

> There's her *thrummed* hat, her muffler too! Run up Sir John!
> > *Shakspeare : Merry Wives of Windsor.*

Thrumble, sometimes written thrimble; to press violently, as a crowd, or into a crowd.

> Peter, who was ever maist sudden, sayes, thou art *thrumbled* and thrusted by the multitude.—*Bruce's Sermons.*

Thrump, to squeeze ; or press violently in a crowd.—(*Jamieson.*)

Thrunk, busy, fussy.

Thrunk-wife, a fussy, meddlesome woman.

Thrunch, much displeased, very angry.

Thrut, the length of the *throw* of a stone ; or of the flight of an arrow.

Thud, a dull, heavy blow.

Neither the Dictionaries of Johnson nor Richardson, nor those of Webster and Worcester, contain this word. Nares, and his most recent editors, make no mention of it; but Mr. Halliwell (Dictionary of Archaic and Provincial Words), defines it to mean a 'heavy blow.' This is scarcely its true signification. A sharp, quick, 'heavy blow,' would be a thump; but a dull, slow, ponderous blow, would be a *thud,* such as the shock of a heavy billow against the side of a ship.

> Fra fearful *thuds* of the tempestuous tide.
> > *Douglas' Eneid.*

> The air grew rough with bousteous (boisterous) *thuds.*
> > *Allan Ramsay.*

> Here Doon pours down his far-fetched floods,
> There, well-fed Irwine stately *thuds.*
> > *Robert Burns.*

Thud—*continued.*

> Loud roars the blast among the woods,
> And tirls the branches aarely,
> On hill and house hear how it *thuds.*
> > *Robert Burns.*

> The brave Lochiel as I heard tell,
> > Led Camerons on in clouds, man ;
> The morning fair, and clear the air,
> > They loos'd with devilish *thuds,* man.
> > > *Ballad of Tranent Muir.*

> Whose thundering with wondering,
> > I heard up through the air ;
> Through cluds so, he *thuds* so,
> > And flew I wist not where.
> > > *The Cherry and the Sloe.*

Thurse, a giant, a spectre.—*Wright's Provincial Dictionary.*

Thurte, might, need.

> As faire a ladye to his wife had he,
> As any earthly creature *thurte* see.
> > *Sir Isumbras.*

Thwaite, a wood cut down, grubbed up, and converted into arable land. This word constantly occurs in the Northern counties, as a termination to the names of places ; as, Mickle*thwaite,* Hemel*thwaite,* Ow*thwaite,* &c.

Thwart, an ill-tempered or cross person, who *thwarts* others. In Berkshire, according to Mr. Halliwell, a ' thurt ' has the same meaning.

> And be a *thwart* disnatured to torment her.
> > *Shakspeare : King Lear.*

Thwartover, contrary, transverse, across.

> And for fifteen long days and nights, the *thwart-over* and cross north easterly wind blew us nothing but lengthening of our sorrow.
> > *Taylor's Works,* 1630.

Tickle, dangerous, difficult; whence the modern phrase, ' a *ticklish* question,' &c.

> A matter dangerous to the state ; and *tickle* to the crown.
> > *Bowe's Correspondence,* 1583.

Tid,
Tyd, } quickly ; from *tide,* time.

> I shall tell thee as *tyd,*
> What this tree hight.
> > *Piers Ploughman.*

Tid—*continued.*

> And he turned him as *tyd*,
> And then took I heede.
>
> *Piers Ploughman.*

If this derivation be correct, it is possible that the modern phrase a 'tid-bit,' or dainty bit, meant originally a bit eaten quickly, on account of its daintiness. Worcester defines ' tid ' to mean ' tender,' ' soft.'

Tidder, tender, soft, frail.

Tidderness, tenderness, frailty.

Tide, to happen, to befall. This word survives in the intensitive form to ' be*tide*,' and in the exclamation : ' Woe be*tide* you.'

Tidde, happened ; preterite of tide.

Tiff, a slight quarrel ; a fit of ill-humour.

Johnson asserts this to be ' a low word,' and supposes it to be without etymology. None of his successors appear to have been more successful than himself in tracing the word to its roots. It has long ceased to be 'low.'

Tift, a slight blow, an impulsion.

> Five-and-twenty silver bells
> Were a' tyed to his mane,
> And at ae *tift* of the norland wind
> They twinkled ane by ane.
>
> *Ritson's Ancient Songs.*

Tifty, quarrelsome.

> Then up spake one, a maid forlorn
> With supple tongue and tifty.
>
> *A Scott's Poems, Jamieson.*

Tilt, violence.

He's in a *tilt*, (of passion) ; probably derived from a *tilt* at a tournament, when a person rides violently against an opposing object.

Tilty, violent, unreasonably ill-tempered.—*Barnes's Roots and Stems of the English as a Teutonic Tongue.*

Tilth, tillage, cultivated land ; the produce of tilling.

> So that the *tilthe* is nigh forlorn,
> Which Christ sewe (sowed) with his own hande.
>
> *Gower.*

Tilth—*continued.*

Full *tilth* and husbandry.

> *Shakspeare : Measure for Measure.*

Give the fallow land their seasons and their *tilth.*

> *Drayton.*

O'er the rough *tilth* he casts his eyes around.

> *Fawkes.*

Look where the full-eared sheaves of rye,
Grow wavy on the *tilth.*

> *Philips.*

In Northamptonshire, according to Sternberg's Glossary, *tilth* means a ploughing. 'That piece of land must have a fresh *tilth* over.' 'That farm is in good *tilth*,' i. e. well cultivated.

Tine, to lose, or be lost.

Tint, lost.

This ancient English word has survived in Scotland. Mr. Halliwell quotes several examples of its use from the Harleian MSS., and from the Cursor Mundi, and other MSS., in Trinity College, Cambridge.

> What was *tint* through tree,
> Tree shall it win.
>> *Piers Ploughman.*

> The turtle that *tynes* her make (mate).
>> *MS. Harl.*

> That is our God so gracious,
> And is so loth man's soul to *tyne.*
>> *Cursor Mundi.*

> It rained fire fra heaven and brimstane,
> And *tynt* all that there was.
>> *MS. Cott.*

> His knife was *tint*, his sheath was ta'en,
> His scabbard from his thigh was gane.
>> *Metrical Romance of Sir Eger, Sir Grahame, and his Gray Steel.*

> I never saw a fairer,
> I never loved a dearer,
> And next my heart I'll wear her,
> For fear my jewel *tine.*
>> *Burns : My wife's a winsome wee thing.*

Allan Ramsay's Collection of Scotch proverbs contains several examples of its use ; among others, the following :

Tint—*continued.*

Where there is nothing, the king *tines* his right.

All's not *tint* that's in danger.

Better spoil your joke than *tine* your friend.

Give *tining* gamesters leave to grumble.

He never *tint* a cow that grat (wept) for a needle.

He wad *tine* his ears if they were na' tacked (fastened) to him.

Time *tint* is ne'er found again.

Tine heart and all's gone.

Tin, ⎫ a fire; to kindle a fire; whence Bel*tin*, or Bel*taine*, the
Tind, ⎬ fire kindled three times a year to Bel, the Sun, by
Tine, ⎭ the Celtic nations; whence also the modern word
tinder.

Coals of contention, and hot vengeance *tined.*
Spenser's Faerie Queene.

If my pufft life be out, give leave to *tine,*
My shameless snuff at that bright light of thine.
Quarles' Emblems.

One candle *tindeth* a thousand.
Sanderson's Sermons, 1689.

Tindles, fires made by children in Derbyshire on the night of All Souls.—*Halliwell.*

Ting, to sound; whence the diminutive tingle or *tinkle,* a small or soft sound; whence also *tang,* the preterite, q.v.; and tongue (*tung*) that which makes the sound.

Tinsel, signifying anything shining with false lustre, is generally supposed to have its origin from the French *etincelle,* a spark; or from the Latin *scintilla.* More probably the true derivation is to be sought in the Anglo-Saxon *tyne,* to lose; whence *tynsail, tinsal,* and *tynsal,* defined in Jamieson's Dictionary, as 'loss of whatever kind.' In this sense, the small pieces and remnants thrown off in the manufacture of articles of gold, silver, and precious stones, originally called *tinsel,* and afterwards used up, or applied to the orna-

Tinsel—*continued.*

mentations of cloths, silks, and velvets, may have led to the secondary meaning of the word; as signifying the appearance, rather than the reality of gold. Beaumont and Fletcher speak of 'tinsel affections,' i.e., affections that were not of the real gold of love, though they might shine like it.

> Goodly apparel of *tinsel*, cloth of gold, and velvet.
> *Strype.*

> Nothing can be more contemptible than that *tinsel* splendour of language, which some writers continually affect.
> *Blair.*

> My profit is not your *tinsel*.
> *Allan Ramsay's Scotch Proverbs.*

Tireling, one who is easily tired or worn out with work or exercise.

Tirl, to spin round, to put in motion; to twist at the knob, pin, or fastening of a door. This is a very common word in ancient ballads, both English and Scotch.

> Oh he's gone round and round about,
> And *tirled* at the pin.
> *Willie and May Margaret:*

Tirl, to unroof, to uncover, to take the top off.

> While in the strong-winged tempest flyin',
> *Tirlin'* the kirks.
> *Burns: Address to the Deil.*

Tirly; rotatory, that which has a spinning motion.

Tith, tight, taut, strong, vigorous.

> She's good mettle; of a good stirring strain,
> She goes *tith*.
> *Beaumont and Fletcher.*

> Take a widow,
> A good stanch wench, that's *tith*.
> *Idem.*

Titte, } quickly; from *tide*, time.
Tytte, }

> Lord, that I have done, forgive me *tytte*.
> *MS. Harleian, (Halliwell.)*

Toare, grass and rubbish, or corn land after the corn is reaped, the long sour grass in pasture fields.—*Halliwell.*

Tocher, a dowry; a word principally applied to the fortunes of persons in the middle and lower ranks of life; who are too poor to give to their daughters *dowries*. A *tocher* stands in about the same relation to a dowry, as a house does to a mansion.

> A cow and a calf,
> An ox and a half,
> Forty good shillings and three,
> Is not that enough *tocher*
> For a shoemaker's daughter?
> *Nursery Rhymes of England; by J. O. Halliwell.*

The bonnie lass *tocherless*, has mair wooers than chances of a husband.

The greatest *tochers* make not ever the greatest testaments.

Marry a beggar, and get a louse for your *tocher*.

Better a *tocher* in her than on her.

Maiden's *tochers*, and minister's stipends, are aye less than they are ca'd.—*Allan Ramsay's Scotch Proverbs.*

> Oh meikle thinks my love o' my beauty,
> And meikle thinks my love o' my kin,
> But little thinks my love I ken brawly,
> My *tocher's* the jewel has charms for him.
> *Burns.*

Tod, a large tuft, bunch, or bush of ivy.

> At length within the ivy *tod*,
> There shrouded was the little god.
> I heard a busy bustling.
> *Spenser : Shepherd's Kalendar.*

> There valiant and approved men of Britain,
> Like boding owls creep into *tods* of ivy,
> And hoot their fears to one another nightly.
> *Beaumont and Fletcher.*

> The owle, till then, 'tis thought, full well could sing,
> And tune her voice to every bubbling spring,
> But when she heard those plaints, then forth she yode,
> Out of the covert of an ivy *tod*,
> And hallooing for aid, so strained her throat,
> That since, she clean forgot her former note.
> *Brown : Britania's Pastorals.*

Tod—*continued.*

> How Cain in the land of Nod,
> When the rascal was all alone,
> Like an owl in an ivy *tod*,
> Built a city as large as Roan.
> *Nares.*

In Suffolk, according to Mr. Halliwell, any bush at the top of a pollard, is called a *tod.*

Tod, the common name for a fox in Scotland; and formerly in England.

> Driv'st hence the wolf, the *tod*, the brock,
> And other vermin from the flock.
> *Ben Jonson.*

Toit, a fit of ill-humour; whence, *hoity-toity!* an exclamation of surprise at seeing a person in a passion.

Toitish, ill-tempered, snappish.

Tole,) to draw, or pull, whence '*toll* the bell,' i.e., pull the
Toll,) bell; and '*toll*-gate,' where the driver or horseman has to *draw* or pull up, to pay the road money.

> Who like the bee, *tolling* from every flower
> The virtuous sweets.
> *Shakspeare: Henry IV.,* pt. ii.
> A dog is *tolled* with a bone.
> *Nares.*
> Be sure to *tole* him on by insensible degrees.
> *Of Education, quoted by Nares.*
> Curvets, runs, whistles, waves, and *toles* him on.
> *Fairfax: Tasso.*

Tolt, to give yourself a blow by striking your head against a beam.—*Baker's Northamptonshire Glossary.*

Tolter, to move heavily and clumsily.

> From cottage-door, farm-house, and dusty lane,
> Where home the cart-horse *tolters* with the wain.
> *Clare's Village Minstrel.*

Toten, to peep.

> With his knopped shoon,
> Clouted full thick,
> His toen (toes) *toteden* out.
> *Piers Ploughman.*
> Then *toted* I into a tavern,
> And there I espied,
> Two frere Carmes,
> With a full coppe.
> *Ibid.*

Touse, ⎱ to pull, to struggle; whence the modern word
Touze, ⎰ 'tussle.'

> In feats of arms, and life's dread desperation,
> I *touse* to gain me fame and reputation.
> *Ford*, 1606.

Towser, ⎱ a rude, violent person, who pulls others about;
Touzer, ⎰ whence the common name for a dog, who is a good
ratter.

> But let him loose among the kitchen maids; never was seen so
> termagant a *towzer.—Otway*, 1684.

Tousie, disordered, dishevelled, uncombed.

'A *tousie* head,' one that has not been combed.

> His *towsie* back,
> Was glossy black.
> *The twa dogs : Robert Burns.*

Tout, ⎱ to blow upon a horn; whence the modern word, 'a
Toot, ⎰ *touter*,' a man who stands at the door of a shop, to entice people in. To blow one's own trumpet; or to *tout*
one's own abilities, is an expression that conveys a similar
meaning.

In Wickliffe's translation of the Bible, the word '*tooter*'
is used to express a spy, or scout: a man stationed on a
tower to blow a horn as a signal of danger.

In Scotland it is said of an old story revived, and told in
a new manner, that 'it is an auld *tout* in a new horn.'

Tout-hill, ⎱ a hill or eminence, on which, in time of danger or
Tote-hill, ⎰ war, a man was stationed to *tout* or blow a horn
as a signal.

Tow, a rope, whence to *tow*, to pull with a rope.

Tozy, soft, tender.

Toziness, softness, tenderness.—*Wright's Provincial Dictionary*.

Traik, to go idly about, from place to place; to wander without purpose; to lose one's self for want of thought whither
one is going; to follow after women.

> He's none of the birds that *traik;* i.e., he will not wander from the
> right way, he can take care of himself.
> *Northern Proverb.*

> There is not a huzzy on this side of thirty that ye can bring within
> your doors, but there will be chiels, writer lads, 'prentice lads, and
> what not, come *traiking* after them for their destruction.
> *Sir Walter Scott : Heart of Mid-Lothian.*

Trail, a term of reproach for a slatternly woman who lets her garments *trail* in the mire; a draggle-tailed slut. *A trull.*

Traily, slovenly.

Traipse, to trail or draggle in the dirt or slush; applied to a slovenly woman.

Trame, treachery, deceit.

Trangle, one's own idea, device, way, or will.

> Let them take their own *trangle.*
> > *Leicestershire*: *Wright's Provincial Dictionary.*

Trant, trade, barter; also a trick or stratagem.

Tranter, a pedlar, a hawker of small wares; a carrier.

> And had some *tranting* merchant to his sire.
> That trafficked both by water and by fire.
> > *Hall's Satires.*

Trantles, articles of little value; toys; petty articles of furniture.—*Jamieson.*

Tranty, tricky, crotchetty, applied to a child that is wise and forward beyond its years. — *Barnes' Roots and Stems of English.*

Treddle, a street walker.

Treen, the old plural of tree; also wooden, or made of a tree.

> Ane *treene* truncheon, ane ramshorne spoone.
> > *Bannatyne.*

Sir Thomas Rokeby being controlled for first suffering himself to be served in *treene* cuppes; answered: these homely cups and dishes pay truly for that they containe. I had rather drink out of *treene*, and pay gold and silver, than drink out of gold and silver, and make wooden payment.—*Camden's Remains.*

> Erminia's steed the while his mistress bore,
> Under safe shelter of the shadie *treen.*
> > *Fairfax* : *Tasso.*

Trend, to make a considerable bend or turn.

> Not far beneath, i' the' valley as she *trends,*
> Her silver stream.
> > *Brown* : *Britannia's Pastorals.*

Trendency, a strong deviation.

Trice, from thrice. A space of time in which you can count three. 'A brace of shakes,' a similar phrase, means while you can count two, or sing two notes, shakes or trills.

> In this *trice* of time,
> Commit a thing so monstrous.
> *Shakspeare : King Lear.*

Trichard, a cheat, a trickster; from the French *tricher*, to cheat, to trick.

> Richard, that thou be ever *trichard*.
> *Song against the Emperor of Almaigne ; Temp. Chaucer.*

Trig, neat, fine, well-dressed, well made; also a fop, or a person giving too much attention to his personal appearance.

> It is my humour, you are a pimp and a *trig*,
> An Amadis de Gaul, a Don Quixote.
> *Ben Jonson, The Alchemist.*

> And you among them a' John,
> Sae *trig* from top to toe.
> *Burns : John Anderson.*

Triple-trine, three times three; applied by the Elizabethan poets to the nine muses.

Trod, a footpath.

Troggin, pedlers' wares, or any miscellaneous collection. The words *troke* and *truck*, to barter, are from the same root. *Truck*, in the Eastern Counties of England signifies odds and ends: and in America, a load of miscellaneous vegetables or other articles.

> They purchased homespun calico, salt, rum, tobacco, and such other *truck* as their necessities called for.—*Chronicles of Penneville.*

> Buy braw *troggin*,
> Frae the banks o' Dee ;
> Wha wants *troggin*,
> Let him come to me.
> *Robert Burns.*

Troke, } to barter; from whence the '*truck* system' in the
Truck, } manufacturing districts.

Troll, to pass round the bottle at table; to troll or trundle a hoop.

> Then doth she *troll* to me the bowl,
> Ev'n as a mault worm shoulde,
> And saith, sweet heart, I take my part,
> Of this jolly good ale and old.
> *Gammer Gurton's Needle.*

> *Troll* about the bridal bowl,
> And divide the broad bride cake.
> *Ben Jonson.*

> Nappy ale,
> Good and stale;
> In a brown bowl,
> Which did about the board merrily *trowl.*
> *Percy's Reliques; the King and the Miller of Mansfield.*

Troth-plight, the passing of a solemn vow or pledge of faith; the person who is security for the fidelity of another.

> As rank as any flax-wench, that puts to before her *troth-plight.*
> *Shakspeare: Winter's Tale.*

> Nay! and to him my *troth-plight,* and my friend.
> *Heywood.*

Trull, a term of contempt for a woman; from trowl or troll, to run, to trundle; whence, one that runs or walks the streets, a prostitute.

Trundle, a wheel. 'You must take your *trundle,*' (i.e., your chance or turn at the wheel of Fate): *Northamptonshire.*

Tryste, a place of meeting; a rendezvous. A purely English word, from the Anglo-Saxon *trwsian,* to confide, whence, trust, trustful, and mistrustful. When two persons, appointed to meet at a designated spot on a future day, each *trusted* or *trysted* that the other would be true to the hour and place; and thus such phrases as a 'trysting tree,' and a 'trysting bower,' for the meeting of lovers; and Falkirk *tryste,* where the great cattle drovers of the North and South of Scotland, agreed to assemble every year, and thus established a fair. Chaucer uses the word in Troilus and Cressida, in the sense of a rendezvous, though the etymology of the word was not clear to 'Urry,' his editor.

> Lo! holde thee at thy *triste.*

In the Ballad of the Reid Squair, (1576), preserved in a MS. in the Cotton Library, and printed by Ritson, occurs:

> On July seventh this suthe to say,
> At the Reid Squair the *tryst* was set.

The word did not survive the days of Chaucer in English poetry. Neither Spenser nor Shakspeare used, or, appear to have been acquainted with it. But it remained

Tryste—*continued.*

a living flower in Scottish verse and parlance. Its obvious beauty and convenience, rendered it familiar to all the readers of Burns and Scott; and it has since been adopted by some of the purest English writers, and partially restored to that place in the English Dictionary, which it ought never to have lost.

> George Douglas caused a *trist* (tryste) to be set between him and the Cardinal and four lords, at the which *trist*, he and the Cardinal agreed finally without the Queen's advice.
> *Letter dated September,* 1543 ; *quoted by Nares.*

> The tenderest hearted maid,
> That ever bided *tryst* at village stile.
> *Tennyson.*

> By the wine-god he swore it.
> And named a *trysting* day.
> *Macaulay.*

Tuggle, from ' tug,' to pull by short, sharp, repeated jerks.

> *Tuggling* and struggling how to get him free.
> *Ross's Heleonore.*

Tussock, a tuft of feathers ; whence *tussock*-grass, a grass with a feathery and tufty crest.

Tuz, a knot of hair or wool ; an entanglement.

Twattle, to talk loudly and idly, and several persons at a time ; *betwattled* is a common expression in many parts of England and in America, to signify the condition of a person whose brain has been confused by contradictory opinions, and loud speaking.

Twiddle, to be busy about nothing ; whence the phrase, ' to *twiddle* one's thumbs,' expressive of the useless activity of an idle person.

Twime, ⎱ a couplet.
Thrime, ⎰ a triplet.

These words are written in an old hand, on the margin of a copy of Blount's Glossographia. No authority for their use is given ; but the words are consonant with the structure of the language ; and would be useful if favored with literary acceptance.

Twine, to deprive.

> To *twine* me o' my gear.
> > *Allan Ramsay.*

> *Twines* many a poor doylt drunken carle,
> Of half his days.
> > *Burns: Scotch Drink.*

Twingle, to twine round.

Twink, this word has been almost wholly superseded by its diminutive *twinkle.*

> Aye, with a *twink,*
> Before you can say come and go.
> > *Shakspeare: Twelfth Night.*

Twire, to turn round, to peep out, whence the diminutive twirl, to round round rapidly.

> When sparkling stars *twire* out.
> > *Shakspeare: Sonnet* xxxiv.

> I saw the wench that *twired* and twinkled at them.
> > *Beaumont and Fletcher.*

Twissle, ⎫ that part of the tree where the branch separates
Twistle, ⎭ from the trunk or bole.

Twissle, one of two apples, two cherries, or any other fruit growing on a single stem.

> As from a tree, we sundrey times espy,
> A *twissle* grown by nature's subtle might.
> > *Turberville, (quoted by Nares).*

Twist, a crotchet, a perverse idea.

Twisty, contentious, ill-humored, capricious.

Twitch, to tie tightly.

Twitch-grass, a species of long grass, so named from its tenacity or stringiness.

Twychild, a man or woman in extreme old age or second childhood; from twy, *twice.*

> And when thou shalt grow *twychilde,* she shall be,
> Careful and kind, religiously to thee.
> > *Davies: Scourge of Folly, (Halliwell.)*

Tyke, a rough, shaggy, mongrel dog.

> Jesus they despised,
> Bote his love and law,
> > *　　　*　　　*　　　*

Tyke—*continued.*

> Now are they lowe cherles,
> *Tikes* and cherles.
>> *Piers Ploughman.*

> Base *tike*, call'st thou me host?
>> *Shakspeare ; Henry V.*

> Bobtail *tike*, or trundle-tail.
>> *Shakspeare : King Lear.*

> You have lost your own stomach, and found a *tyke's*.

> I'm as tired of it, as a *tyke* of lang kale.
>> *Allan Ramsay's Scotch Proverbs.*

Luath in the Twa Dogs, by Robert Burns, was 'a gash and faithful *tyke*, as ever leaped a ditch or dyke;' and the Deil in Tam o' Shanter, 'sat on a window sill in the shape of

> A towsy *tyke*, black, grim, and large.'

Ug, to feel abhorrence, or disgust at.

This word is one of the many derived from natural sounds. The exclamation *ugh*, which people involuntarily make when any frightfully disagreeable object starts up before them, is apparently its root. In England, as well as in America, the word *ugly* has recently acquired a new meaning—i.e., vicious, ill-tempered—than which nothing can be more *ugsome* or provocative of disgust.

> The rattling drum, and trumpets' tout,
> Delight young swankies that are stout,
> What his kind frighted mother *ugs*,
> Is music to the soldier's lugs.
> > *Jamieson's Dictionary.*

Ugsome, ugly.

> The hornid bird which we clepe the night owl';
> *Ugsome* to hear was her wild eldritch shreik.
> > *Douglas: Translation of Virgil.*

> The *ugsomeness* and silence of the night.
> > *Idem.*

> May chains then, and pains then,
> Infernal be his hire,
> Who dang us, and flang us,
> Into this *ugsome* mire.
> > *Allan Ramsay: The Vision.*

Similar to *ug* and *ugsome* in the source of its derivation, is the Gaelic *oich*, an exclamation expressive of weariness and exhaustion consequent upon great bodily effort; as when a porter lays down a heavy load, and can go no further without resting; or when a man climbs a hill, and is compelled to take breath. On the bank of Loch Ness in Invernesshire, is a very steep ascent in the road, which has acquired the name of Craig *Oich* from the country people, in consequence of the usual exclamation, *oich! oich!* of travellers when they reach the top.

Um, round, or around. This prefix was once as common to English as it still is to German verbs.

Um-be-clippe, to clasp round or embrace.

Um-be-grippe, to seize, or grip round.

Um-be-lappe, to wrap round.

Um-be-set, to beset on every side.

Um-besiege, to besiege round about ; to encompass a city with armed men.

Um-be-thinke, to bethink one's self of all surroundings (or circumstances), to remember.

> He *um-be-thoughte* him of ane slight.
>> *Barbour.*

Tim Bobbin gives *um-be-thought,* as used in Lancashire, in the sense of remembered.—*Jamieson.*

Umgang, circuit, circumference.

Umgrip, to seize.

Umlap, to enfold.

Umset, to surround.

Umwhile, formerly, ci-devant.

Unbuxom, uncomely ; the reverse of buxom. Some lexicographers derive this word from the German *beugsam,* obedient, pliable ; and others from buck, a bosom, whence bucksome, having a large or full bosom, plump, hearty looking, comely.

> To storm and to scolde,
> Sclaunders to make,
> Both *unbuxome* and bolde.
>> *Piers Ploughman.*

Uncanny, unlucky. A word common in the North of England and Scotland.

> ' Captain !' said Dinmont in a half whisper, ' I wish she binna *uncanny.*'—*Scott : Guy Mannering.*

> I was, by this experience of his watchful Providence over this great cause, made hopeful he would not suffer it to be spoiled by the imprudence of many *uncanny* hands which are about it.
>> *Baillie's Letters.*

This Northern word seems to have been corrupted in the literature of the seventeenth century in England, to '*in-*

Uncanny—*continued.*

cony.' Nares was quite at a loss to understand this last word, and says that it means 'sweet, pretty, delicate,' and that the derivation is from the northern word 'canny,' in which he is right and that the 'in,' is intensive, and means *very* canny, in which he seems to be wrong. He cites the following examples :

> My sweet ounce of flesh, my *incony* hand.
>> *Shakspeare : Love's Labour Lost.*
> Love me little, love me long, let music rumble,
> While I in thy *incony* lap do tumble.
>> *Jew of Malta.*
> Farewell Dr. Doddy,
> In mind and in body,
> An excellent noddy,
> A coxcomb *incony.*
>> *Dr. Doddipol.*

Unchancy, bringing ill-luck.

> Down the gate, in faith they're worse,
> And mair *unchancy.*
>> *Robert Burns : Epistle to John Kennedy.*

Unchary, not careful, not chary.

> I have said too much unto a heart of stone,
> And laid mine honor too *unchary* on't.
>> *Shakspeare : Twelfth Night.*

Undergrub, to underdig or undermine. This is a purer compound than its modern synonyme, both words being English ; whereas, undermine is half English, half French.

Under-sort, the lower-class ; the mob, the vulgar.

Under-skinker, an under-waiter, or drawer.

> I give thee this pennyworth of sugar, clapped even now into my hand, by an *underskinker*, one that never spake other English in his life, than 'eight and sixpence,' or ' you are welcome.'
>> *Shakspeare : 1st part Henry VI.*

Under-wrought, undermined, underdug, or undergrubbed.

Uneared, unploughed, untilled ; uncultivated.

> In where is she so fair, whose *uneared* womb,
> Disdains the tillage of thy husbandry.
>> *Shakspeare's Sonnets.*

Unease, uneasiness, vexation, trouble.

> Shun thou the seas,
> Which breed *unease*, and quiet live on land.
>> *Kendall's Flowers of Epigrams,* 1577.

Uneath, uneasily.

> Uneath may she endure the flinty streets.
> > *Shakspeare: 2nd part of Henry VI.*

Uneith, scarcely, with difficulty.

> Whether 'twas day or night uneith wist we.
> > *Douglas: Eneid.*

Unfast, loose, unfastened.

Unfurthersome, a term applied in the North to unfavorable weather; that does not *further* or advance the ripening of the crops.

Ungentleman, a churl, a boor, a low person; one not a gentleman.

> A strict observance of the niceties of speech, was more important as an indication of breeding (in the fifteenth century), or in the words of Dame Juliana Berners (the reputed author of the Book of St. Albans), as a means of distinguishing 'gentylmen from *ungentylmen*,' than a rigorous conformity to the rules of grammar, or even to the moral law.—*Marsh's Lectures on the English Language.*

Unhale, not in a hale or hearty condition; sick, unwell.

Unheartsome, melancholy.

> It is an *unheartsome* thing to see our father and mother agree so ill.
> > *Rutherford's Letters.*

Unhearty, timid, listless; without zeal or heart.

Unhouselled, not having received the last sacrament; from housell, to receive the sacrament.

> A priest, a priest, says Aldingar,
> Me for to *housle* and shrive.
> > *Percy's Reliques, Sir Aldinger.*

> Cut off even in the blossom of my sin.
> *Unhousell'd.*
> > *Shakspeare: Hamlet.*

Unleal, disloyal, dishonest.

Unlifty, not to be easily lifted; unwieldy.

Unloveable, ⎱
Unlovesome, ⎰ unamiable.

Unsneck, to draw the sneck, latch, or bolt of a door.

> Tip-toe she tripped it o'er the floor,
> She drew the bar, *unsneck'd* the door.
> > *Jamieson's Popular Ballads.*

Unsnod, rough, not smooth, in disorder.

> My claes aye *unsnod*,
> And my face seldom clean.
> > *Hector MacNeil.*

Unsonsy, unfortunate.

Unsodden, unboiled.

Untholeable, intolerable; not to be *tholed* or endured.

Untrowable, incredible, not to be *trowed* or believed.

Unwinnable, impregnable.

> This crag, *unwynnable* by ingine of man.
> > *Boethius.*

Unwinsome, not or engaging in manners; ugly, affected.

Unwit, ignorance, folly, want of sense.

Unwroken, unavenged.

> *Unwroken* shall we die?
> > *Douglas : Eneid.*

pgang, an ascent, an acclivity.

Uphoven, past participle of *upheave.*

This word occurs in Wicliffe's translation of the Bible, and merits re-introduction, as not only more correct, but more easily pronounceable, than upheaved.

Upstir, to rouse, to excite.

Upstirring, an excitement or insurrection of the people.

Ure, chance, fate, fortune.   From the French heur or heure, a word now only used with the adjectives ' bon ' and ' mal,' to signify good and evil fortune.

> Drive the thing right to the end,
> And take the *ure* that God will send.
> > *Barbour.*

Urf, a stunted, ill-grown child, nearly synonymous with *urk.*

> Ye useless weasel like *urf*, that ye are.
> > *Hogg, The Brownie of Bodsbeck.*

Urk, a small, undergrown child ; whence the diminutive *urchin.*

Vade, to fade quickly, to go to death or decay; possibly of Latin derivation. This word is not exactly synonymous with fade, as appears from its use by Shakspeare and other writers who employ both *vade* and *fade* in the same sentence.

> Sweet rose, fair flower, untimely pluck'd, soon *vaded*.
> Pluck'd in the bud; and faded in the spring.
> *Shakspeare: Sonnets.*

> Beauty is but a vain and doubtful good,
> A shining gloss that *vadeth* suddenly;
> *   *   *   *   *
> A doubtful good, a gloss, a glass, a flower,
> Lost, broken, *vaded*, dead within an hour.
> *Idem.*

> No fading, *vading* flower.
> *Brathwait, Strappado for the Devil,* 1615.

Vady, damp, musty; decaying.

Vap, vapidity, refuse, dregs.

> In vain it is to wash a goblet, if you mean to put nothing into it, but the dead lees and *vap* of wine.
> *Bishop Taylor.*

Veck, an old woman; from the Italian, *vecchia.*

> Which hath ordained Jealousie,
> Yon olde *Veck*, for to espie
> The manner of his governance.
> *Chaucer: The Romance of the Rose.*

Venn, slush, mud.

Vennel, a gutter to carry off the slush.

Both of these words are used in the North, but have disappeared from Southern English.

> Trailing on the *venne*.
> *MS. Lansdowne, (Halliwell.)*

Vinewed, mouldy.

> Many of Chaucer's words are become, as it were, *vinewed* and hoarie with over long lying.—*Beaumont : Letter to Speght*, 1602.

The word blue *vinewed*, or blue mouldy, is still current in the south of England.

Virelai,
Virelay, } a round, a catch, a rondeau ; from *virer*, to turn.

> Ballads, *virelays*, and verses vain.
> > *Spenser : Faerie Queene.*
>
> Then slumber not with dull Endymion,
> But tune thy reed to dapper *virelays*.
> > *Drayton : Polyolbion.*

Virr,
Bir, } force, impetus. A man without strength of mind or purpose, is said in the Border Counties and in Scotland, to have no *bir* in him.

> The lads unwilling yet to stir,
> Fire off their monny guns in *virr*.
> > *Beattie's Tales.*
>
> Wi' double *virr* the drummers drum.
> > *Mayne's Siller Gun.*
>
> Come life, come death, I'll fight with all my *bir*.
> > *Hamilton's Wallace.*

V oth, outlawry.

> *Voth* signifies outlawry ;—*utlagium.*
> > *Skene.*

Vothman, an outlaw.—*Jamieson.*

Wad, straw, or a bundle of straw; whence *wadding*, to signify a stuffing with straw; whence also the title of the old song, 'Moll in the Wad,' i.e., Moll in the straw, after childbirth.

> Moll in the *wad* and I fell out.
> I'll tell you what 'twas all about :
> She had money, and I had none,
> That's the way the row begun.
> *Old Song.*

A wispe of rushes, or any *wad* of hay that's next to hand, they'll steal.—*Taylor, The Water Poet.*

Wad,) a wager, a bet, a pledge; from whence a wedding, or
Wed,) pledging of faith at the altar; and also wad-set, a mortgage.

Wadder, a man who makes bets.

> There is no leech in all this land,
> Can put a finger to a hand,
> The finger that he left in *wed.*
> *Sir Eger, Sir Grahame, and Sir Gray Steel.*

> Wishers and *wadders*,
> Were never good househadders.

A *wad* is a fool's argument.

If *wads* were horses, beggars would ride.
> *Allan Ramsay's Scotch Proverbs.*

> What will you wager, Wise William ?
> My lands I'll *wad* with thee.
>   *   *   *   *
> I'll *wad* my head against your land
> Till I get more monie.
> *Redisdale and Wise William ; Motherwell's Ancient Minstrelsy.*

Waft, to beckon; to make a wavy motion with the hand. A word obsolete in this sense; and now employed to signify the action of the wind in impelling a ship to its destination.

> But, soft, who *wafts* us yonder?
> *Shakspeare : Comedy of Errors.*

Waft—*continued.*

> A flag, *wafting* us back again.
> > *Hackluyt.*

This word appears to have sometimes been written *weft*, preterite of *waft;* as in the following passage from Robinson Crusoe:

> She gave three *wefts* with her ancient.

Wafter, a frigate or man-of war that conducts merchant ships to port.—*Blount's Glossographia*, 1681.

Wafture, a signal, a beckoning motion of the hand, from waft.

> But with an angry *wafture* of your hand,
> Gave sign for me to leave you.
> > *Shakspeare : Julius Cæsar.*

Wain, a farmer's waggon.

Wair, to lay out, to expend judiciously.

> The best o' chiels are whiles in want,
> While coofs on countless thousands rant,
> And ken na how to *wair* it.
> > *Burns : Epistle to Davie a brother poet.*

Waits, haut-boy players; musicians generally.

Wale, to choose, to select; from the Anglo-Saxon and German, one of the oldest words in the English Language.

> Then *wale* a virgin, worthy you,
> Worthy your love and martial vow.
> > *Allan Ramsay : Epistle to Robert Yarde of Devonshire.*

> He *wales* a portion wi' judicious care.
> > *Burns: Cotter's Saturday Night.*

> I'd hang you up in good green wood,
> And cause your own hand *wale* the tree.
> > *John Thomson and the Turk.*

> Then o'er again the jovial throng,
> The poet did request,
> To loose his pack, and *wale* as gay
> A ballad as the best.
> > *Burns : The Jolly Beggars.*

Wale, choice; the best of anything.

> There's auld Bob Morris that wons in yon glen,
> The *wale* of good fellows.
> > *Burns.*

> Supple scones, the *wale* o' food.
> > *Burns.*

Walie, } choice.
Waly, }

> There was a winsome wench and *walie*.
> > *Burns : Tam o' Shanter.*
>
> This *waly* boy will be no coof (fool),
> I think we'll ca' him Robin.
> > *Burns.*

Waly, woefully, alas! An exclamation of sorrow.

> Oh *waly ! waly !* up the bank,
> And *waly ! waly !* down the brae.
> > *Percy's Reliques of Ancient English Poetry.*

Wallow, } flat, insipid, tasteless.
Wallowish, }

Wame, the belly. This word, general in Scotland, is used in the Northern Counties of England, as far south as Yorkshire.

Wanchance, misfortune.

Wanchancie, unlucky.

> Woe unto the man who first did shape,
> That vile *wanchancie* thing, a rape.
> > *Burns : Poor Mailie's Elegy.*

Wandle, pliant, nimble.

Wandought, impotence, a silly weak person, wanting strength or doughtiness.

Wandoughty, impotent.

Wandream, } the nightmare.
Wandreme, }

Wandreth, poverty, sorrow.

> The sixth virtue is strength or stalworthiness, not only of body but of heart, to suffer the weal and the woe, wealth or *wandreth*, whichever betide.—*MS. Lincoln, (quoted by Mr. Halliwell, the orthography modernized.)*

Wang, the cheek. In Leicestershire, says Mr. Halliwell, ' *wang*' means a blow on the cheek.

Wanhope, the waning and disappearance of hope preparatory to despair. This word seems to have been derived from the Dutch and Flemish, and not from the Anglo Saxon. The Dutch word for despair is *wanhoop*, or the waning of hope. Chaucer uses both despair and *wanhope* in the same

Wanhope—*continued.*

sentence in the Knighte's Tale; as if the words were not synonymous:

> That I am exiled and barreine,
> Of all grace, and in so great *despaire*;
>
> *   *   *   *   *
>
> Will ought I sterve in *wanhope* and distresse;
> Farewell my life, my lust, and my gladnesse.

> Good men I warne alle,
> That ye in no *wanhope* falle.
> > *MS. Cantab., quoted by Halliwell.*

> Good hope that helpe should,
> To *wanhope* turneth.
> > *Piers Ploughman.*

> Furie and rage, *wanhope,* despair, and woe.
> > *Lodge: Glaucis and Lilla.*

> *Wanhope* poor soul on broken anchor sits,
> Wringing his arms as wanting of his wits.
> > *Idem.*

This word, and several others equally beautiful, have survived in Scotland, and in the Border Counties of England. 'It was in use,' says Dean Trench, in his Lectures on 'English Past and Present,' 'down to the reign of Elizabeth; and was the latest survivor of a whole family or group of words, which continued much longer in Scotland than with us.'

Wanhap, } mischance, misfortune.
Wanluck, }

Wank, preterite of wink.

> Our king on the shepherd *wank*
> Privily with his eye.
> > *MS. Cantab., Halliwell.*

Wanlust, indifference, satiety; the waning away of lust, list, or pleasure.

Wanlusty, indifferently.

Wanrestful, restless, wanting rest.

> And may they never learn the gates,
> Of ither vile *wanrestfu'* pets.
> > *Burns: The Death and Dying Words of Poor Mailie.*

Wanthrift, prodigality.

Wantsome, deficient.

Wantrust, jealousy, suspicion; *waning* or dwindling of trust and belief.

> Oh, *wantrust*, full of false suspicion!
> Where was thy wit and thy discretion?
> *Chaucer: The Manciple's Tale.*

Wantrustful,
Wantrusty, } jealous, suspicious.

Wap,
Whap, } a blow; also to strike, or to beat. This word finds
Whop, } no place in Richardson, but Johnson defines 'whap,' to be a blow, and calls it 'a low' expression. Doubtless it has long been left to schoolboys, and to illiterate people, but it is, nevertheless, of respectable parentage, and from the same root as *weapon*, that with which a blow is struck, the German *wappen*, arms; and the old English and Scottish *weaponshaw* and *wappinshaw*, a tournament or exhibition of arms. In Scottish poetry, '*wap*' sometimes means to throw. Chaucer has '*waped*,' in the sense of astonished; and Spenser *whape*, in the sense of to shock, or deject. Shakspeare in Timon of Athens, speaking of the power of gold; says:

> This it is
> That makes the *wappened* widow wed again.

Much controversy has arisen about the meaning of this word. Nares imagines it to signify 'worn or weakened,' but it is more probable that it is derived from to *whap*, to beat; and that the passage means, a widow *beaten* by sorrow, 'bruised and buffeted by the storms of fate.'

The intensitive or augmentative of this word, with the prefix *a*; and defined by Mr. Wright, in his Provincial Dictionary, as meaning, to confound, to stupefy with fear, occurs in Spenser:

> A wild and salvage man:
> Yet was no man, but only like in shape,
> And eke in stature higher by a span,
> All over-grown with hair that could *awhape*
> An hardy heart.
> *Spenser: Faerie Queen.*

War-gear, accoutrements of war.

Warp, preterite of *werp*, to throw; whence wharf, a place where goods are thrown, and moudie-*warp*, a mole, the *mould thrower*.

> And *warp* off his weeds; i.e., cast off his clothes.
> *Morte Arthur.*

Warth, } the sea-shore; also, a ford over a river.
Wath, }

Warthstead, } the fording place; often erroneously written
Wathstead, } and pronounced *warstead*.

Wasterne, } a desert, a waste place.
Wasteyn, }

> Walked in that *wasterne.*
> *Morte Arthur.*

> In a *wasteyne* far fro' the towne.
> *MS. Harl., (Halliwell.)*

Wastrel, one who wastes his means; an extravagant or profligate person; any waste, or imperfect article in manufacture.

Wasty, consumptive, wasting away.

Wat, preterite of wet.

> O sighing, said, the lady fair,
> I've *wat* my gowden girdle.
> *The Water o' Wearie's Well.*

> And when of me his leave he took,
> The tears they *wat* mine e'e.
> *Gilderoy.*

> Laith, laith, were the good Scots' lords,
> To wet their cork heeled shoon,
> But long ere all the play was played,
> They *wat* their hats aboon.
> *Sir Patrick Spens.*

Watershed, the pent and flow of the water from the higher to the lower lands.

Waterstead, the place, ordinary channel or bed of a river, a smaller stream.

Wathe, injury, severity.

> Woe and *wathe* between them wake.
> *Wright's Provincial Glossary.*

Wathely, severely.

Wax, } to grow.
Wox, } grew.
Woxen, } grown.

The preterite and past participle of *wax*, to grow, have long been obsolete; and 'wax,' as the infinitive, or in the present tense, is only familiar from its occurrence in the Bible.

> Before my breath, like blazing flax,
> Man and his marvels pass away,
> And changing empires wane and *wax*,
> Are founded, flourish, and decay.
> > *Sir Walter Scott.*

> Now they *wax*, and now they dwindle.
> > *Sir Walter Scott's Song of Meg Merrilies.*

Weald, from the German wald, a forest.

Wedbreach, adultery.

Wedbreaker, an adulterer.—*Wicliffe's Bible.*

Wedfellow, a spouse; applied either to husband or wife.

Wee, little, diminutive. The word ' *wee*,' as used by the Scotch implies extreme littleness, and is always employed to express some degree of affection; little dog, and *wee* dog, do not convey the same idea.

Shakspeare in the Merry Wives of Windsor, makes Simple say of Dr. Caius:

> He hath but a little *wee* face, and a little yellow beard ;

thereby implying that the face was something else than little, that it was *wee ;* i.e., very little.

> A *wee* spark, makes meikle wark.

> A *wee* mouse can creep under a great corn stack.
> > *Allan Ramsay's Scotch Proverbs.*

As a diminutive, the word is commonly used in the best colloquial English, 'my little wee daughter,' a 'bonnie wee book,' &c. The following verses are current on both sides of the Tweed:

> A *wee* house well filled,
> A *wee* farm well tilled,
> A *wee* wife well willed,
> > Make a happy man.

Weed, dress, raiment. This word in the singular, has disappeared from literature as well as from ordinary speech, and is only used in the plural to express the very ungraceful head-dress of a widow. In ancient poetry it occurs frequently, both in the singular and in the plural.

> Shining Pallas, all in warlike *weed*.
>> *Earl of Surrey : Translation of the Eneid.*

> Hast thou given him at his nede,
> Mete and drinke, clothe and *wede*.
>> *MS. Cotton. (Halliwell).*

> Putting on both shirt and *weed*.
>> *Chapman's Homer.*

> The knight was lopen on his steed,
> And armed well in iron *weed*.
>> *Metrical Romance of the Seven Wise Masters.*

> It was a friar of orders grey,
>> Went forth to tell his beades,
> And he met with a lady faire,
>> Clad in a pilgrim's *weeds*.
>> *The Friar of Orders Grey, in Percy's Relics.*

> Let fair humanity abhor the deed,
> That spots and stains love's modest snow white *weed*.
>> *Shakspeare : Rape of Lucrece.*

> Such *weeds* as may beseem,
> Some well appointed page.
>> *Shakspeare : Two Gentlemen of Verona.*

> Throngs of knights, and barons bold,
> In *weeds* of peace.
>> *Milton : L'Allegro.*

> Take off, take off, these bridal *weeds*,
> And crown my waeful head wi' willow.
>> *The Braes of Yarrow.*

> Princely is my lover's *weed*,
> Bonnie laddie, highland laddie,
>> *Jacobite Ballad,* 1745.

> Those whom chance may hither lead,
> Be thou clad in russet *weed ;*
> Be thou deck'd in silken stole,
> Grave these maxims on thy soul.
>> *Lines written in Friar's Carse Hermitage on the Banks of the Nith, by Burns.*

> From thee doff the mortal *weed*.
>> *Sir Walter Scott : Song of Meg Merrilies.*

Ween, to think, to imagine ; a word not quite obsolete, but only used in poetic composition, and in mock heroics.

Weft, a waif ; something lost, gone astray, or abandoned.

> The gentle lady loose at random left,
> The greenwood long did walk and wander wide,
> At wild adventure, like a forlorne *weft*.
> > *Spenser : Faerie Queen.*

> For we, the *wefts* and pilgrims of the streams,
> Are only born to sorrow and distress.
> > *Fanshawe's Lusiad.*

Weird, *n.* fortune, fate, destiny.

Weird, *adj.* witch-like ; fated.

> And sayeth it were a wondrous *weirde*,
> To see a kyng become a herde.
> > *Gower MS., Soc. Antiq.*

> The *weird* sisters, hand in hand,
> Posters of the sea and land.
> > *Shakspeare : Macbeth.*

> Thane of Cawdor ! by which title these *weird* sisters saluted me.
> > *Idem.*

> A man may woo where he will ; but wed where his *weird* is.
> > *Allan Ramsay's Scotch Proverbs.*

> She is a wise wife that knows her ain *weird*.
> > *Scotch Proverb.*

> Betide me weal, betide me woe,
> That *weird* shall never daunton me,
> > *Ballad of True Thomas.*

> To the *weird* lady of the woods,
> Full many and long a day,
> Through lonely shades and thickets rough,
> He wends his weary way.
> > *Percy's Reliques.*

> The *weird* her dearest bairn befell,
> By the bonnie mill dams o' Binnorie.
> > *Minstrelsy of the Scottish Border.*

> When we sat by her flickering fire at night, she was most *weird*.
> > *Charles Dickens : Great Expectations.*

Weise, } to direct, to train, to conduct.
Wysse, }

> Lord King, she said of Heaven's blys,
> This day thou me rede and *wysse*.
> > *MS. Cantab. (Halliwell.)*

> Every miller would *weise* to water to his ain mill.
> > *Scotch Proverb.*

Weld,
Welden, } to hold, to possess, to wield, to rule, to govern.

> And he no money *weldeth.*
> > *Piers Ploughman.*
> He had no heir his landes to *weld.*
> > *MS. Cantab., (Wright's Provincial Glossary.*

Welder, a ruler, a governor.

All-welder, the Almighty Ruler.

> I pray to God, *all-weldand.*
> > *Ywaine and Gawin, (Wright's Provincial Glossary.)*

Welful, productive of happiness.

> Unto the cross of Christe thus said she,
> O dere! O *wealful!* * * * holy cross!
> > *Chaucer: The Man of Lawe's Tale.*

Welfulness, health, happiness, prosperity.

Welkin, the sky; from the German wölken, the clouds.

> Amaze the *welkin* with your broken staves.
> > *Shakspeare.*

Well-will, benevolence.

Welwilly, benevolent.

Well-willer, a benevolent person.

Well-willing, benevolent.

> They came in a loving and *well-willing* manner to enquire.
> > *Melville, MS. (Jamieson.)*

Ill-will, malevolence.

Ill-willer, a malevolent person.

Ill-willy, malevolent.

Of this group of words, ill-will, is the only one that has remained in current use, or that has been admitted into literature. The rest have perished without offence, to make room for Latin synonymes, that are neither as beautiful nor as expressive.

> Venus, I mean, the *welwilly* planete.
> > *Chaucer: Troilus and Cressida.*
> To themselves, *well willers.*
> > *Hooker.*

Well-willy—*continued.*

> The calves and kye met in the loan,
> The man ran with ane rung to red,
> Then there comes ane *ill-willy* cow.
>> *The wife of Auchtermuchty, from the Hyndford MS., Lord*
>> *Hailes's Edition, quoted in Ritson's Caledonian Muse.*

Welly,
Wellnigh, } nearly, or very nearly.

> Our Joseph's *welly* blind, poor lad.
>> *Waugh's Lancashire Songs.*

> Tummus, I *welly* lost my mind.
>> *Tim Bobbin,* 1803.

Went, to dwindle, pine, fade away.

Wint, preterite of went, to fade.

> It *wint,* and went away anon.
>> *MS. Digby, Wright's Provincial Glossary.*

Wern, to refuse, to deny.

> That is mete when men hym *werneth,*
> And he no money weldeth.
>> *Piers Ploughman.*

Werp, to throw, to cast.

Wersh,
Werish, } insipid, unsavory, tasteless.

> Her pleasures *werish,* and her amours tasteless.
>> *Translation of Montaigne,* 1613.

> *Weryshe* as meat is that is not well tasted.
>> *Palsgrave.*

> Helicon's *wersh* well.
>> *Allan Ramsay.*

> A kiss and a drink of water, are but a *wersh* breakfast.
>> *Scotch Proverb.*

In Brockett's Glossary of North Country Words, (1825,) this word appears in the corrupted form of *welsh.* Broth and pottage without salt, are said to be *welsh* ; but *wersh* is evidently the proper spelling.

Westlins, from the west.

> Now frae th' east neuk o' Fife the dawn,
> Speel'd *westlins* up the lift.
>> *Allan Ramsay : Christ's Kirk on the Green.*

Weth,
Weeth, } soft, mild. . Mr. Halliwell says this word is used in the Isle of Wight ; and Mr. Barnes quotes it in the sense of pliant, in his 'Roots and Stems of the English as a Teutonic tongue.'

Wevin, a moment; from the Anglo-Saxon, wiffend, a breathing; whence also a *whiff* or breath.

Whang, a large cut or slice; whence *whanger*, one who takes a large cut, slice, or piece; and whence again, the American phrase, a *slang whanger*, a very vulgar, violent person, using slang words in excess.

> Ye cut large *whangs* out of other folk's leather.
> > *Allan Ramsay's Scotch Proverbs.*

> He's ta'en four-and-twenty broad arrows,
> And laced them in a *whang*.
> > *Sweet Willie and Lady Margaret.*

Whaup, a curlew.

> The wild land fowls are plovers, pigeons, curlews, commonly called *whaups.*—*Statistical Account of Scotland ; article, Orkney.*

Wheeple, the cheep or low cry of a bird; also metaphorically, the ineffectual attempt of a man to whistle loudly.

> A Scottish gentleman, who visited England for the first time, and ardently desired to return home to his native hills and moors, was asked by his English host to come out into the garden at night to hear the song of the nightingale, a bird unknown in Scotland. His mind was full of home, and he exclaimed, 'Na! na! I wadna gie the *wheeple* of a whaup (curlew) for a' the nightingales that ever sang.'
> > *Statistical Account of Scotland.*

Whelm, to turn. ' Overwhelm,' is still current, but ' whelm,' is nearly obsolete.

> 'Till billows gape and gales blow hard,
> And *whelm* him o'er.
> > *Burns : To a Mountain Daisy.*

Whiffler, a fifer, or flute-player; from *whiff*, a breath of wind; also a trumpeter; going foremost in a procession, to prepare the way for a king, or great personage.

> Which like a mighty *whiffler* 'fore the king,
> Seems to prepare his way.
> > *Shakspeare : Henry V.*

> But as a poet that's no scholar makes
> Vulgarity his *whiffler*, and so takes
> Passage with ease and state.
> > *Chapman's Homer.*

Whiles, sometimes. This word survives in Scottish speech and literature; but has disappeared from English. Shakspeare uses it in the sense of while, and until.

Whingle, to complain.

> What thou 'rt in love; and *whinglin ?*
> *Cumberland Ballads.*

Whirr, to fly from the ground in affright, and with a loud noise; like a partridge or pheasant. The word is common throughout England and Scotland, though not admitted to the honors of English literature.

> The moorcock springs on *whirring* wings,
> Among the blooming heather.
> *Robert Burns.*

Whish,) silence, or to keep silence; whence the name of the
Whist,) well-known game at cards.

> The other nipt so nigh,
> That *whist* I could not.
> *Sackville : Mirror for Magistrates.*
>
> They *whisted* all with fixed face attent.
> *Surrey's Translation of the Eneid.*
>
> The winds with wonder *whist,*
> Smoothly the waters kiss'd.
> *Milton.*
>
> Hand your *whish,* (i.e., keep silence, or hold your tongue.)
> *Scott : Rob Roy.*

Wishness,) silence.
Wistness,)

Whittle, a pocket or sheath-knife.

> For their knives, care not,
> While ye have throats to answer ; for myself,
> There's not a *whittle* in the unruly camp,
> But I do prize it at my love, before
> The reverend'st throat in Athens.
> *Shakspeare : Timon of Athens.*
>
> Never want a good *whittle* at your belt.
> *Allan Ramsay's Scot's Proverbs.*

In Burns's poem of Death and Dr. Hornbook, Death advises the poet, alarmed at his sudden apparition :

> To put up his *whittle.*

In his Fragment on the American War, the same poet says that Caledonia

> Threw by the drone,
> And did her *whittle* draw man.

Whittle—*continued.*

' The word, as well as the practice of *whittling,* (cutting a stick for amusement,)' says Bartlett, in his Dictionary of Americanisms, ' is so much more common with us, especially in New England, than it is in the old country, that its use may not improperly be regarded as an Americanism.'

> Americans must and will *whittle.*
> *N. P. Willis.*

> No matter where his home may be,
>   What flag may be unfurl'd,
> He'll manage by some 'cute devise,
>   To *whittle* through the world.

Whitster, a laundress ; a bleacher or washer of linen, a person who makes wearing apparel *white,* a *blanchisseuse.*

> Carry it among the *whitsters* in Datchet Mead, and there empty it in the muddy ditch close by the Thames' side.
> *Shakspeare : Merry Wives of Windsor.*

Whommle, to turn over clumsily and suddenly, and with a loud noise.

> Coming to the fire, with the said pan and water therein, and casting the water thereupon, and *whommeling* the pan upon the fire with the pronouncing of these fearful words : ' Bones to the fire, and soul to the devil,' which accomplished the cure.
> *Trial of Alieson Nisbet for Witchcraft,* **1632.**

Whuffle, to doubt.

Whuffler, a doubter ; from the German *zweifeln* and *zweifler.*

In some parliamentary boroughs in the North of England, a *whuffler* is one who will not promise his vote, because he expects a bribe, if he will only remain in doubt until a few minutes before the close of the poll.

Wicker, a twig. This word, as a noun, has lost, except in the North of England and Scotland, its original meaning of twig, but survives as an adjective, in *wicker*-work, and *wicker*-basket.

> As with the wind, waves the *wicker,*
> So waves this world's vanitie.
> *Bannatyne's Poems.*

> Waving like the willow-*wicker.*
> *Burns.*

Widder, } contrary.
Wither, }

Widder-guess, } a guess in the wrong direction.
Wither-guess, }

Widdershins, } in a direction contrary to the course of the
Withershins, } sun. 'To pass the bottle *withershins ;*' i.e. in
the wrong direction.

> The said Alieson past thrice *withershins* about the bed, muttering
> out certain charms in unknown words.
>
> *Trial of Alieson Nisbet for Witchcraft,* 1632.

Widderly, } contrary.
Witherly, }

Widderwin, } an enemy.
Witherwin, }

Wight, brave, a brave man.

Wightly, bravely.

It would have been strange indeed, if the Anglo-Saxons
had not had a word in their language to express bravery and
courage, without going to the Norman French to borrow it.
Brave is a word of comparatively recent introduction. The
ancient word *wight*, now used in literature as a substantive,
is still current as an adjective in the North of England and
in Scotland.

'A *wight* man never wanted a weapon,' says the Scotch
Proverb. 'He is as *wight*,' says another, 'as a weaver's
doublet that every day takes a thief by the neck.'

The word occurs in the Metrical Romance of Merlin,
where the young Arthur is described as

> Curteus, faire, and gent,
> And *wight*, and hardy, verament.

In the same poem the word is applied to war-horses going
into battle:

> The stedes so noble and so *wight*,
> Lopen and neighed.

In the 'King's Quair,' written by James I. of Scotland
during his captivity in Windsor Castle, and in the choicest
English of the time—that of Chaucer—he bewails that he
has none to love him, and that he is more unhappy than the
birds:

Wight—*continued.*

> For if he (love) be of so great excellence,
> That he of every *wight* hath cures and charge,
> What have I gilt to him a dire offence,
> That I am thrall and birdis gone at large.

The 'Wallace Wight,' is a title of nobility given by the people of Scotland to their favourite hero. But in England the adjective has become quite obsolete, and the substantive is only used in mock heroics.

Wilding, a wild flower or fruit.

Wilt, to wither and shrivel up. This word common in Lincolnshire and in Kent has been carried by English emigrants to the United States, where it has taken root and flourished to such an extent as almost to have superseded its synonyme wither. Neither Johnson nor Richardson admits it to the honours of the language, but Webster, who denies that it is synonymous with wither, declares it to be a legitimate word for which there is no substitute in the language, and defines it to mean, 'to begin to wither, to lose freshness, and become flaccid as a plant when exposed to great heat in a dry day.' 'A *wilted* plant,' he says, 'often revives and becomes fresh ; not so a *withered* plant.' He quotes as an instance of its use, a sentence from Dwight's Theology :

> Despots have *wilted* the human race into sloth and imbecility.

In Bartlett's Dictionary of Americanisms, it is said, that to *wilt down,* means to look sheepish ; and the author quotes Robb's Squatter Life :

> Some cotton fellow bid sixty dollars for the slave ; and she *wilted* right down.

In Sternberg's Northamptonshire Glossary, *wilt* or *wilter,* is defined as meaning to wither or dry up. The corrupt form of the preterite, used in the same county, is *wilkt.*

Wimble, to shift to and fro.

Wimple, to wind or meander like a brook or river ; to hang in folds, like a drooping flag or pendant.

> When *wimpling* waters make their way.
> *Allan Ramsay.*

Wimple—*continued.*

> Whiles owre the linn the burnie plays,
> As through the glen it *wimplet.*
>> *Burns : Halloween.*

> Ye hazel shaws, and briery dens,
> Ye burnies *wimpling* down the glens.
>> *Burns : On Captain Matthew Henderson.*

Wimple, a veil.

> And as she ran her *wimple* let she fall,
> And took more hede.
>> *Chaucer : Legend of Tisbe of Babylon.*

Windle, to turn in the wind, like a leaf; or to drift before the wind like snow, sleet, or rain.

Windling, a branch blown down by the wind.

> He starts at straws, and lets the *windlings* go.
>> *Northern Proverb.*

Winly, pleasantly, winsomely.—*Halliwell.*

Winsel, an unexpected profit, winning, or turn of luck ; a term of endearment to a bride ; or a child, implying something that is won and highly thought of.

Wishworthy, desirable.

Wis, to know.

Wist, known.

> I *wis* your grandam had a worser match.
>> *Shakspeare.*

> But had I *wist* before I kissed.
> That love had been so ill to win.
>> *Lady Anne Bothwell's Lament.*

Wit, knowledge ; whence mother*wit,* natural or common sense.

Witch-thimble, the popular name in the North for the fox-glove, or digitalis purpurea. This word helps to prove that fox-glove, as has been supposed, is a corruption or perversion of *folk's*-glove ; i.e., the glove of the fairies, popularly called the 'folk.'

Witcraft, logic, argumentation.

Witterly, consciously, truly.

> No man, as I leeve,
> Should ever wit *witterly*,
> What day was to mean.
> *Piers Ploughman.*

Within-forth, in doors, at home.—(*Wycliffe's Bible.*) *Scottice ben*, or be in.

Without-forth, out of doors, not at home. *Scottice but*, or be out.

Withy, a tree of which the branches and twigs can be made easily into *withes ;* a willow, a sallow.

Witnessfully, evidently ; that which can be fully proved by many witnesses.

Wittal, ⎫ from ' wit all,' or know all; the husband of an un-
Wittol, ⎭ faithful wife, who knows all his wife's shame, and his own dishonour.

> Cuckold ! *wittol* cuckold !
> The devil himself hath not such a name !
> *Shakspeare : Merry Wives of Windsor.*

Wive, to marry. This word is not quite obsolete ; ' Wive and thrive,' is a common colloquialism.

> Her whom the first man did *wive.*
> *Donne's Satires.*

Wode, ⎫
Wood, ⎬ mad, furious, wild, from the German *wuth.*
Wud, ⎭

The old Saxon English, as preserved in the Lowlands of Scotland, and the English Border Counties, was particuarly rich in words expressive of the various shades and degrees of madness and lunacy. Wowf, wud, daft, and doited, still remain in Scottish parlance, while the English retains mad, silly, crazy, cracked, moonstruck.

> Well loved he garlick, onions, and lekes,
> And for to drink, strong wine as red as blood,
> Then would he speke, and cry as he were *wode,*
> And when that he had drunken wel the wine,
> Then would he speken no word but Latine.
> *Chaucer : Prologue to the Canterbury Tales.*

Wode—*continued.*

> On Monday next at quarter night,
> Shall fall a rain, and that so wild and *wud*,
> That half so great was never Noe's flood.
> > *Chaucer : The Miller's Tale.*

> And here am I and *wode* within this wood.
> > *Shakspeare : Midsummer Night's Dream.*

> Life poisoning pestilence and frenzies *wud*,
> The marrow eating sickness, whose attaint
> Disorder breeds by heating of the blood.
> > *Shakspeare : Venus and Adonis.*

> Ance *wode*, aye waur.
> > *Allan Ramsay's Scotch Proverbs.*

> Oppression will drive a wise man *wode*.
> > *Northern Proverb.*

> When neighbours anger at a plea,
> And just as *wud* as *wud* can be,
> How easy can the barley bree,
> > Cement the quarrel,
> It's aye the cheapest lawyer's fee,
> > To taste the barrel.
> > *Burns : Scotch Drink.*

> We shall be married on Monday,
> > And will not that be good ?
> What, shall we be married no sooner ?
> > Why sure the man's gone *woode.*
> > *Nursery Rhymes of England, by J. O. Halliwell.*

Wode, to grow mad.

> He stareth and *wodeth.*
> > *Chaucer : The Second Nonnes' Tale.*

Wodeness, }
Woodness, } madness.

> *Wodenes* laughing in his rage.
> > *Chaucer.*

Wofare, sorrow ; the opposite of welfare.

Wold, an open country, whether hill or plain, without wood.

> St. Withold footed thrice the *wold*,
> He met the night-mare and her nine foals.
> > *Shakspeare : King Lear.*

Won,   to dwell, inhabit ; whence the modern word 'wont,'
Wone,   'a person's *wont*, usage, or habit ;' from the German,
Wonen,   *wohnen.*

> Antony and Egidie,
> And other holy fadres,
> *Woneden* in wilderness,
> Among wild beastes.
> > *Piers Ploughman.*

> Merrie it is in time of June.
> > *   *   *   *   *

> Violet and rose flower,
> *Wonneth* then in maiden's bower,
> The sun is hot, the day is long.
> > *Metrical Romance of Merlin.*

> A sturdy pas down to the court he goth,
> Whereas there *won'd* a man of great honour,
> To whom that he was always confessour.
> > *Chaucer: The Sompnoure's Tale.*

> Not far away, quothe he, he hence doth *wonne.*
> > *Spenser: Faerie Queene.*

> A people near the northern pole that *wonne.*
> > *Fairfax: Tasso.*

> There's auld Rob Morris that *wons* in yon glen,
> The king of good fellows.
> > *Robert Burns.*

Woning, a dwelling.

> Tell me, sir, what is thy name, and where thy *woning* is.
> > *MS. Cantab, Halliwell.*

Wontless, without wont, unaccustomed.

> What *wontless* courage dost thou still inspire.
> > *Spenser: Faerie Queene.*

Wood-ward, a forester, warder, or keeper of a wood.

Woodweel, the woodpecker.

Woolsted, corrupted into the modern word, *worsted*, made of wool.

Wordfast, true to one's word. An excellent form of speech, packing in the shortest compass, the proverb that, ' his word is as good as his bond.'

Wordridden, to be a slave to words without understanding their meaning; to be overawed by a word rather than an argument ; like the fishwife of the story, who allowed Daniel O'Connell to call her a thief, a liar, and a prostitute, but who would not submit to be called ' a parallelogram.'

Wordridden—*continued.*

A member of Parliament, an illiterate but enterprising man, started a daily newspaper in London. It was not successful at first ; few such enterprises are. He speedily lost courage, cursed the public, himself, and his editor. Desirous of fixing a quarrel on the latter, and having no real cause, he suddenly pounced upon the word ' *bureaucracy,*' which appeared very frequently in the leading articles. He made notes of the times in which the word was used; and found it in no less than eleven instances in one week. Walking up to the Editor's room in a towering passion he pointed out the peccant word. ' Bureaucracy, sir, bureaucracy, *that* is the word which has ruined the paper. That word is the death of it. I shall carry it on no longer. The thing shall stop next Saturday.' And the M.P. was as good—or bad —as his threat, and the paper came to a sudden and ignominious end, after an existence of three months.

Word-wanton, obscene in speech.

Word-wantonly, obscenely.

Word-wantonness, obscenity of conversation.

Worksome, active, laborious, industrious.

Worksomeness, activity, laboriousness.

Worm, a serpent.

> With the grace of God Almighty,
> With the *worm* yet shall I fight.
> *Halliwell.*

> The venom'd *worm*
> Had belched his poison out.
> *Turberville,* 1587.

Worrysome, exasperating, irritating, troublesome, annoying.

Worsen, to grow worse, to make worse.

Wort, a root or herb ; from the German *wurz.*

Wortle, a little root.

These words have almost disappeared from the language, except in combination. Mr. Halliwell defines 'wort' as meaning a vegetable or a cabbage ; but the signification is wider, as may be seen from the following list of herbs and flowers, in the popular speech, a list that might be greatly extended.

Wort—*continued.*

Adder-*wort*, the snake weed.

Bairn-*wort*, the children's flower, the daisy.

Ban-*wort*, the wood violet.

Bane-*wort*, the deadly nightshade.

Bell-*wort*, the convolvulus.

Birth-*wort*.

Bishop's-*wort*, or St. Catherine's flower.

Blood-*wort*, the wall-flower, sometimes called the bleeding heart. Close to Hatton Garden, London, a street that takes its name from and was part of the domain of Sir Christopher Hatton, Lord Chancellor of England, in the time of Queen Elizabeth, is a now squalid and wretched court, called Bleeding Heart Yard. Probably the name is as old as the days of Sir Christopher, and may have been descriptive of a portion of the garden overgrown with *blood-wort*, wall-flower, or *bleeding heart*. Popular superstition, however, has not been content with this innocent meaning, but has built up a ghastly story of the heart of Lady Hatton, torn out of her body on that spot, by the great Enemy of mankind, to whom, when a poor flower-girl, she had sold her soul, after the fashion of Dr. Faustus, for worldly wealth and position, and who claimed her, on the expiration of three times seven years, after the signing of the contract. The legend goes, that the Fiend came for her when she was dancing in a brilliant assemblage at Hatton House, and carried her off to her doom.

Bride-*wort*, the meadow-sweet.

Brose-*wort*, hyoscyamus or henbane.

Brother-*wort*, penny royal.

Culver-*wort*, the columbine.

Drunk-*wort*, an old name for tobacco.

Ers-*wort*, the mouse ear.

Felon-*wort*, the woody nightshade.

Field-*wort*, gentian.

Laser-*wort*, from whence assafœtida is extracted for medicinal purposes.

Lithe-*wort*, the forget-me-not.

Liver-*wort*.

Wort—*continued.*

>   Lubber-*wort*, any root of which the decoction makes a person idle or stupid, applied metaphorically to ' barley ' and ' malt.'
>
>   Moon-*wort*, lunary.
>
>   Nail-*wort*, or whitlow grass, so called from its supposed efficacy in the cure of whitlows.
>
>   Palsy-*wort*, the cowslip or paigle.
>
>   Pile-*wort*, cud weed.
>
>   Rag-*wort*.
>
>   St. John's-*wort*.
>
>   Short-*wort*.
>
>   Smere-*wort*.
>
>   Sneeze-*wort*, or goose tongue.
>
>   Spleen-*wort*.
>
>   Starch-*wort*.
>
>   Youth-*wort*, the plant *ros solis*.

Would.   This word in certain cases where its use is essential to grammatical correctness, threatens to be superseded by a clumsy colloquialism ; as in the following extracts.

>   If a son is really capable of managing his own affairs, *his* father *had* best let him do so.—*Times, May* 8, 1861. *I.e.*, If a son is really capable of managing his own affairs, it would be better if his father *would* let him do so.
>
>   People in the responsible position of ministers *had* better *take* time.—*Times, May* 13, 1861. *I.e.*, It *would* be better for people in the responsible position of ministers to take time.
>
>   Interesting as is the subject—eloquent as are the speakers, we *had* (*would*) much rather hear them descant upon some other theme.—*Times, May* 13, 1861.
>
>   A gentleman of such delicate sensibilities (as Mr. Walpole), *had* better not *have* trusted himself to a personal interview with Mr. Beales.—*Saturday Review, July* 28, 1866 ; *on the Hyde Park Riots.* *I.e.*, It *would have been* better, if a gentleman of such delicate susceptibilities *had* not trusted himself, &c.
>
>   The man who touches them *had* better *have* put his head into a hornet's nest.—*Rereward the Wake, by the Rev. Charles Kingsley*, vol. i., page 299. *I.e.*, It *would* be better for the man who touches them to have put his head into a hornet's nest.

In a review of ' Travels not far from Home,' in the ' Morning Post ' of September 14, 1860, the critic says, ' but the preface *had* better not *have* been written,' instead of ' it *would* have been better if the preface had not been written.'

Would—*continued.*

Mr. Leigh Hunt, in his 'Old Court Suburb,' vol. ii., page 14, says, 'But the acount of it *had* better be given in his own words,' instead of 'it *would* be better if the account were given, &c.' Mr. Thackeray, in 'The Virginians,' vol. i., page 138, says, 'I *had* rather have lost an arm almost,' so obvious a mistake for 'I *would* rather,' as to suggest a misprint rather than a deliberate inelegancy; if it were not that in the same work, he repeats the error (page 667), and says, 'the affair *had* better be settled,' instead of 'it *would* be better if the affair were settled.' Mr. Carlyle in his pamphlet on the Negro question, 'edition, 1853, page 39, speaks of 'a doom for Quashee, which I *had* (would) rather not contemplate.'

Wouth, wrong, harm, madness; sometimes written, '*wothe,* and *wuth.*'

Wowf, partially deranged.   'Having a bee in one's bonnet.'

It is very odd, Lord Allan, who between ourselves, is a little *wowf,* seems at times to have more sense than all of us put together.
Sir Walter Scott : Tales of my Landlord.

Wraith, the supposed apparition of the soul, about to quit the body of a dying person. *Water wraith,* a water spirit.

Wrathe, to incense, to anger, to make wrathful.—(*Halliwell.*)

Wraw, peevish.

Wrawl, to quarrel, to dispute, to wrangle.

Wreak, }
Wroke, } vengeance, to avenge.

Wroken, avenged.

In our time, the substantive 'wreak' has wholly dropped out of use; and the verb is never employed without substantive, originally implied in the meaning; as to *wreak* displeasure, wrath, or vengeance. In Anglo-Saxon, *wreaker* signified an avenger. In the Shakspearian era of literature, and in the ancient romances, both substantive and verb were used as single words. Thus:

His soul to hell so mote it wend!
Hounds gnaw him to the bone!
So *wreak* us, God, of all our foes.
Metrical Romance of Sir Bevis of Hampton.

Wroken—*continued.*

> Render me now to the Greeks' sight again,
> And let me see the fight begun of new,
> We shall not all *unwroken* die this day.
>> *Earl of Surrey's translation of the Eneid.*

> Till I be *wroken* of Saladyne,
> Certes my joy shall I tyne!
>> *Metrical Romance of Richard Cœur de Lion.*

> Then if thou hast,
> A heart of *wreak* in thee, that will revenge
> Thine own particular wrongs.
>> *Shakspeare : Coriolanus,* act iv., scene 5.

> 'Tis not my fault, the boar provoked my tongue,
> Be *wreaked* on him.
>> *Shakspeare: Venus and Adonis.*

> Lend me your helping hand,
> To *wreak* the parricide.
>> *Beaumont and Fletcher.*

> Come, *wreak* his loss, whom bootless ye deplore.
>> *Fairfax.*

> And soon in the Gordon's foul heart's blood,
> He's *wroken* his dear ladye!
>> *Border Ballad of Edom o' Gordon.*

> When years shall *wreak* my wrong.
>> *S. Daniel.*

To have *wroken* himself of such wrongs as were done and offered to him by the French king.—*Hollinshed.*

Wrench,⎫ a stratagem.
Wrenck,⎰

> Old men are fell and quent,
> And wicked *wrenches* can attent.
>> *Metrical Romance of the Seven Wise Masters.*

> For all her *wrench*,
> The more love she might not win.
>> *Idem.*

> This was one of woman's *wrenches.*
>> *Idem.*

> For it leaves a man with *wrencks* and wyles,
> And at the last it him beguiles.
>> *Hampole MS., Bowes, quoted by Halliwell.*

Wright, an artificer or artizan. In Scotland and the North of England, 'wright' means a carpenter, and stone-*wright*, a mason. In English, as admitted into the Dictionaries, the word is only retained in combination as Shipwright, Millwright. The words 'Cartwright,' and 'Wheelwright,' exist as surnames; but are still used by the peasantry for cartmaker, and wheelmaker.

Wrine, a deep line in the face, a furrow; whence the diminutive wrinkle, a small wrine.

Writh, the stalk of a plant.—*Wright's Provincial Glossary.*

Wrox, to begin to decay.

Wry, to twist, to turn; whence the modern words, awry; wry-mouth, and wry-neck.

> Seeing plainly
> That Fortune doth *wry,*
> All contrary,
> From mine intent.
> *Ellis's Ancient Songs and Ballads,* 1483.

Wush, preterite of wash.

> He *wush* his face and kamed his hair.
> *The Dowie Dens o' Yarrow.*

Wyte, ⎫ to blame; an ancient English word anterior to the time,
Wite, ⎭ when blame was introduced into the language from the Norman French.

> And but, I do sirs, let me have the *wite.*
> *Chaucer: The Chanones Yeman's Tale.*

> And though that I be jealous, *wite* me not!
> *Chaucer: The Merchant's Tale.*

> And therefore if that I mis-speak or say,
> *Wite* it (the ale of Southwark), I you pray.
> *The Miller's Prologue.*

> Fortune,
> Thy false wheel, all my woe, I well may *wite.*
> *The Miller's Tale.*

> Ane does the skaith, and another gets the *wyte.*

> Deem warily, ye know not who *wytes* yoursel'.

> Many *wyte* their wives,
> For their own thriftless lives.

> Ye need not *wyte* your teeth because your tail is small.
> *Allan Ramsay's Scotch Proverbs.*

> Alas! that e'er my muse had reason,
> To *wyte* my countryman wi' treason
> *Burns: Scotch Drink.*

Yack, a smart blow. ' A yack *i' th' ear,*' a box on the ears. ' A *yack* on the head.'

Yal, preterite of *yell,* to cry out like a man in rage ; or like a wild beast.

Yald, vigorous, lively, alert.

> Being *yald* and stout, he wheel'd about,
> And clove his head in twain.
> > *Hogg's Mountain Bard.*

Yalloch, a shout, a yell ; a wild halloo.—(*Jamieson.*)

Yammer, *v.* to yearn or desire.

> And the little things *yammering* round.
> > *Lancashire Songs by Edwin Waugh.*

> I *yammer* to hear how things turned eawt.
> > *Tim Bobbin.*

> And the worm *yammers* for us i' th' ground.
> > *Waugh's Lancashire Songs.*

Yammerly, piteously.—*Gawayne.*

Yamph, to bark, like a small dog.

Yanks, leggings, or leather gaiters.

Yap,
Yaup, } hungry ; having an eager desire for anything.
Yappy,

> As glad, as gay, as young, as *yap* as˘ ye·
> > (*Jamieson.*)
> Right *yap* she yoked to the ready feast.
> > *Ross's Helenore*

' Come away, Mr. Dunshunner,' said the Provost, 'I hope ye are *yaup,* for ye have a lang day's work before ye.'
> > *W. E. Aytoun, Blackwood's Magazine.*

Yare, } brisk, nimble.
Yary,

Yarely, briskly, nimbly.

> Be *yare* in thy preparations, for thy assailant is quick, skilful, and deadly.—*Shakspeare : Twelfth Night.*

> Speak to the mariners! Fall to 't *yarely,* or we see ourselves aground! Bestir! Bestir!—*Shakspeare : Tempest.*

> In Cæsar's fleet,
> Are those that often have against Pompey fought,
> Their ships are *yare.*
> > *Shakspeare : Antony and Cleopatra.*

This word is common to all the Northern and Eastern counties, and seems to be the original root of *early,* after early had superseded *rathe.* In Lancashire, in 1540, according to a quotation from *Palsgrave's Acolastus,* in Halliwell's Dictionary, early and yarely, were synonymous.

Yarm, to scream.

> The fiend began to cry and *yarm.*
> > *MS. Lincoln, (quoted by Halliwell.)*

Yarn, preterite of the Anglo-Saxon yerne, to grow, to spin out, to run. The sailor's phrase, a ' yarn,' or long story, run out to inordinate length, is thus pure English, of an ancient stock.

> Till I forget youth,
> And *yarn* into eld.
> > *Piers Ploughman.*

Yarrow, the achillea millefolium.

> He fumitory gets, and eye-light for the eye,
> The *yarrow,* wherewithal he stops the wound-made gore.
> > *Drayton : Polyalbion.*

Yatter, to talk in a peevish and querulous manner.

Yaup, to make a loud noise in talking; also to laugh vulgarly.

Yaw, to roll from one side to another; whence ' yawl,' a heavy barge.

Yawney, a sleepy, stupid person.

Yea, signifies positive assent; yes is a weakened and attenuated variety of the same word, signfying acquiescence in a proposition that it is unnecessary to refute.

Ask a country man if two and two are four? and he replies, ' *Yea,* that they be.' Ask him, are you in good health? and he says, ' *Yes,* that I be.'

Year, to grow old, to increase in years.

Year-day, an anniversary of birth, death, or marriage, **or any** memorable event in a family or nation.

Yearth, the earth ; that which yeareth or maketh the years.

Yeather, a flexible twig, strip of ash, birch, used for binding faggots.

Yeavy, moist.

Ye, to go, from the German gehen.

Yede, preterite of ye, to go.

> So they washed and *yede* to meat,
> The Bishop the grace did say.
> > *MS. Cantab.* (*Halliwell*).

Yeep, }
Yep, } active, nimble.

> Thou art young and *yepe*.
> > *Piers Ploughman.*
> They weren *yep*.
> > *Arthur and Merlin.*
> In alle Egypte is none so *yep*.
> > *Cursor Mundi,* (*Halliwell*.)

Yeld, barren ; a *yeld* cow, that yields no milk.

Yelf, a hay-fork, a dung-fork.

Yelm, a portion of straw, as much as can be carried under the arm ; to lay out straw in convenient sheaves for the thatcher.

Yeme, heed, attention.

> This was the texte timely,
> I took ful good *yeme*,
> The glose was gloriously written
> With a gilt pin.
> > *Piers Ploughman.*

Yeme, to govern.

> *Yeme* well thyself.
> > *Idem.*
> To *yemen*
> Both young and old.
> > *Idem.*
> Full faire shall I him feede,
> And *yeme* him with our own childe,
> And clothe them in one weed.
> > *MS. Lincoln, Halliwell.*

Yerne, to run.

Yepely,
Yeply, } actively, sharply, nimbly.

> And *yepelike* spake
> Pride——
>
> *Piers Ploughman.*

Yernful, full of yearning and desire; melancholy, full of
fancies, conceits, and crotchets.

> But oh, Musick, as in joyful tunes,
> Thy merry notes I did borrow,
> So now lend me thy *yernful* tunes,
> To utter all my sorrow.
>
> *Damon and Pythias, (Wright's Provincial Dictionary.)*

Yespen, }
Yaspen, } as much of any thing as can be taken up in both
hands joined; a double handful.

Yester, the period of time last past, This word is now only
used in combination with ' day,' as *yesterday.* It is a common colloquialism to talk of last night, as *yesterday-night*
instead of yester-night. The words yester-morn, yester-
een, are still allowed in English poetry, and common in
Northern and Scottish parlance. *Yester*-month, *yester*-
week, and *yester*-minute, are not incorrect, though scarcely
ever employed in modern composition.

> In my sleep *yestereen,*
> The figure of Cassandra, prophetess.
>
> *Douglas : Translation of Virgil.*

> *Yestreen* I rode this water deep,
> And my gude lord beside me.
>
> *Gipsy Davie, Scottish Minstrelsy.*

> In hope that you would come here *yestere'en.*
>
> *Ben Jonson.*

> And shall the wretch, whom *yester*-sun beheld
> Waiting my nod,
> Presume to-day to plead audacious love?
>
> *Congreve : Mourning Bride.*

> I gaed a rueful gate *yestreen.*
>
> *Burns.*

In like sort we have such plentie of fish upon our several coasts,
that although millions of them be taken in a day, yet on the next, their
loss will be so supplied with new store, that nothing shall be missing
of the *yester* fang.—*Holinshed : Description of Scotland.*

Yeth-hounds, hounds without heads, supposed to be animated by the spirits of children who have died without baptism. 'These hounds are believed,' says Mr. Halliwell, who quotes a superstition current in Devonshire, 'to ramble among the woods at night, making wailing noises.'

Yewen, formed of the wood of the yew-tree.

> With *yewen* bow.
> > *Spenser.*

Yex, to cough, hiccough.

> And *yexen* in their mirth.
> > *Shakspeare : Midsummer Night's Dream.*

> His prayer a rhapsody of holy hiccoughs, sanctified barkings, illuminated goggles, sighs, sobs, *yexes*, gasps, and groans.
> > *Character of a Fanatic, Harleian Miscellany.*

Yox, preterite of yex.

Yoxen, past participle of yex.

Yode, preterite of ye, and yede, to go.

> Before them *yode* a lusty taberere.
> > *Chaucer.*

> The king of France before him *yode*.
> > *MS. Lincoln, Halliwell.*

Yold, preterite of yield.

> The earth *yold* its fruits.
> > *Wicliffe's Bible.*

> The child they to Clement *yold*.
> > *Halliwell.*

Yoly, handsome, smart, young ; possibly the same as, or a misprint for, the French *joli*, whence the modern 'jolly.'

> Towards her came a knight,
> Gentyle she thought and a *yoly* man.
> > *MS. Cantab. Halliwell.*

Yow, to reap, gathering the corn under the arm.—(*Halliwell.*)

Yon, that or those, as distinguished from this and these ; whence *yonder*, or yon-there, that which is there,

> What hills are *yon*,
> *Yon* pleasant hills ;
> The sun shines sweetly on.
> > *The Demon Lover.*

Yond, distant, strange.

Nares defines this word to mean 'furious, savage,' a total miscomprehension of the meaning.

Yonderly, shy, timid, retiring.

Yonste, grace, favor, affection ; from the German *gunst*.

The very *yonste* and good will that I bear to you.
Caxton's Reynard the Foxe.

Yore, the preterite of year, to increase in years, to grow old ; whence *yore*, the days of old, the olden time, the time that yeared, or *yore*.

Yorne, aged, of the days of old, or of *yore*. Mr. Halliwell defines the word to mean 'long,' and 'hastened.' Nares's Glossary makes no mention of it. It is not uncommon in Scotland and the North of England in the sense, not of long, but of 'long ago,' antique, venerable.

Yoten, a giant, from the Norse *jotun*.

Youthy, having the false and affected appearance of youthfulness ; applied to an old person of either sex, who dresses in the style, or talks and otherwise behaves as if still young.

I warrant she 's no less than three score : but she's as *youthy* as if she were na out o' her teens.—*Jamieson.*

Yowe, a ewe, Northern and Scottish.

The death and dying words of poor Mailie, the author's only pet *yowe.*—*Robert Burns.*

Yowf, to bark in a gruff manner, as distinguished from yelp, to bark in a shrill, sharp manner.

Then Jowler he began to *yowff*.
The Gruesome Carl, Blackwood's Magazine.

An unco (i.e. strange) dog coming in among them, they all set up a barking, with their faces up to heaven, howling, yelling, and *yowffing*.
Law's Memorials.

Yowl, to howl vehemently.

The greyhound arose, and began to *yowl* upon them.
MS. Bodleian, Halliwell.

The young priest began to stare at the windows, and the men in green baize began to set up a *yowl* so dismal, that you might have fancied them the very dogs.
Letters from Rome, Daily Telegraph, December 29, 1866.

Yoyster, to frolic, to laugh loudly.

Yuck,
Yuke, } to itch.

Yuky, itchy.

> My lug's *youky ;* i.e., my ear itches.
> *Allan Ramsay.*

Yule, Christmas ; from the Norse and Icelandic Ule, a *wheel,* and signifying that the wheel of the world had completed its annual revolution.

Yule, to keep Christmas.

Yuling, keeping Christmas.—(*Halliwell.*)

Yuly, beautiful.

> A captain's wife most *yuly.*
> *Wright's Provincial Glossary.*

A LIST OF BOOKS

PUBLISHED BY

CHATTO & WINDUS

(Successors to John Camden Hotten),

74 & 75, PICCADILLY, LONDON, W.

THE FAMOUS FRASER PORTRAITS.

MACLISE'S GALLERY OF

ILLUSTRIOUS LITERARY CHARACTERS.

With Notes by the late WILLIAM MAGINN, LL.D.

Edited, with copious Notes, by WILLIAM BATES, B.A., Professor of Classics in Queen's College, Birmingham. The volume contains the whole 83 SPLENDID AND MOST CHARACTERISTIC PORTRAITS, now first issued in a complete form. In demy 4to, over 400 pages, cloth gilt and gilt edges, 31*s.* 6*d.* ; or, in morocco elegant, 70*s.*

" What a truly charming book of pictures and prose, the quintessence, as it were, of Maclise and Maginn, giving the very form and pressure of their literary time, would this century of illustrious characters make."—*Notes and Queries.*

74 & 75, *PICCADILLY, LONDON, W.*

THE PRINCE OF CARICATURISTS.

—◆◆◆—

THE WORKS OF
JAMES GILLRAY,
The Caricaturist,

With the Story of his Life and Times, and full and Anecdotal Descriptions of his Engravings.

Edited by THOS. WRIGHT, Esq., M.A., F.S.A.

Illustrated with 90 full-page Plates, and about 400 Wood Engravings. Demy 4to, 600 pages, cloth extra, 31*s.* 6*d.*; or, in morocco elegant, 70*s.*

BEAUTIFUL PICTURES
BY BRITISH ARTISTS.

A Gathering of Favourites from our Picture Galleries, 1800—1870. By WILKIE, CONSTABLE, J. M. W. TURNER, MULREADY, Sir EDWIN LANDSEER, MACLISE, LESLIE, E. M. WARD, FRITH, Sir JOHN GILBERT, ANSDELL, MARCUS STONE, Sir NOEL PATON, EYRE CROWE, FAED, MADOX BROWN. All Engraved in the highest style of Art. With Notices of the Artists by SYDNEY ARMYTAGE, M.A. A New Edition. Imperial 4to, cloth gilt and gilt edges, 21*s.*; or, in morocco elegant, 65*s.*

UNIFORM WITH "BEAUTIFUL PICTURES."

COURT BEAUTIES OF THE
REIGN OF CHARLES II.

From the Originals in the Royal Gallery at Windsor, by Sir PETER LELY. Engraved in the highest style of Art by THOMSON, WRIGHT, SCRIVEN, B. HOLL, WAGSTAFF, and T. A. DEANE. With Memoirs by Mrs. JAMESON, Author of "Legends of the Madonna." New and sumptuous "Presentation Edition." Imp. 4to, cloth gilt and gilt edges, 21*s.*; or, in morocco elegant, 65*s.*

"This truly beautiful and splendid production is equally a gem among the **Fine** Arts and in Literature."—*Quarterly Review.*

---

74 & 75, *PICCADILLY, LONDON, W.*

COMPANION TO THE "HISTORY OF SIGNBOARDS."

Advertising: its History, in all Ages and
Countries, with many very Amusing Anecdotes and Examples of
Successful Advertisers. Crown 8vo, with numerous Illustrations,
coloured and plain, cloth extra, 7s. 6d. [*In preparation.*

ARE YOU ENGAGED? IF SO, GET

Advice to Parties
About to Marry. A Series
of Instructions in Jest and
Earnest. By the Hon. HUGH
ROWLEY. With Humorous Il-
lustrations. Price 3s. 6d., elegantly bound, and enclosed in
tinted wrapper, beautifully
scented by RIMMEL.

* Before taking the "awful plunge"
be sure to consult this little work. If it
is not a guarantee against life-long
misery, it will at least be found of
great assistance in selecting a partner
for life.*

American Happy Thoughts. The
finest collection of American Humour ever made. Foolscap 8vo,
illustrated covers, 1s. [*Preparing.*

Anacreon. Illustrated by
the Exquisite Designs of GIRODET. Translated by THOMAS MOORE. Bound in vellum
cloth and Etruscan gold, 12s. 6d.

* A beautiful and captivating volume. The
well-known Paris house, Firmin Didot, a few years
since produced a miniature edition of these exquisite
designs by photography, and sold a large number at
£2 per copy. The Designs have been universally
admired by both artists and poets.*

Armorial Register of the Order of
the Garter, from Edward III. to the Present Time. The several
Shields beautifully emblazoned in Gold and Colours from the Original
Stall Plates in St. George's Chapel, Windsor. All emblazoned by
hand. A sumptuous volume, bound in crimson morocco, gilt, £20.

ARTEMUS WARD'S WORKS.

Artemus Ward,

Complete. The Works of CHARLES FARRER BROWNE, better known as "ARTEMUS WARD," now first collected. Crown 8vo, with fine Portrait, facsimile of handwriting, &c., 540 pages, cloth neat, 7s. 6d.

* *Comprises all that the humourist has written in England or America. Admirers of Artemus Ward will be glad to possess his writings in a complete form.*

Artemus Ward's

Lecture at the Egyptian Hall, with the Panorama. Edited by the late T. W. ROBERTSON, Author of "Caste," &c., and E. P. HINGSTON. Small 4to, exquisitely printed, bound in green and gold, with NUMEROUS TINTED ILLUSTRATIONS, 6s.

Artemus Ward: his Book. With Notes

and Introduction by the Editor of the "Biglow Papers." One of the wittiest books published for many years. Fcap, 8vo, illustrated cover, 1s.

The *Saturday Review* says:—"The author combines the powers of Thackeray with those of Albert Smith. The salt is rubbed in by a native hand—one which has the gift of tickling."

Artemus Ward: his Travels among

the Mormons and on the Rampage. Edited by E. P. HINGSTON, the Agent and Companion of A. WARD whilst "on the Rampage." New Edition, price 1s.

* *Some of Artemus's most mirth-provoking papers are to be found in this book. The chapters on the Mormons will unbend the sternest countenance. As bits of fun they are* IMMENSE!

Artemus Ward's Letters to "Punch,"

Among the Witches, and other Sketches. Cheap Popular Edition. Fcap. 8vo, in illustrated cover, 1s.; or, 16mo, bound in cloth extra, 2s.

* *The volume contains, in addition, some quaint and humorous compositions which were found upon the author's table after his decease.*

Artemus Ward among the Fenians:

with the Showman's Experiences of Life at Washington, and Military Ardour at Baldinsville. Toned paper, price 6d.

Army Lists of the Roundheads and

Cavaliers in the Civil War, 1642. Second Edition, considerably Enlarged and Corrected. Edited, with Notes, by EDWARD PEACOCK, F.S.A. 4to, half-Roxburghe, 7s. 6d.

** *Very interesting to Antiquaries and Genealogists.*

The Art of Amusing.

A Collection of Graceful Arts, Games, Tricks, Puzzles, and Charades, intended to amuse everybody, and enable all to amuse everybody else. By FRANK BELLEW. With nearly 300 Illustrations. Crown 8vo, 4s. 6d.

** *One of the most entertaining hand-books of amusements ever published.*

AwfulCrammers.

A New American Joke Book. Edited by TITUS A. BRICK, Author of "Shaving Them." Fcap. 8vo, with numerous curious Illustrations, 1s.

A FINE EDITION is also published, in crown 8vo, printed on toned paper, and bound in cloth gilt, at 3s. 6d.

" Rarer than the phœnix is the virtuous man who will consent to lose a good anecdote because it isn't true."—DE QUINCY.

Babies and Ladders :

Essays on Things in General. By EMMANUEL KINK. A New Work of Irresistible Humour (not American), which has excited considerable attention. Fcap. 8vo, with numerous Vignettes by W. S. GILBERT and others. 1s.

Bayard Taylor's Diversions of the

Echo Club. A Delightful Volume of Refined Literary Humour. In 16mo, paper cover, with Portrait of the Author, 1s. 6d. ; cloth extra, 2s.

UNIFORM WITH MR. RUSKIN'S EDITION OF "GRIMM."

Bechstein's As Pretty as Seven, and

other Popular German Stories. Collected by LUDWIG BECHSTEIN. With Additional Tales by the Brothers GRIMM. 100 Illustrations by RICHTER. Small 4to, green and gold, 6s. 6d. ; gilt edges, 7s. 6d.

※ *One of the most delightful books for children ever published. It is, in every way, a Companion to the German Stories of the Brothers Grimm, and the tales are equally pure and healthful. The quaint simplicity of Richter's engravings will charm every lover of legendary lore.*

The Biglow Papers. By JAMES RUSSELL

LOWELL. The Best Edition, with full Glossary, of these extraordinary Verses. Fcap. 8vo, illustrated cover, 1s.

UNIFORM WITH OUR "RABELAIS."

Boccaccio's Decameron.

Now fully translated into English, with Introduction by THOMAS WRIGHT, F.S.A. Crown 8vo, with the BEAUTIFUL ENGRAVINGS by STOTHARD which adorned Pickering's fine Edition, published at £2 12s. 6d. This New Edition is only 7s. 6d.

※ *A faithful translation, in which are restored many passages omitted in former Editions.*

Book of Hall-Marks ; or, Manual of

Reference for the Goldsmith and Silversmith. By ALFRED LUTSCHAUNIG, Manager of the Liverpool Assay Office. Crown 8vo, with 46 Plates of the Hall-Marks of the different Assay Towns of the United Kingdom, as now stamped on Plate and Jewellery, 7s. 6d.

※ *This work gives practical methods for testing the quality of gold and silver. It was compiled by the author for his own use, and as a Supplement to "Chaffers."*

Booksellers, A History of. A Work

giving full Accounts of the Great Publishing Houses and their Founders, both in London and the Provinces, the History of their Rise and Progress, and descriptions of the special class of Literature dealt in by each. Crown 8vo, over 500 pages, with frontispiece and numerous Portraits and Illustrations, cloth extra, 7s. 6d.

" In these days, ten ordinary Histories of Kings and Courtiers were well exchanged against the tenth part of one good History of Booksellers."—THOMAS CARLYLE.

Booth's Epigrams : Ancient and Modern,

Humorous, Witty, Satirical, Moral, and Panegyrical. Edited by the Rev. JOHN BOOTH, B.A. A New Edition. Pott 8vo, cloth gilt, 6s.

" Is our civilization a failure, or is the Caucasian played out?"

BRET HARTE'S WORKS.

Widely known for their Exquisite Pathos and Delightful Humour.

Bret Harte's Complete Works, in Prose

and Poetry. Now First Collected. With Introductory Essay by J. M. BELLEW, Portrait of the Author, and 50 Illustrations. Crown 8vo, 650 pages, cloth extra, 7s. 6d.

74 & 75, *PICCADILLY, LONDON, W.*

BRET HARTE'S WORKS—*continued.*

Bret Harte's Luck of Roaring Camp,

and other Stories. Fcap. 8vo, illustrated cover, 1*s.*

Bret Harte's That Heathen Chinee,

and other Humorous Poems. Fcap. 8vo, illustrated cover, 1*s.* 6*d.*

Bret Harte's Sensation Novels Con-

densed. Fcap. 8vo, illustrated cover, 1*s.* 6*d.*

*** *A most enjoyable book, only surpassed, in its special class, by Thackeray's Burlesque Novels.*

Bret Harte's Lothaw ; or, The Adventures

of a Young Gentleman in Search of a Religion. By Mr. BEN-JAMINS (*Bret Harte*). Price 6*d.* Curiously Illustrated.

Bret Harte's East and West. Fcap.

8vo, illustrated cover, 1*s.*

Bret Harte's Stories of the Sierras, and

other Sketches. With a Wild Story of Western Life by JOAQUIN MILLER, Author of "Songs of the Sierras." Illustrated cover, 1*s.*

NEW EDITIONS OF SIR DAVID BREWSTER'S WORKS.

Brewster's More Worlds than One,

the Creed of the Philosopher and the Hope of the Christian. Eleventh Edition. Crown 8vo, cloth, very neat, 4*s.* 6*d.*

Brewster's Martyrs of Science :

Galileo, Tycho Brahe, Kepler. Crown 8vo, cloth, very neat, 4*s.* 6*d.*

Brewster's The Kaleidoscope Prac-

tically Described. Crown 8vo, with numerous Illustrations, cloth, very neat, 4*s.* 6*d.*

Brewster's The Stereoscope Prac-

tically Described. Crown 8vo, numerous Illustrations, cloth neat, 4*s.* 6*d.*

*** *This was the great philosopher's last contribution to practical science.*

Bright's (Rt. Hon. J., M.P.) Speeches

on Public Affairs of the last Twenty Years. Collated with the
best Public Reports. Royal 16mo, 370 pages, cloth extra, 1s.

⁎ *A book of special interest at the present time, and wonderfully cheap.*

COLMAN'S HUMOROUS WORKS.

Broad Grins. My Nightgown and Slippers,

and other Humorous Works, Prose and Poetical, of GEORGE COL-
MAN the Younger. Now first collected, with Life and Anecdotes of
the Author, by GEORGE B. BUCKSTONE. Crown 8vo, 500 pp., 7s. 6d.

⁎ *Admirers of genuine English wit and humour will be delighted with this
edition of George Colman's humorous works. As a wit, he has had no equal in
our time; and a man with a tithe of his ability could, at the present day, make
the fortune of any one of our so-called "comic journals," and bankrupt the rest.*

NEW BOOK FOR BOYS.

The Conquest of the Sea: A History

of Divers and Diving, from the Earliest Times to the Present Day.
By HENRY SIEBE. Profusely Illustrated with fine Wood Engravings.
Small crown 8vo, cloth extra, 4s. 6d.

74 & 75, *PICCADILLY, LONDON, W.*

Uniform with the 2s. Edition of his Works.

Carlyle (T.) on the Choice of Books.

With a New Life and Anecdotes of the Author. Brown cloth, 1s. 6d. ; paper cover, 1s.

Chips from a Rough Log. Fcap. 8vo,

illustrated cover, 1s.

Christmas Songs and Ballads. Selected

and Edited by JOSHUA SYLVESTER. A New Edition, beautifully printed and bound in cloth, extra gilt, gilt edges, 3s. 6d.

Clerical Anecdotes and Pulpit Eccen-

tricities. An entirely New Gathering. Square 16mo, in illustrated paper wrapper, 1s. 4d. ; or cloth neat, 1s. 10d.

The Country of the Dwarfs. By PAUL

DU CHAILLU. A Book of Startling Interest. Fcap. 8vo, illustrated with full-page Engravings, in fancy wrapper, 1s.

Cruikshank's Comic Almanack.

FIRST SERIES, 1835-43. A Gathering of the BEST HUMOUR, the WITTIEST SAYINGS, the Drollest Quips, and the Best Things of THACKERAY, HOOD, MAYHEW, ALBERT SMITH, A'BECKETT, ROBERT BROUGH, &c. With about One Thousand Woodcuts and Steel Engravings by the inimitable CRUIKSHANK, HINE, LANDELLS, &c. Crown 8vo, cloth gilt, a very thick volume, price 7s. 6d.

Cruikshank's Comic Almanack.

SECOND SERIES, 1844-53, Completing the work. Uniform with the FIRST SERIES, and written and illustrated by the same humorists. Crown 8vo, cloth gilt, a very thick volume, price 7s. 6d.

** The two volumes (each sold separately) form a most extraordinary gathering of the best wit and humour of the past half-century. The work forms a "Comic History of England" for twenty years.

THE BEST GUIDE TO HERALDRY.

Cussans' Handbook of

Heraldry; with Instructions for Tracing Pedigrees and Deciphering Ancient MSS.; also, Rules for the Appointment of Liveries, &c., &c. By JOHN E. CUSSANS. Illustrated with 360 Plates and Woodcuts. Cr. 8vo, cloth extra, gilt and emblazoned, 7s.6d.

** This volume, beautifully printed on toned paper, contains not only the ordinary matter to be found in the best books on the science of Armory, but several other subjects hitherto unnoticed. Amongst these may be mentioned:—1. DIRECTIONS FOR TRACING PEDIGREES. 2. DECIPHERING ANCIENT MSS., ILLUSTRATED BY ALPHABETS AND FAC-SIMILES. 3. THE APPOINTMENT OF LIVERIES. 4. CONTINENTAL AND AMERICAN HERALDRY, &c.

VERY IMPORTANT COUNTY HISTORY.

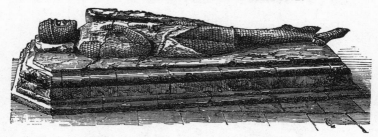

Cussans' History of Hertfordshire.

A County History, got up in a very superior manner, and ranging with the finest works of its class. Illustrated with full-page Plates on Copper and Stone, and a profusion of small Woodcuts. Parts I. to VI. are now ready, price **21s.** each.

*** *An entirely new History of this important County, great attention being given to all matters pertaining to the Fami y History of the locality.*

UNIFORM WITH THE "CHARLES DICKENS EDITION."

Dickens : The Story

of his Life. By THEODORE TAY-LOR, Author of the "Life of Thackeray." Uniform with the "Charles Dickens Edition" of his Works, and forming a Supplementary Volume to that Issue. Cr. 8vo, crimson cloth, 3s. 6d.

"Anecdotes seem to have poured in upon the author from all quarters. . . Turn where we will through these 370 pleasant pages, something worth reading is sure to meet the eye."—*The Standard.*

Also Published :

THE "BEST EDITION" of the above Work, illustrated by Photographic Frontispiece of "Dickens as Captain Bobadil," Portraits, Facsimiles, &c. Crown 8vo, cloth extra, 7s. 6d.

THE "CHEAP EDITION," in 16mo, paper wrapper, with Frontispiece and Vignette, 2s.

---

74 & 75, *PICCADILLY, LONDON, W.*

Dickens' Speeches, Social and Literary,

now first collected. Uniform with, and forming a Supplementary Volume to, the "CHARLES DICKENS EDITION." Crown 8vo, crimson cloth, 3s. 6d.

"His speeches are as good as any of his printed writings."—*The Times.*

Also Published:

THE "BEST EDITION," in crown 8vo, with fine Portrait by Count D'ORSAY, cloth extra, 7s. 6d.

THE "CHEAP EDITION," without Portrait, in 16mo, paper wrapper, 2s.

Dickens' Life and Speeches, in One Volume, 16mo, cloth extra, 2s. 6d.

BALZAC'S CONTES DROLATIQUES.

Droll Stories, collected from the

Abbeys of Touraine. Now FIRST TRANSLATED INTO ENGLISH, COMPLETE AND UNABRIDGED, with the whole 425 Marvellous, Extravagant, and Fantastic Illustrations (the finest he has ever done) by GUSTAVE DORÉ. Beautifully printed, in 8vo, cloth extra, gilt, gilt top, 12s. 6d.

. *The most singular designs ever attempted by any artist. So crammed is the book with pictures, that even the contents are adorned with thirty-three Illustrations.*

A few copies of the FRENCH ORIGINAL are still on sale, bound half-Roxburghe, gilt top—a very handsome book—price 12s. 6d.

The Danbury Newsman. A Brief but

Comprehensive Record of the Doings of a Remarkable People, under more Remarkable Circumstances, and Chronicled in a most Remarkable Manner. By JAMES M. BAILEY. Uniform with Twain's " Screamers." Fcap. 8vo, illustrated cover, 1s.

"A real American humorist."—*Figaro.*

The Derby Day. A Sporting Novel of

intense interest, by a well-known writer. Fcap. 8vo, illustrated cover, 1s.

Disraeli's (Rt. Hon. B.) Speeches

on the Conservative Policy of the last Thirty Years, including the Speech at the Literary Fund Dinner, specially revised by the Author. Royal 16mo, paper cover, with Portrait, 1s. 4d. ; in cloth, 1s. 10d.

D'Urfey's ("Tom") Wit and Mirth ;

or, PILLS TO PURGE MELANCHOLY : Being a Collection of the best Merry Ballads and Songs, Old and New. Fitted to all Humours, having each their proper Tune for either Voice or Instrument : most of the Songs being new set. London : Printed by W. Pearson, for J. Tonson, at Shakespeare's Head, over-against Catherine Street in the Strand, 1719.

An exact and beautiful reprint of this much-prized work, with the Music to the Songs, just as in the rare original. In 6 vols., large fcap. 8vo, antique boards, edges uncut, beautifully printed on laid paper, made expressly for the work, price £3 3s. ; or LARGE PAPER COPIES (a limited number only printed), price £5 5s.

*** The PILLS TO PURGE MELANCHOLY *have now retained their celebrity for a century and a half. The difficulty of obtaining a copy has of late years raised sets to a fabulous price, and has made even odd volumes costly. Considering the classical reputation which the book has thus obtained, and its very high interest as illustrative of the manners, customs, and amusements of English life during the half century following the Restoration, no apology is needed for placing such a work more within the reach of general readers and students by re-issuing it for the first time since its original appearance, and at about a tithe of the price for which the old edition could now be obtained.*

For drinking-songs and love-songs, sprightly ballads, merry stories, and political squibs, there are none to surpass these in the language. In improvising such pieces, and in singing them, D'URFEY *was perhaps never equalled, except in our own century by* THEODORE HOOK. *The sallies of his wit amused and delighted three successive English sovereigns ; and while his plays are forgotten, his songs and ballads still retain the light* abandon *and joyous freshness that recommended them to the wits and beaux of Queen Anne's days. Nor can the warm and affectionate eulogy of Steele and Addison be forgotten, and* D'URFEY *may now take his place on the bookshelves of the curious, side by side with the other worthies of his age.*

The Earthward Pilgrimage, from the

Next World to that which now is. By MONCURE D. CONWAY. Crown 8vo, beautifully printed and bound, 7s. 6d.

Edgar Allan Poe's Prose and Poetical

Works; including Additional Tales and the fine Essays by this great Genius, now FIRST PUBLISHED IN THIS COUNTRY. With a Translation of CHARLES BAUDELAIRE'S "Essay on Poe." 750 pages, crown 8vo, with fine Portrait and Illustrations, cloth extra, 7s. 6d.

POE'S COTTAGE AT FORDHAM.

Mrs. Ellis's Mothers of Great Men.

A New Edition of this well-known Work, with numerous very beau-ful Portraits. Crown 8vo, cloth gilt, over 500 pages, 7s. 6d.

[In preparation.

THE STANDARD WORK ON THE SUBJECT.

Emanuel on Diamonds and Precious

Stones; Their History, Value, and Properties; with Simple Tests for ascertaining their Reality. By HARRY EMANUEL, F.R.G.S. With numerous Illustrations, Tinted and Plain. A New Edition, with the Prices brought down to the Present Time. Crown 8vo, full gilt, 6s.

" Will be acceptable to many readers."—*Times.*
" An invaluable work for buyers and sellers."—*Spectator.*

*** *The present, which is greatly superior to the first edition, gives the latest market value for Diamonds and Precious Stones of every size.*

74 & 75, *PICCADILLY, LONDON, W.*

The Englishman's House, from a Cot-
tage to a Mansion.   A Practical Guide to Members of Building
Societies, and all interested in Selecting or Building a House.   By
C. J. RICHARDSON, Architect, Author of "Old English Mansions,"
&c.   Second Edition, Corrected and Enlarged, with nearly 600
Illustrations.   Crown 8vo, 550 pages, cloth, 7s. 6d.

₊ *This Work might not inappropriately be termed "A Book of Houses." It
gives every variety of house, from a workman's cottage to a nobleman's palace.
The book is intended to supply a want long felt, viz., a plain, non-technical
account of every style of house, with the cost and manner of building.*

Our English Surnames: Their Sources
and Significations.   By CHARLES WAREING BARDSLEY, M.A.
Crown 8vo, about 600 pages, cloth extra, 9s.

INDISPENSABLE TO EVERY HOUSEHOLD:

Everybody Answered.   A Handy Book
for All; and a Guide to the Housewife, the Servant, the Cook, the
Tradesman, the Workman, the Professional Man, the Clerk, &c.,
&c., in the Duties belonging to their respective Callings.   One
thick volume, crown 8vo, cloth gilt, 4s. 6d.   [*In preparation.*

Family Fairy Tales; or, Glimpses of Elf-
land at Heatherstone Hall.   Edited by CHOLMONDELEY PENNELL,
Author of "Puck on Pegasus," &c.   Adorned with beautiful
Pictures of "My Lord Lion," "King Uggermugger," and other
Great Folks, by M. ELLEN EDWARDS, and other artists.   Handsomely printed on toned paper, in cloth, green and gold, price 4s. 6d.
plain, 5s. 6d. coloured.

Faraday's Chemical History of a Candle.
Lectures delivered to a Juvenile Audience. A New Edition of this well-known volume, which has been so long out of print, Edited by W. CROOKES, Esq., F.S.A., &c. Crown 8vo, cloth extra, with all the Original Illustrations, price 4s. 6d.

Faraday's Various Forces of Nature.
A New Edition, with all the Original Illustrations, Edited by W. CROOKES, Esq., F.S.A., &c. Crown 8vo, cloth extra, 4s. 6d.

FLAGELLATION AND THE FLAGELLANTS.

A History of the Rod in all Countries,
from the Earliest Period to the Present Time. The use of the Rod in the Church, Convent, Monastery, Prison, Army, Navy, in public and private ; the use of the Birch in the Family, Ladies' Seminaries, Boys' Schools, Colleges, the Boudoir, Ancient and Modern. By the Rev. W. COOPER, B.A. Second Edition, revised and corrected, with numerous Illustrations. Thick crown 8vo, cloth extra gilt, 12s. 6d.

"A remarkable, and certainly a very readable volume."—*Daily Telegraph.*

The Fiend's Delight: A "Cold Collation"

of Atrocities.   By DOD GRILE.   New Edition, in illustrated wrapper, fcap. 8vo, 1s. ; or crown 8vo, cloth extra, 3s. 6d.

"A specimen of 'American Humour' as unlike that of all other American humourists, as the play of young human Merry-Andrews is unlike that of a young and energetic demon whose horns are well budded."—*New York Nation.*

The Finish to Life in and out of

London ; or, The Final Adventures of Tom, Jerry, and Logic. By PIERCE EGAN.   Royal 8vo, cloth extra, with Spirited Coloured Illustrations by CRUIKSHANK, 21s.

*** *An extraordinary picture of* "LONDON BY NIGHT" *in the Days of George the Fourth.   All the strange places of amusement in the neighbourhood of Covent Garden and St. James's are fully described, and very queer places they were too !*

WALK UP ! WALK UP ! AND SEE THE

Fools' Paradise ; with the Many Wonder-

ful Adventures there, as seen in the strange, surprising

PEEP-SHOW OF PROFESSOR WOLLEY COBBLE,

Raree Showman these Five-and-Twenty Years.

Crown 4to, with nearly 200 immensely funny Pictures, all beautifully coloured, bound in extra cloth gilt, price 7s. 6d.

THE PROFESSOR'S LEETLE MUSIC LESSON.

A SECOND SERIES IS NOW READY, CALLED

Further Adventures in Fools' Paradise,

with the Many Wonderful Doings, as seen in the

PEEP-SHOW OF PROFESSOR WOLLEY COBBLE.

Crown 4to, with the Pictures beautifully Coloured, uniform with the FIRST SERIES, in extra cloth gilt, price 7s. 6d.

74 & 75, *PICCADILLY, LONDON, W.*

THE ONLY COMPLETE HOGARTH EVER PUBLISHED.

Hogarth's Works ; with Life and Anecdotal

Descriptions of the Pictures, by JOHN IRELAND and JOHN NICHOLS. The Work includes 150 Engravings, reduced in exact facsimile of the Original Plates, specimens of which have now become very scarce. The whole in Three Series, 8vo, cloth, gilt, 22s. 6d. Each series is, however, Complete in itself, and is sold separately at 7s. 6d.

Hogarth's Five Days' Frolic ; or, Pere-

grinations by Land and Water. Illustrated with Tinted Drawings, made by HOGARTH and SCOTT during the Journey. 4to, beautifully printed, cloth, extra gilt, 10s. 6d.

** A graphic and most extraordinary picture of the hearty English times in which these merry artists lived.

Hood's Whims and Oddities. The

Entire Work. Now issued Complete, the Two Parts in One Volume, with all the Humorous Designs. Royal 16mo, paper cover, 1s. ; cloth neat, 1s. 6d.

Hunt's (Leigh) Tale for a Chimney

Corner, and other charming Essays. With Introduction by EDMUND OLLIER, and Portrait supplied by the late THORNTON HUNT. Royal 16mo, paper cover, 1s. 4d.; cloth neat, 1s. 10d.

Hunt's (Robert, F.R.S.) Drolls of Old

Cornwall; or, POPULAR ROMANCES OF THE WEST OF ENGLAND. New Edition, Complete in One Volume, with Illustrations by GEORGE CRUIKSHANK. Crown 8vo, extra cloth gilt, 7s. 6d.

*** "Mr. Hunt's charming book on the Drolls and Stories of the West of England."—*Saturday Review.*

Jennings' (Hargrave)

One of the Thirty. With curious Illustrations. Crown 8vo, cloth extra, 10s. 6d.

*** *An extraordinary narrative, tracing down one of the accursed pieces of silver for which Jesus of Nazareth was sold. Through eighteen centuries is this fated coin tracked, now in the possession of the innocent, now in the grasp of the guilty, but everywhere carrying with it the evil that fell upon Judas.*

Jennings' (Hargrave)

The Rosicrucians: Their Rites and Mysteries. With chapters on the Ancient Fire and Serpent Worshippers, and Explanations of the Mystic Symbols represented in the Monuments and Talismans of the Primeval Philosophers. Crown 8vo, cloth extra, with about 300 Illustrations, 10s. 6d.

Joe Miller's Jests; or, The Wit's Vade

Mecum. Being a collection of the most brilliant Jests, the politest Repartees, the most elegant Bon-Mots, and most pleasant short Stories in the English Language. London: Printed by T. Read, 1739. A remarkable facsimile of the very rare ORIGINAL EDITION. 8vo, half-Roxburghe, 9s. 6d.

*** *Only a very few copies of this humorous and racy old book have been reproduced.*

Josh Billings: His Book of Sayings.

With Introduction by E. P. HINGSTON, Companion of Artemus Ward when on his "Travels." Fcap. 8vo, illustrated cover, 1s.

Kalendars of Gwynedd ; or, Chrono-

logical Lists of Lords-Lieutenant, Sheriffs and Knights for Anglesey, Caernarvon, and Merioneth. With Lists of the Lords-Presidents of Wales, and the Constables of the Castles of Beaumaris, Caernarvon, Conway, and Harlech. Compiled by EDWARD BREESE, F.S.A. With Notes by WILLIAM WATKIN EDWARD WYNNE, Esq., F.S.A., of Penairth. Only a limited number printed. One volume, demy 4to, cloth extra, 28s.

Lamb's (Charles) Essays of Elia. The

Complete Work. Beautifully printed, and uniform with the "Essays of Leigh Hunt." Royal 16mo, paper cover, 1s.; cloth neat, 1s. 6d.

Leigh's Carols of Cockayne. Vers de

Société, mostly descriptive of London Life. By HENRY S. LEIGH. With numerous exquisite Designs by ALFRED CONCANEN and the late JOHN LEECH. Small 4to, elegant, uniform with "Puniana," 6s.

UNIFORM WITH "DR. SYNTAX."

Life in London ; or,

The Day and Night Scenes of Jerry Hawthorn and Corinthian Tom. WITH THE WHOLE OF CRUIKSHANK'S VERY DROLL ILLUSTRATIONS, in Colours, after the Originals. Crown 8vo, cloth extra, 7s. 6d.

*** *One of the most popular books ever issued. It was an immense favourite with George IV., and as a picture of London life fifty years ago was often quoted by Thackeray, who devotes one of his "Roundabout Papers" to a description of it.*

Literary Scraps. A Folio Scrap-Book of

340 columns, with guards, for the reception of Cuttings from Newspapers, Extracts, Miscellanea, &c. A very useful book. In folio, half-roan, cloth sides, 7s. 6d.

Little Breeches, and other Pieces (PIKE

COUNTY BALLADS). By Colonel JOHN HAY. Foolscap 8vo, illustrated cover, 1s. 6d.

The Little London Directory of 1677.

The Oldest Printed List of the Merchants and Bankers of London. Reprinted from the Exceedingly Rare Original, with an Introduction by JOHN CAMDEN HOTTEN. 16mo, in a beautiful binding, after the original, 6s. 6d.

The Log of the Water Lily, during Three

Cruises on the Rhine, Neckar, Main, Moselle, Danube, Saone, and Rhone. By R. B. MANSFIELD, B.A. Illustrated by ALFRED THOMPSON, B.A. Fifth Edition, revised and considerably enlarged. Crown 8vo, cloth extra, gilt, 5s.

Longfellow's Prose

Works, Complete, including his Stories and Essays, now for the first time collected. Edited, with a Preface, by the Author of "Tennysoniana." With Portrait and Illustrations, drawn by VALENTINE BROMLEY, and beautifully engraved, 650 pages, crown 8vo, cloth gilt, 7s. 6d.

Lost Beauties of the English Language.

An Appeal to Authors, Poets, Clergymen, and Public Speakers; with an Introductory Essay. By CHARLES MACKAY, LL.D. In crown 8vo, cloth extra, uniform with the "Slang Dictionary," 6s. 6d.

UNIFORM WITH "THE MAGICIAN'S OWN BOOK."

Magic and Mystery. A Splendid Collec-

tion of Tricks with Cards, Dice, Balls, &c., with fully descriptive working Directions. Crown 8vo, with numerous Illustrations, cloth extra, 4s. 6d.   [*Preparing.*

COMPANION TO "THE SECRET OUT."

The Magician's Own Book. Containing

ample Instructions for Performances in Legerdemain with Cups and Balls, Eggs, Hats, Handkerchiefs, &c. All from Actual Experience. Edited by W. H. CREMER, Jun., of Regent Street. Cloth extra, with 200 Illustrations, 4s. 6d.

MARK TWAIN'S WORKS.

Mark Twain's Choice Works. With extra passages to the "Innocents Abroad," now first reprinted, and a Life of the Author. 50 Illustrations by MARK TWAIN and other Artists, and Portrait of the Author. 700 pages, cloth gilt, 7s. 6d.

Mark Twain's Innocents Abroad : The Voyage Out. Crown 8vo, cloth, fine toned paper, 3s. 6d.; or fcap. 8vo, illustrated wrapper, 1s.

Mark Twain's New Pilgrim's Progress : The Voyage Home. Crown 8vo, cloth, fine toned paper, 3s. 6d. ; or fcap. 8vo, illustrated wrapper, 1s.

Mark Twain's Burlesque Autobiography, First Mediæval Romance, and on Children. Fcap. 8vo, illustrated cover, 6d.

Mark Twain's Eye-Openers. A Volume of immensely Funny Sayings, and Stories that will bring a smile upon the gruffest countenance. Fcap. 8vo, illustrated wrapper, 1s.

Mark Twain's Jumping Frog, and other Humorous Sketches. Fcap. 8vo, illustrated cover, 1s.
"An inimitably funny book."—*Saturday Review.*

Mark Twain's Pleasure Trip on the Continent of Europe. (The "Innocents Abroad" and "New Pilgrim's Progress" in one volume.) 500 pages, paper boards, 2s.; or in cloth, 2s. 6d.

Mark Twain's Practical Jokes ; or, Mirth with Artemus Ward, and other Papers. By MARK TWAIN, and other Humorists. Fcap. 8vo, illustrated cover, 1s.

Mark Twain's Screamers. A Gathering of Delicious Bits and Short Stories. Fcap. 8vo, illustrated cover, 1s.

Mayhew's London Characters: Illus-
trations of the Humour, Pathos, and Peculiarities of London Life.
By HENRY MAYHEW, Author of "London Labour and the London
Poor," and other Writers. With nearly 100 graphic Illustrations.
Crown 8vo, cloth gilt, about 500 pages, 7s. 6d.   [*Preparing.*

Magna Charta. An exact Facsimile of the
Original Document, preserved in the British Museum, very carefully
drawn, and printed on fine plate paper, nearly 3 feet long by 2 feet
wide, with the Arms and Seals of the Barons elaborately emblazoned
in Gold and Colours. A.D. 1215.   Price 5s.; or, handsomely framed
and glazed, in carved oak, of an antique pattern, 22s. 6d.
   A full Translation, with Notes, has been prepared, price 6d.

ENTIRELY NEW GAMES.

The Merry Circle, and How the Visitors
were entertained during Twelve Pleasant Evenings. A Book of
New Intellectual Games and Amusements. Edited by Mrs. CLARA
BELLEW.   Crown 8vo, numerous Illustrations, cloth extra, 4s. 6d.
₊ *A capital Book of Household Amusements, which will please both old and
young. It is an excellent book to consult before going to an evening party.*

Monumental Inscriptions of the West
Indies, from the Earliest Date, with Genealogical and Historical
Annotations, &c., from Original, Local, and other Sources. Illustrative of the Histories and Genealogies of the Seventeenth Century,
the Calendars of State Papers, Peerages, and Baronetages.   With
Engravings of the Arms of the principal Families. Chiefly collected
on the spot by the Author, Capt. J. H. LAWRENCE-ARCHER. One
volume, demy 4to, about 300 pages, cloth extra, 21s.

Mr. Brown on the Goings-on of Mrs.

Brown at the Tichborne Trial, &c. Fcap. 8vo, illustrated cover, 1s.

Mr. Sprouts: His Opinions. Fcap. 8vo,

illustrated cover, 1s.

UNIFORM WITH "TOM D'URFEY'S PILLS."

Musarum Deliciæ; or, The Muses' Re-

creation, 1656 ; Wit Restor'd, 1658 ; and Wit's Recreations, 1640.
The whole compared with the originals ; with all the Wood Engravings, Plates, Memoirs, and Notes. A New Edition, in 2 volumes,
post 8vo, beautifully printed on antique laid paper, and bound in
antique boards, 21s. A few Large Paper copies have been prepared,
price 35s.

*** *Of the Poets of the Restoration, there are none whose works are more rare
than those of Sir John Mennis and Dr. James Smith. The small volume entitled
"Musarum Deliciæ; or, The Muses' Recreation," which contains the productions
of these two friends, was not accessible to Mr. Freeman when he compiled his
"Kentish Poets," and has since become so rare that it is only found in the cabinets
of the curious. A reprint of the "Musarum Deliciæ," together with several other
kindred pieces of the period, appeared in 1817, forming two volumes of Facetiæ,
edited by Mr. E. Dubois, author of "The Wreath," &c. These volumes having in
turn become exceedingly scarce, the Publishers venture to put forth the present new
edition, in which, while nothing has been omitted, no pains have been spared to
render it more complete and elegant than any that has yet appeared. The type,
plates, and woodcuts of the originals have been accurately followed ; the notes of
the Editor of 1817 are considerably augmented, and indexes have been added,
together with a portrait of Sir John Mennis, from a painting by Vandyke in Lord
Clarendon's Collection.*

The Mystery of Mr. E. Drood. An

Adaptation. By ORPHEUS C. KERR. Fcap. 8vo, illustrated
cover, 1s.

The Mystery of the Good Old Cause:

Sarcastic Notices of those Members of the Long Parliament that
held Places, both Civil and Military, contrary to the Self-denying
Ordinance of April 3, 1645 ; with the Sums of Money and Lands
they divided among themselves. Small 4to, half-morocco, 7s. 6d.

Never Caught in Blockade-Running.

An exciting book of Adventures during the American Civil War.
Fcap. 8vo, illustrated cover, 1s.

Napoleon III., the Man of His Time;

from Caricatures. PART I. THE STORY OF THE LIFE OF NAPO-.
LEON III., as told by J. M. HASWELL.

PART II. THE SAME STORY, as told by the POPULAR CARICA-
TURES of the past Thirty-five Years. Crown 8vo, with Coloured
Frontispiece and over 100 Caricatures, 400 pp., 7s. 6d.

*** *The object of this Work is to give Both Sides of the Story. The Artist has
gone over the entire ground of Continental and English Caricatures for the last
third of a century, and a very interesting book is the result.*

Nuggets and Dust, panned out in Cali-

fornia by DOD GRILE. Edited by J. MILTON SLOLUCK. A new
style of Humour and Satire. Fcap. 8vo, illustrated cover, 1s.

*** *If Artemus Ward may be considered the Douglas Jerrold, and Mark
Twain the Sydney Smith of America, Dod Grile will rank as their Dean Swift.*

The Old Prose Stories whence TENNYSON'S

"Idylls of the King" were taken. By B. M. RANKING. Royal
16mo, paper cover, 1s. ; cloth extra, 1s. 6d.

THE OLD DRAMATISTS.

Ben Jonson's Works. With Notes, Critical and Explanatory, and a Biographical Memoir by WILLIAM GIFFORD. Edited by Lieut.-Col. FRANCIS CUNNINGHAM. Complete in 3 vols., crown 8vo, Portrait. Cloth, 6s. each; cloth gilt, 6s. 6d. each.

George Chapman's Plays, Complete, from the Original Quartos. With an Introduction by ALGERNON CHARLES SWINBURNE. Crown 8vo, Portrait. Cloth, 6s.; cloth gilt, 6s. 6d.
[*In preparation.*

Christopher Marlowe's Works: Including his Translations. Edited, with Notes and Introduction, by Lieut.-Col. F. CUNNINGHAM. Crown 8vo, Portrait. Cloth, 6s.; cloth gilt, 6s. 6d.

Philip Massinger's Plays. From the Text of WM. GIFFORD. With the addition of the Tragedy of "Believe as You List." Edited by Lieut.-Col. FRANCIS CUNNINGHAM. Crown 8vo, Portrait. Cloth, 6s.; cloth gilt, 6s. 6d.

Original Lists of Persons of Quality;
Emigrants; Religious Exiles; Political Rebels; Serving Men Sold for a Term of Years; Apprentices; Children Stolen; Maidens Pressed; and others who went from Great Britain to the American Plantations, 1600-1700. With their Ages, the Localities where they formerly Lived in the Mother Country, Names of the Ships in which they embarked, and other interesting particulars. From MSS. preserved in the State Paper Department of Her Majesty's Public Record Office, England. Edited by JOHN CAMDEN HOTTEN. A very handsome volume, crown 4to, cloth gilt, 700 pages, 31s. 6d. A few Large Paper copies have been printed, price 50s.

Parochial History of the County of
Cornwall. Compiled from the best authorities, and corrected and improved from actual survey. 4 vols. 4to, cloth extra, £3 3s. the set; or, separately, the first three volumes, 16s. each; the fourth volume, 18s.

COMPANION TO THE "BON GAULTIER BALLADS."

Puck on Pegasus. By H. CHOLMONDELEY

PENNELL. In 4to, printed within an India-paper tone, and elegantly
bound, gilt, gilt edges, price 10*s*. 6*d*.

*⁎⁎ This most amusing work has passed through Five Editions, receiving
everywhere the highest praise as "a clever and brilliant book." In addition
to the designs of* GEORGE CRUIKSHANK, JOHN LEECH, JULIAN PORTCH, "PHIZ,"
and other artists, SIR NOEL PATON, MILLAIS, JOHN TENNIEL, RICHARD
DOYLE, *and* M. ELLEN EDWARDS *have now contributed several exquisite
pictures, thus making the New Edition—which is Twice the Size of the old one
—the best book for the Drawing-room table published.*

By the same Author.

Modern Babylon, and other Poems.

Small crown 8vo, cloth extra, gilt, 4*s*. 6*d*.

COMPANION TO "CUSSANS' HERALDRY."

The Pursuivant of Arms;

or, Heraldry founded upon Facts. A
Popular Guide to the Science of Heraldry.
By J. R. PLANCHÉ, Esq., F.S.A.,
Somerset Herald. To which are added,
Essays on the BADGES OF THE HOUSES OF
LANCASTER AND YORK. A New Edition,
enlarged and revised by the Author, illus-
trated with Coloured Frontispiece, five
full-page Plates, and about 200 Illustra-
tions. Beautifully bound in cloth, with
Emblematic Design, extra gilt, 7*s*. 6*d*.

PICCADILLY ANNUAL FOR 1874.

The Knowing

Ones at Home. Stories
of their Doings at a Local
Science Meeting, at the
Crystal Palace, at St.
Paul's, at a Foresters'
Fête, &c., &c. A New
and entirely Original Hu-
morous Story, crammed
with Fun from the first
page to the last. Pro-
fusely Illustrated by
BRUNTON, MATT MOR-
GAN, and other Artists.
4to, handsome wrapper, 1*s*.

74 & 75, *PICCADILLY, LONDON, W.*

Policeman Y: His Opinions on War

and the Millingtary. With Illustrations by the Author, JOHN
EDWARD SODEN. Cloth, very neat, 2s. 6d. ; in paper, 1s.

FOR GOLD AND SILVERSMITHS.

Private Book of Useful Alloys and

Memoranda for Goldsmiths and Jewellers. By JAMES E.
COLLINS, C.E., of Birmingham. Royal 16mo, 3s. 6d.

* *The secrets of the Gold and Silversmiths' Art are here given, for the benefit
of young Apprentices and Practitioners. It is an invaluable book to the Trade.*

"AN AWFULLY JOLLY BOOK FOR PARTIES."

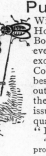

Puniana: Thoughts

Wise and Otherwise. By the
Hon. HUGH ROWLEY. Best
Book of Riddles and Puns
ever formed. With nearly 100
exquisitely Fanciful Drawings.
Contains nearly 3000 of the
best Riddles, and 10,000 most
outrageous Puns, and is one of
the most Popular Books ever
issued. New Edition, small
quarto, uniform with the
"Bab Ballads." Price 6s.

"Enormous burlesque — unap-
proachable and pre-eminent. We
venture to think that this very queer
volume will be a favourite. It
deserves to be so ; and we should
suggest that, to a dull person desirous to get credit with the young holiday
people, it would be good policy to invest in the book, and dole it out by instalments.'
—*Saturday Review.*

By the same Author.

A Second Series of Puniana: Containing

nearly 100 beautifully executed Drawings, and a splendid Collection
of Riddles and Puns, fully equal to those in the First Volume. Small
quarto, uniform with the First Series, cloth gilt, gilt edges, 6s.

[*Nearly ready.*

Remarkable Claimants, Ancient and

Modern. Being the Histories of all the most celebrated Pretenders
and Claimants during the last 600 years. Fcap. 8vo, 300 pages,
illustrated boards, 2s.

74 & 75, *PICCADILLY, LONDON, W.*

GUSTAVE DORÉ'S DESIGNS.

The Works of Rabelais. Faithfully trans-
lated from the French, with variorum Notes, and numerous characteristic Illustrations by GUSTAVE DORÉ. Crown 8vo, cloth extra,
700 pages. Price 7s. 6d.

UNIFORM WITH "WONDERFUL CHARACTERS."

Remarkable Trials and Notorious
Characters. From "Half-Hanged Smith," 1700, to Oxford, who
shot at the Queen, 1840. By Captain L. BENSON. With spirited
full-page Engravings by PHIZ. 8vo, 550 pages, 7s. 6d.

*** *A Complete Library of Sensation Literature! There are plots enough here
to produce a hundred "exciting" Novels, and at least five hundred "powerful"
Magazine-Stories. The book will be appreciated by all readers whose taste lies in
this direction.*

Rochefoucauld's Reflections and
Moral Maxims. With Introductory Essay by SAINTE-BEUVE, and
Explanatory Notes. Royal 16mo, elegantly printed, 1s. ; cloth
neat, 1s. 6d.

74 & 75, *PICCADILLY, LONDON, W.*

Rogues and Vagabonds of the Race-

Course. Full Explanations how they Cheat at Roulette, Three Cards, Thimble-rig; with some Account of the Welsher and Money-Lender. By ALFRED TOULMIN, late 65th Regt. Fcap. 8vo, illustrated cover, 1s.

Roll of Battle Abbey; or, A List of the Prin-

cipal Warriors who came over from Normandy with William the Conqueror, and Settled in this Country, A.D. 1066–7. Carefully drawn, and printed on fine plate paper, nearly three feet by two feet, with the Arms of the principal Barons elaborately emblazoned in Gold and Colours. Price 5s.; or, handsomely framed in carved oak of an antique pattern, 22s. 6d.

Roll of Caerlaverock: the Oldest Heraldic

Roll; including the Original Anglo-Norman Poem, and an English Translation of the MS. in the British Museum. By THOMAS WRIGHT, M.A. The Arms emblazoned in gold and colours. In 4to, very handsomely printed, extra gold cloth, 12s.

Roman Catholics in the County of

York in 1604. Transcribed from the Original MS. in the Bodleian Library, and Edited, with Genealogical Notes, by EDWARD PEACOCK, F.S.A., Editor of "Army Lists of the Roundheads and Cavaliers, 1642." Small 4to, handsomely printed and bound, 15s.

** *Genealogists and Antiquaries will find much new and curious matter in this work. An elaborate Index refers to every name in the volume, among which will be found many of the highest local interest.*

Ross's (Chas. H.) Unlikely Tales and

Wrong-Headed Essays. Fcap. 8vo, with numerous quaint and amusing Illustrations, 1s.

Ross's (Chas. H.) Story of a Honey-

moon. A New Edition of this charmingly humorous book.
Fcap. 8vo, illustrated boards, 2s.
[*Nearly ready.*

School Life at Winchester College;

or, The Reminiscences of a Winchester Junior. By the Author of
"The Log of the Water Lily;" and "The Water Lily on the
Danube." Second Edition, Revised. COLOURED PLATES, 7s. 6d.

The Secret Out; or, One Thousand

Tricks with Cards, and other Recreations; with Entertaining Ex-
periments in Drawing Room or "White Magic." By the Author
of the "Magician's Own Book." Edited by W. H. CREMER, Jun.,
of Regent Street. With 300 Engravings. Crown 8vo, cloth, 4s. 6d.

*** *Under the title of "Le Magicien des Salons," this book has long been a Standard
Magic Book with all French and German Professors of the Art. The tricks are
described so carefully, with engravings to illustrate them, that not the slightest
difficulty can be experienced in performing them.*

Shaving Them; or, The Adventures of

Three Yankees. By TITUS A. BRICK. Fcap. 8vo, illustrated
cover, 1s.

Shelley's Early Life. From Original

Sources. With Curious Incidents, Letters, and Writings, now
First Published or Collected. By DENIS FLORENCE MAC-CARTHY.
Cheaper Edition, crown 8vo, with Illustrations, 440 pages, 7s. 6d.

*** *A most interesting volume of new biographical facts. The work pos-
sesses special interest to Irish readers, as the poet's political pamphlets, advo-
cating Home Rule and other rights, are here for the first time given in a
collected form. These pamphlets Shelley and his wife threw from the balcony
of a window in Sackville Street, as the best means of publishing the poet's
political principles.*

THE POCKET SHELLEY.

SHELLEY, FROM THE GODWIN SKETCH.

Shelley's Poetical Works. Now First

Reprinted from the Author's Original Editions. In Two Series, the FIRST containing "Queen Mab" and the Early Poems; the SECOND, "Laon and Cythna," "The Cenci," and Later Poems. In royal 16mo, over 400 pages in a volume, price 1s. 8d. each, in illustrated cover; 2s. 2d. each in cloth extra.

The Third Series, completing the Work, will shortly be ready.

Sheridan's (Richard Brinsley) Com-

plete Works, with Life and Anecdotes. Including his Dramatic Writings, printed from the Original Editions, his works in Prose and Poetry, Translations, Speeches, Jokes, Puns, &c.; with a Collection of Sheridaniana. Crown 8vo, cloth gilt, with Portrait and Illustrations, 7s. 6d. [*Preparing.*

Shirley Brooks' Amusing Poetry. A

Collection of Humorous Poems. Selected by SHIRLEY BROOKS, Editor of *Punch.* Fcap. 8vo, paper boards, 2s. [*Preparing.*

*** *This work has for many years been out of print, and very scarce.*

Signboards: Their History. With Anecdotes of Famous Taverns and Remarkable Characters. By JACOB LARWOOD and JOHN CAMDEN HOTTEN. SEVENTH EDITION. Crown 8vo, cloth extra, 580 pp., 7s. 6d.

BULL AND MOUTH.

"It is not fair on the part of a reviewer to pick out the plums of an author's book, thus filching away his cream, and leaving little but skim-milk remaining; but, even if we were ever so maliciously inclined, we could not in the present instance pick out all Messrs. Larwood and Hotten's plums, because the good things are so numerous as to defy the most wholesale depredation."—*The Times.*

*** *Nearly 100 most curious illustrations on wood are given, showing the various old signs which were formerly hung from taverns and other houses.*

CHARLES DICKENS' EARLY SKETCHES.

Sketches of Young Couples, Young Ladies and Young Gentlemen. By "QUIZ" (CHARLES DICKENS). With 18 Steel-plate Illustrations by "PHIZ" (H. K. BROWNE). A New Edition, crown 8vo, cloth gilt, 4s. 6d.   [*Preparing.*

The Slang Dictionary: Etymological, Historical, and Anecdotal. An ENTIRELY NEW EDITION, revised throughout, and considerably Enlarged, containing upwards of a thousand more words than the last edition. Crown 8vo, with Curious Illustrations, cloth extra, 6s. 6d.

"Valuable as a work of reference."—*Saturday Review.*

A KEEPSAKE FOR SMOKERS.

The Smoker's Text-Book. By J. Hamer,

F.R.S.L. Exquisitely printed from "silver-faced" type, cloth, very neat, gilt edges, 2s. 6d., post free.

"A pipe is a great comforter, a pleasant soother. The man who smokes, thinks like a sage, and acts like a Samaritan."—*Bulwer.*

"A tiny volume, dedicated to the votaries of the weed; beautifully printed on toned paper, in, we believe, the smallest type ever made (cast especially for show at the Great Exhibition in Hyde Park), but very clear, notwithstanding its minuteness. . . . . The pages sing, in various styles, the praises of tobacco. Amongst the writers laid under contribution are Bulwer, Kingsley, Charles Lamb, Thackeray, Cowper, and Byron."—*The Field.*

WEST-END LIFE AND DOINGS.

The Story of the London Parks. By

Jacob Larwood. With numerous Illustrations, Coloured and Plain. In One thick Volume, crown 8vo, cloth extra, gilt, 7s. 6d.

*** *A most interesting work, giving a complete History of these favourite out-of-door resorts, from the earliest period to the present time, together with the fashions, the promenades, the rides, the reviews, and other displays.*

Summer Cruising in the South Seas.

By C. W. Stoddard. With about Thirty Engravings on Wood, drawn by Wallis Mackay. Crown 8vo, cloth, extra gilt, 5s.

*** *Chapters descriptive of life and adventure in the South Sea Islands, in the style made so popular by " The Earl and the Doctor."*

74 & 75, *PICCADILLY, LONDON, W.*

ALGERNON CHARLES SWINBURNE'S WORKS.

Swinburne's William Blake: A Critical
Essay. With facsimile Paintings, Coloured by Hand, after the Drawings by Blake and his Wife. Thick 8vo, cloth extra, price 16s.

Swinburne's Atalanta in Calydon.
New Edition. Foolscap 8vo, price 6s.

Swinburne's Bothwell. A New Poem.
[*In preparation.*

Swinburne's Chastelard. A Tragedy.
New Edition. Price 7s.

Swinburne's Poems and Ballads.
New Edition. Price 9s.

Swinburne's Notes on his Poems,
and on the Reviews which have appeared upon them. Price 1s.

Swinburne's Queen Mother and Rosa-
mond. New Edition. Foolscap 8vo, price 5s.

Swinburne's Song of Italy. Foolscap
8vo, toned paper, cloth, price 3s. 6d.

WILLIAM COMBE'S BEST WORK.

Dr. Syntax's Three Tours. WITH THE

WHOLE OF ROWLANDSON'S VERY DROLL FULL-PAGE ILLUSTRA-
TIONS, IN COLOURS, AFTER THE ORIGINAL DRAWINGS. Comprising the well-known TOURS—

   1. IN SEARCH OF THE PICTURESQUE.
   2. IN SEARCH OF CONSOLATION.
   3. IN SEARCH OF A WIFE.

The Three Series Complete and Unabridged, with a Life of the
Author by JOHN CAMDEN HOTTEN. 8vo, cloth extra, gilt, in one
handsome volume, price 7s. 6d.

  * *One of the most amusing and laughable books ever published.*

A SMALLER EDITION, with Eight Coloured Plates, the text complete,
price 3s. 6d.

THEODORE HOOK'S HOUSE, NEAR PUTNEY.

Theodore   Hook's   Ramsbottom

Papers. The whole 29 Letters, complete and unabridged,
precisely as they left the pen of their genial and witty Author. Fcap.
8vo, illustrated cover, 1s.

Taylor's History of Playing Cards.

With Sixty curious Illustrations, 550 pp., price 7s. 6d.

** *Ancient and Modern Games, Conjuring, Fortune-Telling, and Card Sharping, Gambling and Calculation, Cartomancy, Old Gaming-Houses, Card Revels and Blind Hookey, Picquet and Vingt-et-un, Whist and Cribbage, Tricks, &c.*

Thackerayana. Notes

and Anecdotes illustrative of Scenes and Characters in the Works of WILLIAM MAKEPEACE THACKERAY. With nearly Four Hundred Illustrations, coloured and plain. In 8vo, uniform with the Library Edition of his works, 7s. 6d.   [*Preparing.*

Theodore Hook's

Choice Humorous Works, with his Ludicrous Adventures, Bons-mots, Puns, and Hoaxes. With a new Life of the Author. PORTRAITS, FACSIMILES, and ILLUSTRATIONS. Cr. 8vo, 600 pages, cloth extra, 7s. 6d.

** "As a wit and humorist of the highest order his name will be preserved. His political songs and *jeux d'esprit,* when the hour comes for collecting them, *will form a volume of sterling and lasting attraction !*"—J. G. LOCKHART.

74 & 75, *PICCADILLY, LONDON, W.*

THE SUBSCRIPTION ROOM AT BROOKES'S.

Timbs' Clubs and Club Life in Lon-

don. With ANECDOTES of its FAMOUS COFFEE HOUSES, HOSTEL-
RIES, and TAVERNS. By JOHN TIMBS, F.S.A. New Edition,
with NUMEROUS ILLUSTRATIONS, drawn expressly. Crown 8vo,
cloth extra, 600 pages, 7s. 6d.

⁎ *A Companion to " The History of Sign-Boards." It abounds in quaint
stories of old London Clubs—the* Blue Stocking, Kit Kat, Beef Steak, Robin Hood,
Mohocks, Scriblerus, One o'Clock, the Civil, *and hundreds of others; together
with* Tom's, Dick's, Button's, Ned's, Will's, *and the famous Coffee Houses of the
last century. A full account of the great modern clubs of Pall Mall and St. James's
is also given. The book is a mine of anecdote.*

Timbs' English Eccentrics and Ec-

centricities. Stories of Wealth and Fashion, Delusions, Impos-
tures and Fanatic Missions, Strange Sights and Sporting Scenes,
Eccentric Artists, Theatrical Folks, Men of Letters, &c. By JOHN
TIMBS, F.S.A. An entirely New Edition, with numerous Illustrations. Crown 8vo, cloth extra, 600 pages, 7s. 6d. [*Preparing.*

74 & 75, *PICCADILLY, LONDON, W.*

"Tom Smith." Reminiscences of the late

THOMAS ASSHETON SMITH, Esq. ; or, The Pursuits of an English Country Gentleman. By Sir J. E. EARDLEY WILMOT, Bart. A New and Revised Edition, with steel-plate Portrait, and plain and coloured Illustrations. Crown 8vo, cloth extra, 7s. 6d.

Vers de Societe. An entirely New Se-

lection, fuller and better than any hitherto made ; introducing all the Old Favourites, and many new ones. Edited by H. CHOLMONDELEY PENNELL, Author of "Puck on Pegasus." Beautifully printed, and bound in cloth, extra gilt, 6s.   [*Preparing*.

Victor Hugo's Les Miserables: Fan-

tine. Now first published in an English Translation, complete and unabridged. Post 8vo, illustrated boards, 2s.   [*Nearly ready*. *The other Stories (each complete in itself) will follow.*

Vyner's Notitia Venatica: A Treatise

on Fox-Hunting, the General Management of Hounds, and the Diseases of Dogs ; Distemper and Rabies ; Kennel Lameness, &c. Sixth Edition, Enlarged. By ROBERT C. VYNER, Esq., of Eathorpe Hall, Warwickshire. WITH SPIRITED ILLUSTRATIONS IN COLOURS, BY ALKEN, OF MEMORABLE FOX-HUNTING SCENES. Royal 8vo, cloth extra, 21s.

*** An entirely new edition of the best work on Fox-Hunting.*

Walt Whitman's Leaves of Grass.

The Complete Work, precisely as issued by the Author in Washington. A thick volume, 8vo, green cloth, price 9s.

"Whitman is a poet who bears and needs to be read as a whole, and then the volume and torrent of his power carry the disfigurements along with it and away. He is really a fine fellow."—*Chambers's Journal.*

Warrant to Execute Charles I. An

exact Facsimile of this important Document, with the Fifty-nine Signatures of the Regicides, and corresponding Seals, admirably executed on paper made to imitate the original document, 22 in. by 14 in. Price 2s. ; or, handsomely framed and glazed in carved oak of antique pattern, 14s. 6d.

Warrant to Execute Mary Queen of

Scots. The Exact Facsimile of this important Document, including the Signature of Queen Elizabeth and Facsimile of the Great Seal, on tinted paper, made to imitate the Original MS. Price 2s. ; or, handsomely framed and glazed in carved oak of antique pattern, 14s. 6d.

Wonderful Characters : Memoirs and

Anecdotes of Remarkable and Eccentric Persons of Every Age and Nation. From the text of HENRY WILSON and JAMES CAULFIELD. Crown 8vo, cloth extra, with Sixty-one full-page Engravings of Extraordinary Persons, 7s. 6d.

** There are so many curious matters discussed in this volume, that any person who takes it up will not readily lay it down until he has read it through. The Introduction is almost entirely devoted to a consideration of Pig-Faced Ladies, and the various stories concerning them.

Wright's (Andrew) Court-Hand Re-

stored ; or, Student's Assistant in Reading Old Deeds, Charters, Records, &c. Half Morocco, a New Edition, 10s. 6d.

** The best guide to the reading of old Records, &c.

Wright's History of Caricature and

the Grotesque in Art, in Literature, Sculpture, and Painting, from the Earliest Times to the Present Day. By THOMAS WRIGHT, Esq., F.S.A. Profusely illustrated by FAIRHOLT. Small 4to, cloth extra gilt, red edges, 21s.

Wright's Caricature History of the

Georges (House of Hanover). A very Entertaining Book of 640 pages, with 400 Pictures, Caricatures, Squibs, Broadsides, Window Pictures, &c. By THOMAS WRIGHT, Esq., F.S.A. Crown 8vo, cloth extra, 7s. 6d. A few copies of a Large Paper Edition are still on sale, with extra Portraits, bound in half-morocco, 30s.

"A set of caricatures such as we have in Mr. Wright's volume brings the surface of the age before us with a vividness that no prose writer, even of the highest power, could emulate. Macaulay's most brilliant sentence is weak by the side of the little woodcut from Gillray, which gives us Burke and Fox."—*Saturday Review.*

ALL THE BEST AMERICAN HUMOUR.

Yankee Drolleries. Edited by GEORGE

AUGUSTUS SALA. Containing ARTEMUS WARD, HIS BOOK; BIGLOW PAPERS; ORPHEUS C. KERR; MAJOR JACK DOWNING; and NASBY PAPERS. 700 pages, cloth, 3s. 6d.

More Yankee Drolleries. A Second

Series of the best American Humorists. Containing ARTEMUS WARD'S TRAVELS; HANS BREITMANN; THE PROFESSOR AT THE BREAKFAST TABLE; BIGLOW PAPERS, Part II.; and JOSH BILLINGS; with an Introduction by GEORGE AUGUSTUS SALA. 700 pages, cloth, 3s. 6d.

A Third Supply of Yankee Drolleries.

Containing ARTEMUS WARD'S FENIANS; THE AUTOCRAT OF THE BREAKFAST TABLE; BRET HARTE'S STORIES; THE INNOCENTS ABROAD; and NEW PILGRIM'S PROGRESS; with an Introduction by GEORGE AUGUSTUS SALA. 700 pages, cloth, 3s. 6d.

Popular Shilling Books, mostly Humorous,

In Illustrated Covers.

(See also under alphabetical arrangement.)

AMERICAN HAPPY THOUGHTS.
ARTEMUS WARD : AMONG THE MORMONS.
——————— HIS BOOK.
——————— LETTERS TO PUNCH.
AWFUL CRAMMERS. By Titus A. Brick.
BABIES AND LADDERS. By Emmanuel Kink.
BIGLOW PAPERS.
BRET HARTE'S EAST AND WEST.
——————— LUCK OF ROARING CAMP.
——————— STORIES OF THE SIERRAS.
BRIGHT'S SPEECHES, cloth.
BROWN (Mr.) ON THE GOINGS ON OF MRS. BROWN.
BYRON IN LOVE. By Howard Paul.
CARLYLE (THOMAS) ON THE CHOICE OF BOOKS.
CHIPS FROM A ROUGH LOG.
DANBURY NEWSMAN. By J. M. Bailey.
DERBY DAY : a Sporting Novel.
DOD GRILE'S FIEND'S DELIGHT.
——————— NUGGETS AND DUST.
DU CHAILLU'S COUNTRY OF THE DWARFS.
FUN FOR THE MILLION. By the best Humorists of the Day.
HANS BREITMANN'S BALLADS.
HATTON'S KITES AND PIGEONS. Illustrated.
HOLMES' AUTOCRAT OF THE BREAKFAST TABLE.
——————— POET AT THE BREAKFAST TABLE.
——————— PROFESSOR AT THE BREAKFAST TABLE.
——————— WIT AND HUMOUR.
HOOD'S WHIMS AND ODDITIES. Both Series, complete.
JOSH BILLINGS : HIS BOOK OF SAYINGS.
LAMB'S ESSAYS OF ELIA. Both Series, complete.
MR. SPROUTS : HIS OPINIONS.
MARK TWAIN'S INNOCENTS ABROAD.
——————— JUMPING FROG.
——————— NEW PILGRIM'S PROGRESS.
——————— PRACTICAL JOKES.
——————— SCREAMERS.

POPULAR SHILLING BOOKS—*continued.*

MYSTERY OF MR. E. DROOD. By O. C. Kerr.
NEVER CAUGHT. The Blockade-runner's Story.
ORPHEUS C. KERR PAPERS.
PICCADILLY ANNUAL FOR 1874: KNOWING ONES AT HOME.
POLICEMAN Y: BALLADS. Illustrated.
ROCHEFOUCAULD'S MAXIMS, with Sainte-Beuve's Essay.
ROGUES AND VAGABONDS OF THE RACECOURSE.
ROSS'S UNLIKELY TALES AND WRONG-HEADED ESSAYS.
SHAVING THEM. By Titus A. Brick.
THEODORE HOOK'S RAMSBOTTOM PAPERS.

The Golden Library of the Best Authors.

₊ *A charming collection of Favourite Works, elegantly printed in Handy Volumes, uniform with the Tauchnitz Series.*

(See also under alphabetical arrangement.)

BAYARD TAYLOR.—DIVERSIONS OF THE ECHO CLUB. 1*s.* 6*d.*; cloth, 2*s.*

CARLYLE.—ON THE CHOICE OF BOOKS. 1*s.*; cloth, 1*s.* 6*d.*

CHARLES LAMB.—THE ESSAYS OF ELIA. Complete. Both Series. 1*s.*; cloth, 1*s.* 6*d.*

HOLMES.—AUTOCRAT OF THE BREAKFAST TABLE. 1*s.*; cloth, 1*s.* 6*d.*

———— PROFESSOR AT THE BREAKFAST TABLE. 1*s.*; cloth, 1*s.* 6*d.*

HOOD.—WHIMS AND ODDITIES. 80 Illustrations. Two Series, complete. 1*s.*; cloth, 1*s.* 6*d.*

LEIGH HUNT.—A TALE FOR A CHIMNEY CORNER, and other Essays. 1*s.* 4*d.*; cloth, 1*s.* 10*d.*

LELAND.—HANS BREITMANN'S BALLADS, Complete. 1*s.*; cloth, 1*s.* 6*d.*

ROCHEFOUCAULD. REFLECTIONS AND MORAL MAXIMS. With Essay by SAINTE-BEUVE. 1*s.*; cloth, 1*s.* 6*d.*

SHELLEY.—POETICAL WORKS. From the Author's Original Editions. First Series, QUEEN MAB and EARLY POEMS. Second Series, LAON AND CYTHNA, the CENCI, and LATER POEMS. Each Series 1*s.* 8*d.*; in cloth, 2*s.* 2*d.*

SIR T. MALLORY.—THE OLD PROSE STORIES from which TENNYSON took his "IDYLLS OF THE KING." 1*s.*; cloth, 1*s.* 6*d.*